PICT O. PALESTINE

A humanitarian blogging from Bethlehem

Palden Jenkins

Coherent visions

Pictures of Palestine
Palden Jenkins

First published
2012

Coherent Visions
BCM Visions
London
WC1N 3XX

ISBN
978-0-9569367-8-3

Typesetting and Layout
Jonathan How
www.coherentvisions.com

Distribution
Edge of Time Ltd
BCM Edge
London
WC1N 3XX
www.edgeoftime.co.uk

Pictures of Palestine website
www.palden.co.uk/pop
includes pictures, comments
and additional material

Note
This book contains the views
and observations of the author, a
British visitor to Palestine.
It was commissioned and
encouraged neither by any
Palestinians nor by the Hope
Flowers School and it does not
officially speak on behalf of
Hope Flowers.
It nevertheless strives to be true
and accurate. Some names have
been altered.
Photograph reproduction in this
book is imperfect. It was a choice
between this and a recession-
unfriendly book. All photos
are to be found in colour and
with annotations on the book's
website. All pictures and maps are
by the author.

For

Julian, Maya, Gwen, Marieka and Tulki

and soul-friends and family everywhere

Pictures of Palestine

Contents

5

Introduction

It wasn't just a question of whether to spend three months in Palestine. It felt like the start of a longterm commitment and an act of faith. Freelance humanitarian work involves *getting engaged* with people, becoming a part of their world, their experience and their families. A fully-fledged feeling of *family* is something Palestinians excel in.

I care for people I know in Palestine. On an earlier trip in 2005 I realised that, if I returned, people would expect me to come back regularly. They would look to me for solutions, give me things ordinary visitors wouldn't receive. I might even die with these people – after all, it's a conflict-zone.

Humanitarian work sounds a bit romantic but it doesn't stop if bullets start flying. People back home have at times implored me to *be sensible*. "Palestinians deserve sympathy but charity begins at home, and really they should sort themselves out." Yet my British forefathers contributed mightily to setting up Palestinians' problem back in the 1920s to the 1940s, leaving a legacy we now prefer to forget.

I'm a Sixties veteran who never quite gave up. My Palestine work started in the 1990s, a new step on what had already been a long life-journey. It's no quick-fix thing and you need a mad streak, a dose of righteous despair to do it.

Perhaps it's in my blood. I was born in a maternity home that had been the WW2 American Generals' HQ in Britain. At school in Liverpool I grew up sandwiched between Catholics and Protestants, taunted for refusing to take sides, for saying they should work things out by means other than violence. I became a hippy with a rainbow vision, and this deepened my understanding of the human condition and the meaning of life. As a student at the London School of Economics I joined in protesting against what was happening in Vietnam and Ulster – all we were saying was to give peace a chance. My father, uncles and grandfathers had been world war combatants, my aunt had helped Alan Turing break the Enigma Codes at Bletchley Park and my mother had hidden under the kitchen table during the Blitz in London. So my genes echoed with the reverberations of explosions and confrontation.

I still believe in peace and love as pragmatic, fundamental solutions to global problems, though of course I know it's not quite so simple. I look at people's furrowed eyebrows and pudgy bellies, at the smog and the chemicalised landscape, at jet fighters screeching overhead, and see that something is not quite right. Whether I have a mental illness or a sound grasp of reality has always been an open question for people who know me.

For the triumph of evil, it is necessary only that good people do nothing. So said the 18th century philosopher Edmund Burke. This is a big statement for our day.

I had been asked to spend three months in Bethlehem at Hope Flowers, a peace school and adult education centre specialising in trauma-recovery and post-conflict community reconstruction. To quote the founder, Hussein Issa, *every act of violence begins with an unhealed wound.* Yes indeed. Humanity is damaged, the damage is still growing and Palestinians and Israelis have a concentrated dose of it. Worldwide, people have come to accept violence as regrettably normal – it's routinely reported on the daily news. Yet Hope Flowers has developed something which can help embed peace-building across the world.

Genuine peace is a national security issue for *all* countries. Governments believe in economic development, civil institution-building and upholding law and order, and there's value in this, but building real peace is about developing a sound social consensus of mutually-assured trust and cooperation at street level, in people's values, in their feelings. It's a healing process. My own country, Britain, has for centuries played a major role in ramping up conflict worldwide and its forces fight in foreign lands today, so I feel a strange sense of personal responsibility to *do* something.

We need to help societies become more liveable, mutually supportive, joined-up, okay with themselves and with each other. Hope Flowers, led by Ibrahim Issa, Hussein's son, gives damaged people a basis by which to turn resentment into understanding and pain into progress, building a decent life and acting constructively, even when living in a difficult situation.

Palestinians have more experience than virtually anyone in dealing with conflict and disaster. Most conflicts last five years, up to ten, and then, when peace comes, everyone tries to forget. They want to

get a job, go shopping, build house extensions and have a new car. They lose the acute and poignant intensity of experience they gained while 'treading the edge' in times of war. But the Palestine conflict has gone on for many decades, and Palestinians are noteworthy in their capacity to survive under duress. They have much to teach the world.

When first I went to Bethlehem, I had big ideas about what I would do. Many of these proved thoroughly irrelevant – the things that were most valued were quite different. Also it wasn't just a matter of *my helping them* but also of *their helping me*. In the West we have material wealth and social poverty, with relatively dysfunctional families and communities, whereas Palestinians have material hardship and social wealth, a strength of society which is exemplary. Their insecurity has given them togetherness.

One of my priorities on this trip was photographic: I wanted to catch Palestine *as it stands* through the camera lens. No stereotypes, just real-life stuff. The media feed us partially-true images of bombed-out buildings, angry youths, masked gunmen, old ladies wailing, grieving fathers carrying dead children, but we have little idea of Palestinians' *real* lives, what they do on Tuesdays, where their kids play, how they do their shopping. Hence the name of this book – *Pictures of Palestine*. It's a bundle of impressions of real life.

Welcome to Bethlehem. This is what it's like, as seen through my goggles and via my antennae. At least, it was like this in 2009, when I wrote a blog about my time there. Some things, such as checkpoints, have lightened up since then and some things, such as Israeli land-grabs, have got worse. Nothing really changes with Palestine's situation, but in another sense it is changing profoundly. I hope this book helps you understand how and why.

Note: most prices are quoted in Israeli shekels or *sheqalim*. In 2009 the value of shekels was roughly six to the UK Pound, five to the Euro and four to the US Dollar. Jordanian Dinars were one to the Pound, 0.8 to the Euro and 0.6 to the US Dollar.

Pictures of Palestine

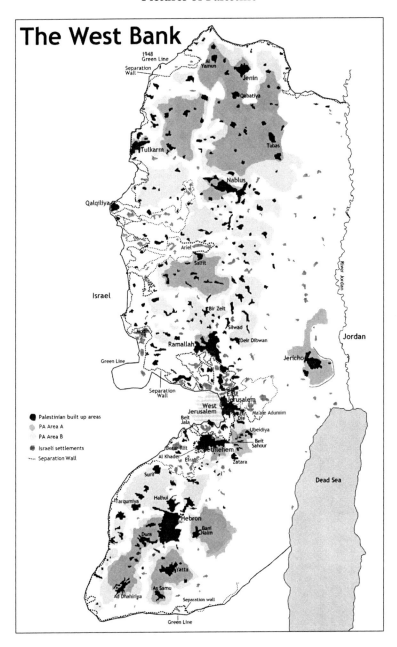

The West Bank

1948 Green Line

Separation Wall

Yarnun

Jenin

Qabatiya

Tulkarm

Tubas

Nablus

Qalqiliya

Ariel

Salfit

Israel

Bir Zeit

Silwad

Ilit

Deir Dibwan

Ramallah

Jericho

Green Line

Jordan

Separation Wall

East Jerusalem

West Jerusalem

Ma'ale Adumim

Abu Dis

Beit Jala

Ubeidiya

Beit Sahour

Betar Illit

Bethlehem

Al Khader

Efrat

Zatara

Surif

Tarqumiya

Halhul

Dead Sea

Hebron

Dura

Bani Naim

Yatta

Ad Dhahiriya

As Samu

Separation wall

Green Line

River Jordan

Legend:
- ● Palestinian built up areas
- PA Area A
- PA Area B
- ⊛ Israeli settlements
- ···· Separation Wall

11

Part One:
East Bank, West Bank

The Old Town of Bethlehem

1 **Amman**
arrival in Jordan

Six in the morning. I was sitting on a street corner in a sleepy daze, waiting for Amman to wake up and to find lodging in a hotel that was locked and silent. Disgorged at 4.30am from the plane into a somnambulant Queen Alia airport, I had been brought at hyper speed along the freeway into the dawn-illuminated city. The accelerator-happy taxi driver kept jabbering at me in Arabic while I nodded, making noises as if I understood. Apart from street cats, birds and a few early morning cars, all was quiet in Amman.

I had felt strangely matter-of-fact about travelling – the anodyne experience of airports and planes made it strangely toneless and unromantic. Yet visiting Palestine seemed a momentous move and I had been through three months of digging in my psyche's favourite fears and doubts to get to this point.

The day before, my cousin had driven me up from Cornwall to London Heathrow. That in itself was a big transition, moving from a land of ocean winds, seals and gulls, cliffs and flower-bedecked country lanes into a high-tech, grey, buzzing reality festooned with motorways, the air heavy with howling metal birds and the walkways crowded with people studiously omitting to eyeball each other.

We ate at a restaurant in Terminal One, I changed some money, hugged my cousin goodbye and then was off, up the escalators, through security, down the ramps and on to the plane. Hours later I emerged, blinking like an owl, at Queen Alia. At least there

15

were none of the queues, the searching questions and uniformed scrutinies you get at Ben Gurion airport in Tel Aviv. During an engaging encounter with an Israeli inquisitor, a small error might find you locked in a room, further questioned at length, then bundled into a plane heading home with the wrong stamp in your passport. No, at Queen Alia it was just a cursory glance from the immigration man, ten dinars for a visa and fifteen for a taxi.

So there I was on a street corner, the sun rising and the balmy air warming rapidly. Over the road was the enormous, graceful Malik Abdullah Mosque, memorialising Allah in concrete and glass. I sat writing on my laptop as birds twittered wildly and doves tried mating in the middle of the road.

I had last been in the Middle East in 2005 and had waited too long to return. Now, I had a sense of coming home, yet in that moment I also felt rather alien, out of sorts. Must give myself time to adjust. I needed the hotel to open so that I could drop my stuff, take a rest and then explore the city. And I needed to cogitate, reorientate.

Pam Perry started me on this malarky, back in 1998. We worked together on humanitarian support missions for some years until in 2007 Pam died of complications from a lung transplant that didn't work. Now she's up in heaven and, in my early-morning daze, I felt as if she might be gazing down, happy I was back in the Middle East and carrying on our work. "Spirit has a plan", she would say. Well, yes, indeed. Sometimes we are but chess-pieces in a bigger game.

Together with Eliyahu Maclean, an observant Jew, and Sheikh Bukhari, a Central Asian Muslim, both of them from Jerusalem, Pam and I had helped found Jerusalem Peacemakers in 2004. It aimed to support eight spiritually-oriented peacemakers working on both sides in the conflict, by arranging funding, backup and speaking tours for them in the West. After Pam died, Jerusalem Peacemakers was handed over to the peacemakers to run.

One of them was Ibrahim Issa of the Hope Flowers School in Bethlehem. I had visited the school in 2005 and met him. By

Pictures of Palestine

2009 he had to leave Jerusalem Peacemakers to allay Palestinian suspicions of collaboration with the Israelis. Such is the way of things. He was the only member from the West Bank, while all the others, both Jewish and Muslim, lived in Israel. I liked Ibrahim and, before long, I began to serve Hope Flowers as its webmaster and outreach editor. Ibrahim felt like a brother. We developed an allegiance, a soul-friendship.

Last time I entered Israel through the Israeli Ben Gurion airport but this time I had opted to enter through Jordan. I wanted to go into Palestine via the King Hussein Bridge, sneaking in round the back entrance.

Sitting in the sun tapping on my keyboard, blowing away the occasional exploring ant and enjoying bathing in the balmy morning warmth, I thought of my loved ones back home with moist eyes and a fond smile. Then the sound of the hotel door opening rattled along the street. Time to find some breakfast.

2 The First Circle
Impressions of Amman

Amman is likeable, busily laid-back and riddled with contradictions. Grand, modern banks are interspersed with scrappy old Arabic buildings, sitting quite comfortably alongside each other. The city is built on a series of hills, with Downtown literally down in a valley amidst them. Downtown, you're definitely at a loss if you're unfamiliar with Arabic since few signs are in English – this is the traditional, historic centre of Amman. But up in modern West Amman there are high, impressive buildings worthy of Dubai, wide boulevards and flyovers where a Bedouin's garb is strangely out of place.

The traditional part of Amman is crowded with shops and markets stacked with goods. Men sit around talking or busying themselves, yet seem not to be selling much. This of course astounds the Western mind, preoccupied with productivity, sales, turnover and profit. But things are cheap: I had a taxi ride for a dollar and a luscious fruit drink of fresh orange, banana and melon for 70 cents. How the economy works I do not know but it's clearly vibrant and the only signs of hardship are occasional beggars from the refugee camps out of town.

Most people seem not to lack for much. They love driving around in their cars and yellow taxis. Taxi-drivers honk horns at you, slowing down to solicit your business, failing to understand that you might actually *want* to walk. Modernity and convenience are seen as unequivocally good things, so the idea that one might *enjoy walking* is inconceivable, outdated. But we Brits have our strange ways.

Modern Amman is proudly contemporary and architecturally adventurous. When Arabs get going on architecture they knock spots off the British and our patchy attempts at civic artistry. Everywhere there are portraits of King Abdullah and the late King Hussein, proudly viewing their people from posters, murals and mosaics – though Abdullah's noble grimace could do with an American-style image consultant's input. Jordan is a semi-democratic country with a proactive king who plays a key role in government, but it shares a problem endemic in Arabic countries with a small, rich elite dominating a large population – and this was the main issue here during the Arab revolutions of 2011. Jordan is fairer and more reformist than most of its neighbours, so changing the regime wasn't an issue – people just wanted improvements in economic opportunity, rights and democratic standards.

The king gives the country a sense of identity and moderation. Jordan, located between everywhere else, is defined mainly by what it's not. It's not Iraq, Syria or Turkey, neither is it Saudi Arabia, nor Palestine, and it's certainly not Israel. This said, only 30% of the population is Jordanian. The rest are Palestinians, Iraqis, Lebanese, Arabians, Circassians and internationals. Surrounding countries have for decades scored high in ethnic cleansing, injustice and ruinous mayhem, but Jordan offers relative sanity.

Its multinational composition arises from the fact that these countries were set up in the 1920s by the British and the French, before which they were ethnically intermingled provinces of the Ottoman empire. The national identity of Middle Eastern countries is nowadays rigorously reinforced by their ruling elites but, underneath, they have a complex ethnic mix going back millennia, crossing the national borders established only 90 years ago.

While there are plenty of migrants in Amman there aren't hordes of foreign tourists, apart from some who cannonade round with cameras and *Lonely Planet* guides, visiting Jerash, Madaba, Petra and the Dead Sea resorts. Many Ammanis naturally assumed I was a tourist, trogging around with a conspicuous Nikon camera. But I was uninterested in tourist sites, spending much of the day planting myself in discreet spots and telephotoing the rich panoply of faces in the crowds. I just love Arab streets, full of people with lively expressions and a strong presence. I like to photograph people's thoughts and conversations – for me, a photo without an implicit thought-bubble is no photograph.

I met a Brazilian with whom I chatted at some length. He had had a nightmare in Israel, having gone there for a few days after visiting Iran and Syria – which, to Israelis, is exactly the wrong thing to do. He was upset by the five hour wait he'd endured entering the country and the six hour process of getting out. He hadn't studied his *Lonely Planet*, which warns about this. Were it not for the border between them – a substantial hurdle – Amman and Jerusalem would be just over an hour's bus ride apart.

A friend of his had been detained overnight at Ben Gurion airport. Given the names of Israeli contacts, border bureaucrats had become suspicious because none were at home when rung up – they were probably out at work. One contact, though Israeli, was discounted because, according to the computer, she had visited England three times. We Brits are prejudiced extremists in some Israelis' eyes.

So my Brazilian friend had spent just one day in Jerusalem, returning to Jordan disgruntled, and landing up drinking juice with me. Had he been naive about Israel or did he suffer that peculiar malaise of expecting to be treated normally and decently in Israel? He had a very positive impression, meanwhile, of Iran, where he had felt welcomed. Well, the hand of God moves in strange ways.

One of my tasks was to find an internet café in order to upload my blog, written in stages throughout the day. I found a coffee shop in the First Circle on Jabal Amman (a hill), where I drank China tea and, to my surprise, was blasted with Beatles and Eric Clapton oldies, while watching young Ammanis and internationals sitting round chattering in style. Little did they know I was a vintage Liverpool brother of their rock heroes.

Pictures of Palestine

Having blogged and uploaded, I sallied forth into the busy streets. At nine in the evening, Arabic cities heave with activity and the roads are choked. I tried finding a taxi; no chance. Walking Downtown, I found a streetside bar where I bought a glass of tamarind cordial, then heaved up the long hill towards the Abdullah Mosque.

The streets were all rather surreal – I was slightly drunk on sleeplessness. Eventually I sank into bed and disappeared into dreamland with the sounds of the city leaking in through the window. How lovely to sleep with just a sheet on top – it was in the middle twenties even at night.

3 **Afternoon Prayers**
Glubb Pasha and a free lunch

The next day, a bit frazzled and peopled-out after trudging too many streets, I went into a mosque. Inside was a big, open, carpeted courtyard with men on the far side, heads to the ground. Others came in and out, taking off shoes to do private prayers for five minutes – a commendably quiet break to reorientate heart and mind before getting on with a busy life.

I sat at the threshold, closed my eyes and went into meditation, leaning against the wall. It was tranquil here, the sounds of the street outside oozing in without being disturbing. Floating off into quite a deep state, I must have been gone for a while. When I emerged, slowly opening my eyes, an old man was standing there quietly in front of me, looking at me intently.

"Just like Glubb Pasha, you, sir!" Sir John Bagot Glubb was an English military man and historian of the 1920s-1950s. An officer in the Arab Legion, he had founded the Bedouin Desert Patrol, later to be a major mover in the 1940s in the newly-independent Jordan. He loved Arabs and Bedouin and wrote books about them.

"You Muslim? You come with me?" indicating I should join him in prayers.

"No, I'm not a Muslim". Then I used my easy get-out excuse which usually resolves this kind of situation, and isn't untrue. "I'm Buddhist."

"Ah, you good man. Where you from, Canada?"

"No, England."

"Ah, Glubb Pasha, he from Ingaland. Good man, he lived in Amman, yes." There was a short silence. "You going to Petra?"

Pictures of Palestine

"No, I'm not a tourist. Just staying in Amman a few days."

"Where you going then, afterwards?"

"Beit Lahem." That's the Arabic name of Bethlehem.

"Ah, you Christian?"

"No, Buddhist."

"Oh... You visiting Beit Lahem then for what?"

"I work in a school, I'm a humanitarian worker."

"Ah, that is good." He paused. "Falastin, it's not good there. People so suffering. It's good you go to Falastin. They need help."

"Yes, the wall, the checkpoints, the occupation..." By this time there was a small crowd standing around. "It's important to go."

Arabs have deep frustration over Palestine. Most cannot visit, for visa reasons, and some care not to because they find the situation upsetting or they have bad memories – many people in Amman originate from the West Bank. A friend I met the day before, who lent me a mobile phone, had been jailed and then thrown out of Palestine by the Israelis twenty years earlier because, like Ibrahim, he'd been a rock-throwing youth in the first *intifada*. He grew up just outside Ramallah. He's distinctly a man of peace now.

Pictures of Palestine

There might be some hand-wringing hypocrisy to it, since Jordanians lament Palestine's fate yet they don't necessarily do much about it – though, commendably, they do host 2.7 million Palestinian refugees, which perhaps is enough. But Jordanians appreciate a Westerner being committed to Palestine. Yet they don't understand why someone like me should be so motivated, since I'm neither Muslim nor Arab and, therefore, surely I wouldn't bother. But Palestinians are humans, and so am I, and that's the main connection. I would want someone to help my own people if we were in dire need.

After charmingly being accused of resembling Glubb Pasha I headed off to take more photos and look for food. There he was again, my old Muslim friend, standing at the entrance to an alleyway. "You eat here, it's good here." I'm not sure how he figured out I was hungry. Either these guys have ways of reading us off or the café owner was his son-in-law.

That's how I landed up in the courtyard of the Hashem restaurant, eating falafel, pitta, hummus and salad, with mint tea, all for free. He had tipped them off, and they wanted to hear my story. They hauled in someone who spoke passable English, who translated as they asked questions. *Why are you going to Falastin? What will you do there? How many children do you have? How old are you? Where is your wife? What is this school in Beit Lahem? How will you get there? How long will you stay? You coming back to Amman?*

I shed a few tears when I told them of the children there, feeling quite emotional about what I was heading into, and secretly wondering what was in store. In the West I keep my feelings more buttoned down, but these people's interest and enthusiasm made my heart wobble. It stirred me to see the concern and feeling these guys had about Palestine.

God is great, he gave me a free lunch. And many of these people are exiled Palestinians, unable to return or even visit. I felt that I had just unintentionally become a proxy for them. A few of them might even have included me in their prayers.

4 Israel's Longterm Survival
introducing Israel's situation

One of my daughters wrote me an e-mail asking whether the blog I was writing, on which this book is based, would be biased. Well, yes, I was portraying a Palestinian perspective, if that's what 'biased' means. Yet I care about the survival and future of Israel too, and Palestine's success doesn't have to mean Israel's failure. Many people don't get this.

'If you're not with us, you're against us'. Crossing that gulf is a difficult aspect of working with both sides – you can get the splitz. The two sides aren't just arguing about different aspects of the same debate – they're not even in the same conflict. There aren't just two sides, and it's not a straight black-and-white issue – it involves lots of variegated nuances and complexities. To be for one lot doesn't have to mean you're against the other lot. The real battle lies between those who encourage polarisation and violence and those on the receiving end of them. Both sides can live together, and they shall. They do live together, even though they are strangely divided.

Palestinians aren't angels and they've made mistakes but the power and the burden of error weighs heavily on the Israeli side. Israel has long had superiority in weapons, money, connections, PR, foreign backers, *chutzpah* and forcefulness. Israelis don't see things this way, seeing themselves as endangered victims, thus explaining the hardship, punishment and violence they assert on others in self-defence. This is not unique amongst nations, but for Israel it's extreme and the effects impact heavily on their victims and on the wider world.

Pictures of Palestine

The Israeli project – to provide a safe haven for Jews where they may live by their own norms – is a noble thing. Historically, Jews have suffered immensely, especially from the actions of Europeans. But this doesn't justify their oppressing or punishing Arabs today or doing to others many of the things that once were done to them. Israelis don't see themselves as oppressors – they are the oppressed, busy protecting themselves. They don't see themselves as colonisers but as a people with an entitlement to what they feel is theirs.

Israelis have a lot to be proud of. They built a nation in six decades. From their perspective, Arabs have attacked and menaced them and Israelis have bravely held off such threats. This was the narrative I learned as a teenager in 1967 at the time of the Six Day War, during which the Israelis occupied the Palestinian territories as if by accident, pre-emptively defending themselves. In later life, I discovered that this invasion, like the previous one of 1948, involved severe ethnic cleansing and uprooting of Palestinians, razing and occupying villages and parts of towns and killing of thousands of largely defenceless people. The awful fate visited on Jews by Europeans was visited by Jews on Palestinians.

Only some Jews were perpetrators. Many were accomplices who shut their eyes, went along with things or obeyed orders, to an extent tricked by their leaders. Some protested but didn't get far; others felt that the ills taking place were regrettable but unavoidable, believing Israel to be in mortal danger when Arab armies, somewhat incompetently, solely sought to protect Palestinians against overwhelming Israeli force. The Israeli project was driven by a caucus of Zionists who branded Palestinians as barbarians. Zionists drove the occupation in ways which decisively defined Israel's character and future as a state locked in a military vortex.

It could have been done differently. As they immigrated in the first half of the 20th Century, Jews could have integrated much more with Palestinians – there would have been difficulties, certainly, though arguably fewer difficulties than actually arose. The British administration of the 1920s-1940s could have exercised less of a divide-and-rule approach, driving people against one another. When the UN partitioned Palestine, favouring Jews in the process, the Israelis could have made do with the territory they were allocated, without such rabid ethnic cleansing of the land. They could have traded land for peace in the 1970s or 1990s. None of these options would have been perfect, but some sort of peaceful and productive coexistence could have arisen, leading to a sounder long term future for Israelis. But the path Israel has chosen is deeply flawed, and the results are coming back to haunt them.

Israeli feelings of existential threat arose from deep-seated and justified feelings of vulnerability following the Jews' terrible history in Europe. But the threat from Palestinians and other Arabs has been less a conquering aggression, more an ineffective response to Israeli force and expansion. A sense of threat does not have to be the case now, even in these days of Arab revolutions. When Israel upsets its neighbours, causing great loss and damage, or when during negotiations it refuses to budge on issues crucial to Palestinians and neighbouring Arabs, it naturally creates an unhappy response.

Thus, Israel becomes its own worst enemy: while intending to reinforce Israeli security, it generates ill-feeling and threats instead, undermining that security. The ethnic cleansing of 1948 would be consigned to history if such cleansing didn't continue today. Hezbollah in Lebanon would be no threat if Israel hadn't invaded and bombarded Lebanon so devastatingly on several occasions in the last 30 years. Hamas and other militias in Gaza would not fire rockets if Israel let up on its siege of Gaza. Action creates a reaction.

Zionism sees Israel's own interests and expansion as paramount. Whatever means are used toward this end, and whatever costs are incurred or imposed, Israel's growth must go on. Zionists like to reinforce the belief that the world stands against the Jewish people. The notion that Israelis' needs and security could be helped by acknowledging the needs and security of others doesn't enter the equation, except amongst a much-dwindled Israeli peace camp. In the long term, if anything weakens Israel, it is Zionism, since it undermines the sympathy the world might have toward Jews. Only a proportion of Israelis actively subscribe to Zionist sentiments, though acquiescence to such sentiments increases when Israel feels threatened, and this happens regularly, and Zionism is a norm drummed into Israelis from an early age.

This strong-minded agenda doesn't even really accord with Judaism's core tenets: Judaism is one thing and Zionism another. The laws of Moses' ten commandments – not to kill, not to steal – aren't being followed, and the nobler, more tolerant aspects of the Jewish faith are sidestepped. It's considered heretical to say this. The

Ma'ale Adumim, an Israeli settlement on the West Bank, east of Jerusalem

Pictures of Palestine

Zionist mentality builds concrete walls and fences around Israelis in self-protection, and in so doing they become separated from the world and increasingly fail to see the wider world's viewpoint. Zionists accuse critics of anti-Semitism (though Arabs are Semites too) and it labels Jewish detractors as 'self-hating Jews'.

But here comes a key proposition. If Israelis saw things another way, opening up to the notion that their fellow humans sit in the same boat as they, and if Israel ramped down its military expansionism and permitted some restitution of the ills which

have occurred since 1948, then, over time, threats to Israel would subside, and the country and its population would become more safe and secure.

One Jewish extremist I know is so way-out that he's right off the political map. Menachem Froman is an 'ultra-orthodox' (strictly observant) rabbi. He regards the state of Israel as scripturally premature and illegitimate, since the arising of such a state is prophesied to follow the coming of the Messiah. To him, the founding of Israel is supposed to make manifest a Holy Israel, a state of divine perfection and peace – what Christians call Heaven on Earth. To Jews the Messiah hasn't yet come, and in Froman's view Israel is thus manifestly unholy, both theologically and in everyday life. He's the rabbi of an illegal West Bank settlement south-east of Bethlehem, and he's also a member of Jerusalem Peacemakers.

But, get this. He hobnobs with sheikhs, imams, bishops, Tibetan lamas, Native Americans and oddbods like me. He also makes friends with 'the enemy'. When Yasser Arafat was holed up under bombardment by the Israelis in Ramallah in 2002, during the second *intifada*, Froman walked through the lines, using his rabbinical authority to confound the Israeli troops seeking to stop him, and he visited Arafat repeatedly, becoming a close personal friend. Later, he walked into Gaza to make friends with Ismael Haniyeh, the Hamas prime minister. Israeli troops can't quite shoot a rabbi if he breaks the rules since rabbis are by definition ordained by Jewish tradition to define the rules.

Palestinians like him: he's the kind of Jew they can talk with. He considers Jews no more nor less special than anyone else. He doesn't mind living under an Israeli or a Palestinian administration as long as he can live in *Eretz Yisrael*, the holy realm of Israel, where he was born. His own proposed peace settlement states simply that if Arabs can live in Israel (which they do) then Jews can live in Palestine, so let's just divide it up and get on with life, or live equally under one single government and shared land. But Froman, a memorable, charismatic character, does not represent mainstream Israel.

Pictures of Palestine

Most Palestinians and Arabs don't want to fight. The idea that they want to destroy Israel is nowadays a myth, or voiced by Arabs only when tempers are hot. Arab extremists say they want to eliminate Israel and, equally, Israeli extremists want all Palestinians to be driven out of the land, but neither kind of extremist represents a majority, and such exclusion would charge a heavy price to the victorious left behind. Germany, for example, has paid heavily in compensation and guilt for its exclusion of Jews 60-80 years ago.

Most Palestinians and Arabs accept the existence of an Israel within the pre-1967 borders – an enormous concession they signed up to in the 1993 Oslo Accords. Even Hamas, which Israelis perceive as the arch-enemy, has stated that it will recognise Israel within such boundaries. Palestinians just want a fair deal and a decent life. Peace will never be a perfect deal for everyone, but it will be better than the current situation.

Israel cannot afford to remain militarised forever: it has poor people and social problems of its own, enormous water-shortages, a risk of coastal flooding, toxicity, pollution and all the kinds of problems that pervade most modern countries. It also shares the West's dwindling prestige and power. And it is isolated.

Even if Israel won every war it undertakes, this doesn't make for a happy, healthy nation. Israel needs to make friends with its neighbours because it *needs* them, and they need Israel. Israelis can't drive to Damascus, Beirut or Amman for the weekend – they are hemmed into their own country. Arabs can't visit Tel Aviv for business or shopping or easily visit Jerusalem to pray in its Muslim holy places. It's crazy. They all have a lot to offer each other. They share Middle Eastern space.

Israelis need a safe and peaceful future. Many are not fully aware of what's going on in their name, or they shruggingly accept the 'security reasons' they are given when their army tramples on Palestinians. Many feel powerless, or they maintain an indifference by 'living inside the bubble'. Others adopt extreme, partisan views, as if everyone is against them and deserves a strident response. Since the late 1990s, the centre of gravity of Israeli politics has headed toward the hard right, and a harsh minority nowadays dominates the public dialogue. Zionist minority interests place their priorities above those of the nation. The rule of dominant interests, while not unique to Israel, maintains a perpetual state of near-conflict.

I support a neighbourly Israel and its gradual integration into the Middle East. But I have difficulty going along with the way this nation behaves today. I know plenty of remarkable Israelis whose humanity and conduct of character are impressive, but these people's voices do not prevail.

Israel acts against its own longterm best interests and could come to regret many aspects of the last sixty years. It soils its nest by pushing its case uncompromisingly, thus creating enemies and the opposite longterm effects to what it genuinely seeks. Its reliance on force, bombing, assassinations, land-grabs, ill-treatment and dehumanisation of Arabs builds up new, avoidable problems, fostering new generations of opponents. We need a new habit of peaceful coexistence. This will take a generation or two, but it is important.

Looking down on Tel Aviv and the Mediterranean from up in the Palestinian West Bank near Bir Zeit

Pictures of Palestine

Israel's great danger is the risk of truth breaking out amongst its own Jewish inhabitants, causing the Zionist world-view to be deconstructed. Disillusionment and uncertainty could one day cause many Israelis to decide that other countries offer greater peace and security. There's even a risk of fighting breaking out between dissonant Israeli communities, or between 'Israel proper' and 'Israel of the settlements'.

Palestinians don't have to fight Israelis – they just need to stand firm. Gradually, they will simply out-populate Israelis, and changing wider-world circumstances will redefine the situation in Palestine and Israel. Palestinians want dialogue and a fair deal. They're remarkably patient but they still need a sense of *progress*. So do many Israelis, living in a small, walled-in country with an army that's slowly losing its mojo and a government dominated by minority interests.

The Holy Land is a multi-ethnic, multifaith land and a fascinating place. Sanctity is elusive and faiths define it differently, but it's safe to say that ongoing conflict is not one of its characteristics. Positive change matters for the whole world – Israel and Palestine form a bottleneck in the world's process of change.

Security is developed by building up a nation's internal feelings of alrightness, community and integrity. It is built by cultivating collective happiness and creativity, giving people a sense of a positive, mutually-beneficial future. This is the *real* national interest, the guarantee of Israel's future.

5 Crossing the Threshold
travelling from Amman to Jericho

First, you catch a taxi to Tabar Boor, Amman's North Station. It's a big bus and taxi station buzzing with people and shared taxis that go to designated destinations, leaving when filled. To the King Hussein Bridge it costs five dinars – at least, on that day and with that taxi.

Off we went, fast-cruising along the freeways through Amman and out into the country – a dry, brown, upland landscape with houses and settlements dotted around, interspersed with trees and shrubby bushes. The road is bordered by farms, villages, agricultural institutes, stylish country clubs and sedate out-of-town estates owned by rich Middle Eastern tycoons set in a pleasant, wide-open upland landscape.

Then suddenly we cruised over a brow and started going down. Not just an ordinary incline which soon ends, but down, down, down, ears increasingly impacted. Amman is 700m (2,000ft) up and the Dead Sea valley is nearly 400m (1,200ft) below sea level, so it's a big drop of over 1,100m or 3,200ft. The landscape is hauntingly beautiful with amazing white-gold-brown sedimentary rock formations, some rounded, some jagged, and lunar, otherworldly in character.

Trucks laboured up the other side of the road, belching diesel fumes, but we sailed down the dramatically sweeping road as it hugged the side of a high slope, with hills to the left and a wide valley vista to the right. The guys in the car were elated, singing and chattering loudly. They looked at me to see whether I was getting uptight – after all, Jordanian driving is somewhat, shall we say, free-style – but I was smiling and didn't care, and if this was my last moment of life, there are worse ways to go! It was uplifting to the soul. Here we were in biblical territory, stark, beautiful, inspiring, Planet Earth in unearthly glory.

In due course, we saw the bottom of the Jordan valley, Earth's lowest place. It's green and agricultural on the Jordanian side, with trees, occasional pools and channels of open water, farm workers in the fields and horticultural tunnels for vegetable-growing. The guys were having a ball, singing, and the driver did dramatic overtaking manoeuvres as we careered through this vast grandeur – the top end of the tectonic African Rift Valley, a major rip in the ancient geo-continent of Pangaea. "Earth's greatest rift", my Palestinian geologist friend Fareed calls it, alluding also to the Israeli-Jordanian border that follows the River Jordan, a bristling border far more significant than most.

Eventually we reached the Jordanian crossing complex. Now, one thing about the Middle East is that there aren't all the organised signs and instructions we know of in the West – you have to follow your nose and hope for the best. The guys tumbled

out at one place and the driver indicated, with monosyllabic English and classic Arab hand-signals, "You stay". So I stayed while they nattered awhile. Then we were off to another compound, and I got out, dragging my bag into a building where other foreigners seemed to be gravitating, into a queue that appeared to be the right place to be. No, not a queue, a throng. But everyone was pleasant and patient.

I met a tall German traveller, thirtyish, and we started talking. He had overlanded from Germany through Romania and Turkey, Syria and Jordan, and was now heading into Israel to return home by air from Tel Aviv. Nice chap. Eventually they took our passports and disappeared with a huge pile of them. An American academic in the throng joked, "Hell is a place where Arabs are administrators".

The officials obviously operated with quite a bit of administrative discretion – rules and regulations exist in suitable profusion but, well, reality unfolds as it will, and head office is way back in Amman. The man leafed through your passport, handing it to someone else who took it away, and you were left wondering what would happen next. But a big wodge of passports eventually returned and names were called.

"Eh, Breeteesh, go get stamp for departure tax, five dinars, over there, sir". I bet he had at least six kids. Over to another counter. A lady in a colourful, modern veil doled out stamps in exchange for a five dinar note, and you took your stamp back to the man, eventually getting your passport back.

What next? The German and I went the only way that figured. Outside were some buses, but which one? A Japanese guy gave us a look and pointed. Bags in the stowage, and into the bus. Three dinars eighty – hmm, a bit steep for a short journey. Air conditioning – phew, a relief! The temperature outside was in the upper thirties. We waited and the Berliner and I talked about the Iron Curtain. He said that when you crossed it in Berlin they would put passports and papers on a long conveyor belt to the other side, and you trotted across the Iron Curtain, anxiously chasing your passport in fear that you might stop existing if you lost it.

Pictures of Palestine

In our case a modern bus was to carry us through no man's land. When full, it pulled out and drove through a series of seemingly pointless checkpoint barriers, then over the Jordan – not an impressive river, neither is its bridge an impressive bridge. The Allenby Bridge is one of those mythic names you hear when you're young, but it's not a bridge that lodges in your memory for very long. Yet this still felt like a major threshold to cross, more significant a border than many. Suddenly the signs were in Hebrew with Arabic below and the bus stopped at a checkpoint. Out we all climbed. Passports checked by a woman in military uniform, in a glass-fronted booth with a hard-working old air conditioner grinding away behind her, gun propped beside it, and a radio device and a bottle of water. Her posting was a lonely one. God, it's hot, now hitting forty.

Back in, start up. Another bridge, another barrier which eventually raised and then, suddenly, we were in the developed world, approaching a modern terminal surrounded with green, irrigated grass. Disconcertingly we had moved from the Middle East to the West in a few hundred metres.

Out of the bus, get the baggage, load it on conveyors, and it disappears. The Israeli soldiers watching over us were quite friendly, machine guns hanging languidly off shoulders. Emptying pockets for security, walking through the scanners, into another contraption with a computer voice that said "Stop", while I was weirdly puffed by jets of air, or something, for some purpose, and then came "Pass through the barrier" in an American techno-accent. Some invisible dude was presumably seeing through my clothes, checking for all the weapons in my underpants. Or perhaps I was being sprayed against diseases. Re-fill pockets. Into the building, and there were hundreds of people, mostly Palestinian, gaggled in queues before a line of high desks with army-uniformed women officials, parked behind thick glass screens.

It took a while for my German friend and I to realise we were in the wrong queue. A nice Palestinian lady pointed at a queue for foreign visitors, and we moved over to line up at a desk marked

Pictures of Palestine

'VIP' – we were presumably more important than Palestinians. But only just: we were nevertheless treated in what, to a European, was a mildly intimidating way.

We stood there for *four hours* – a back-breaking, mind-numbing wait. Israeli officials and soldiers can have a delightfully obstructive attitude, with no notion at all of 'customer experience'. In the queue next to ours, the official disappeared for half an hour, and a Canadian gentleman quite reasonably asked the remaining official when their own official would return. Diffidently, without raising her head from her paperwork, she said in an American accent, "That queue is no longer open. Go join the back of this one". The seventy-something and his wife looked wearily exasperated, realising they could do nothing except incur trouble if they complained, so they obeyed, having lost about ten places in the queue in the process.

The young female officials in army uniform took about twenty minutes with each person, asking questions, going away, coming back, tapping on the computer, asking more questions. Even the most innocuous travellers were intensely questioned. *How many times have you visited Israel? Why do you wish to enter? Are you visiting the Palestinian Territories? Why did you visit Syria? Where will you stay? What is the name of your father? Do you know anyone in Israel? Are they Jewish or Arab?* Other soldiers, all males, nonchalantly sat behind them watching, looking important, occasionally picking up the phone and yet more officials went in and out of noisy, banging doors.

Our fellow travellers stood there, some patient, some tired, others trying to suppress annoyance. I talked to two French women on a study year in Beirut, who wished to see Israel – they were beginning to have regrets, realising Lebanon is another of the wrong places to have been in Israelis' eyes. My German friend was looking a bit faint so I gave him a pastry I had bought in Amman. He had no shekels yet, so he saved my place and I went to procure two cans of iced coffee. We both revived.

Pictures of Palestine

Eventually my turn came. When the official looked up I smiled and said *Shalom*, giving her my passport. She leafed through it and the questions started up. I spun a story about having recently retired, taking a break in the Holy Land and writing a book about Christian holy places – hence my need to visit Bethlehem on the West Bank, as well as Jerusalem and Nazareth in 'Israel proper'. I implied I would stay a month or so, knowing I'd get a three-month visa, and rattled off names of Jews I knew. A long pause as she tapped on the computer, concentrating. I kept my cool and did my English gentleman-traveller act.

"Welcome to Israel", she eventually said, with a rather sweet smile. She seemed to enjoy saying that. Evidently I was not registered a suspect on the computer. Bang, down went the stamp on my passport. *Is that it?* It seemed I was through. I buried a smile of glee and said *Shalom* again. Most of the others in my queue had been given extra forms to fill in, leading to further queuing and processing – but I was free to go. How did I manage that?

Where next? I headed through a gap, eyeballed by bored soldiers, to another hall and another queue. Wait, show passport again, then into the baggage claim, where mountains of bags lay in chaotic groups. A small panic as, worn out, I couldn't find mine. Well, at least my baggage was unlikely to have been sent to Rio, Johannesburg or Phuket. Eventually I found it and staggered out of the building. My German friend was back there filling in extra forms – goodbye Dieter. Phew, out here the temperature was now in the mid-forties.

I sat down and took a break. *Relax, Palden, you're through!* What next? Buses, taxis, people going here and there, most buses and taxis heading for Jerusalem. Eventually I saw a Palestinian bus company sales window: *Shaheen Bus.*

"Bus to Beit Lahem?"

"No, you take bus to Jericho, then service to Beit Lahem. Fifteen shekels to Jericho." He tore off and handed me a ticket.

The bus was nearly full. I was the only foreigner, though some émigré Palestinians were on board, visiting home. Along the modern Israeli roads we went, following Jericho signs, finally turning off and arriving at a barrier. *Now entering Palestinian Authority Territory*, said a sign. *Israelis not allowed.* That's an Israeli, not a Palestinian sign – Israelis imposing *apartheid* on themselves. A few miles more, then another terminal, but we didn't have to get out.

A smartly-uniformed Palestine Authority official came on board, collected everyone's passports and disappeared into the building. For twenty minutes we sat in the bus, with air-conditioning noisily blasting away, then he returned. "Welcome to Palestine, here's your passport", he said to me with a smile, and I knew his smile was genuine – foreigners visiting the Palestinian Territories mean a lot to them and they don't come in floods.

Eventually we reached Jericho bus station. I bundled out into the heat, breathing in the thick, hot, Jordan valley air, and spontaneously started crying. *I'm back! At last I'm back!* I went down on my knees and put my forehead to the hot tarmac in the Muslim prayer style, gushing tears. A man came to me, helping me up. "You wilcome here, sir. Wilcome to Falastin."

I was welcome, and I felt it. I was so happy and relieved, my heart was fluttering. It had been a rather long four years.

6 The Back-roads of Palestine
arriving in Bethlehem

"Where you want go?" "Beit Lahem".
"Where you from?" "Britaniyya."
"Ah, my son, he in Leicester, doctor in hospital." I'm never sure whether to be happy or sad when they say things like this, but most Palestinians seem quite happy that at least someone in the family is chasing a future abroad. It's their family insurance policy.

I was the first to the yellow eight-seater VW service bus, so I would have to wait for more passengers to appear. That was fine – I wanted to assimilate being in Jericho again. Everyone was friendly.

If ever you come to Palestine, be ready to be overwhelmed with hospitality – it's quite moving and takes a while to get used to. It's not a front. People come up and shake your hand, saying "Wilcome, wilcome to Falastin", and they really mean it. They know it takes some resolve to get here.

I went off and found some Egyptian mango juice and Jericho springwater to guzzle. The dense Jordan valley heat was like an engulfing blanket but, being thin, I'm fine with that – it's chilly, damp British weather I have a problem with! I went over to some guys standing around talking. The usual friendly questions. *Where you from? What your name? Where you going? How many children you have? What you doing here?* They're often interested in my age, and eyebrows raise when I tell them – Palestinian men of my age often look older and more worn than I do.

41

Pictures of Palestine

I took photos of some of them – they seemed to love it. But some didn't want it, gesticulating 'No' with a quick wave of the finger, and I knew why. It's politics and security: they or their family have had trouble with the Israelis, or they supported Hamas or another faction, or they had a history, or their brother was in jail, or... Long ago I had been in similar straits and I know what it's like: it's not just that you want to avoid the gaze of the powers that be, but also that you don't want to keep reminding your friends or even yourself that, rightly or wrongly, you're toxic property.

Eventually the service taxi-van was full and we were off through the streets of Jericho, an ancient city with an 8,000 year history. We left the town, driving some miles up to the main Jerusalem highway and then turning right, following the road as it ascends through the Judean desert hills. It sweeps through the valleys, climbing up and up just to reach sea level, marked by a sign in Hebrew, Arabic and English. After making good progress, still uphill, we suddenly slowed down and pulled off near the Ma'ale Adumim interchange onto a bumpy, crowded road and into a scrappy Palestinian township near Al Azariya.

Pictures of Palestine

[Here's a little reading tip. An apostrophe (') in the middle of an Israeli or Arabic word signifies a 'glottal stop', a definite, clipped non-sound separating two syllables. Thus, *Ma'ale* is pronounced Ma-aleh and Modi'in is pronounced *Modi-een*.]

Ma'ale Adumim is one of the biggest Israeli West Bank settlements, a Jerusalem orbital town and an asset Israel is unlikely to abandon, whatever foreign politicians want. This new town and the roads servicing it, built on confiscated Palestinian land, split the West Bank into northern and southern halves, rendering Palestine territorially sub-functional as a nation.

But we were not going to Ma'ale Adumim. Instead, we hit a bumpy side-road which, for Palestinians, is a key trunk road linking the northern and southern West Bank. It weaves through a small town, then weaving along valleys and up and down the high hills, with sharp switchbacks, steep inclines and loads of traffic. In Britain we'd regard it as a back-country 'B' road, but actually it is 'Palestine Route One'. Nowadays it is being modernised but in 2009 the only sign of its trunk road status was the density of traffic.

Some of the areas it drives through are poor and dilapidated, the houses quite scrappy, the land stony and dry. Garbage, wrecks and piles of rubble are heaped here and there – an alienated landscape where the locals have lost their care and pride. They're probably rural refugees, thrown off land the Israelis have taken, such as at Ma'ale Adumim. It's one of the tragic aspects of this country. But then, many Palestinians harbour little hope, so they're unlikely to invest in longterm improvements. They half-expect the Israelis to come in some day, wreck everything again or drive them out, and they do have reason to anticipate that.

Yet there are some pretty nice houses along the road too, in other locations. Palestinians who are go-getters or beneficiaries of the PA or foreign agencies take great pride in their new-builds, many of which have a fine vista and attractive courtyards with flowering trees and bushes. It's as if their optimism compensates for their others' lack of it. It also reveals an emerging class divide between those who benefit from foreign subsidies and advantages and those who do not. Palestine has its haves and have-nots and they nowadays live in quite distinct economies.

The road is exciting to travel as it climbs up steep hills and tips into deep valleys, weaving through an impressive limestone upland landscape, passing through hilltop villages with prominent mosques and affording views stretching many miles. Yes, this is a trunk road – but it's heartbreaking too. Privileged Israelis drive along their fast, wide highways while Palestinians have to heave up, down and around on side-roads like this: transportation *apartheid*. Although the West Bank is occupied by Israel, its cars have different number-plates from those of Israelis, conferring different driving and access rights. Go up the wrong road and you could, on a bad day, experience a sudden hail of bullets at worst, or interrogation at best.

We passed through only one checkpoint, which today was open. The Israeli soldiers leaned against their booths and bollards, talking to each other and idly gazing at passing traffic. Poor guys – what a job. There they stood sweating, posted in an unfriendly spot next to

a Palestinian hilltop village, perpetually on guard against a foe who nowadays rarely materialises and might hardly exist.

In the distance I could see the Herodeon, near Bethlehem, a prominent conical hill and ancient site going back millennia. It looks like a volcano but it was shape-enhanced in ancient times and contains, allegedly, the tomb of Herod the king. Naturally, we didn't head straight toward it – our route was still sinuous and tortuous. After another twenty minutes we pulled into Beit Sahour – Shepherds' Fields, referring to the Christmas story – near Bethlehem. The family that made up most of the passengers in the bus was dropped off right outside their gate. The remaining woman asked me, on behalf of the driver, where I wanted to be dropped. I decided to go to Manger Square in central Bethlehem to catch some food, take a rest and ascertain where Ibrahim Issa was to be found.

There I bundled out of the bus dragging my wheeled bag, my precious technology bag over my shoulder. Containing a netbook computer, camera and lenses, digital sound recording equipment, DVD and card readers, cables, plugs and adaptors, with room for travel papers, passport and a bottle of water, this technology bag is neat – but rather a wrench on the shoulder muscles.

The Christian taxi-drivers near the Nativity Church, seeing a Westerner – who of course must be rich – started hollering at me for my custom. You learn how to gesticulate 'No'. One bright young driver with a pleasant face got my attention, though I still said no to him. I wanted to sit down and have something to eat. He shepherded me to a nearby café and within seconds a pitta stuffed with salad and falafel was set in front of me, along with fresh carrot juice. What a relief! All the taxi-drivers stood round asking questions and smiling, all very amiable once they'd realised I was no source of business for them right now.

I rang Ibrahim, but no answer. Did I have the right number? Hmmm, what next? Leaving my bag at the café, I went wandering. As I returned, the young taxi-driver signalled me: "I help you. What your name?"

Pictures of Palestine

He took me to the Hope Flowers School at the far end of Al Khader, west of Bethlehem, but it was locked and deserted. On the way I noticed that the town was in visibly better shape than on my last trip in 2005, just after the second *intifada*, during which the Israelis had wrecked Bethlehem and still then staged periodic incursions and searches. But now the separation wall had been built and Bethlehem, imprisoned behind it, was safer and more relaxed. The security wall protects Palestinians from Israelis as well as vice versa. This relaxation of tension was visible on the streets. Another sign of progress was the condition of the trees in the central reservation of the Hebron road leading to Al Khader.

These trees, planted in 2005 by the Earth Stewards, were all intact and growing! I had joined them – mostly Dutch, German and Austrian green activists – in a tree-planting project organised by Hope Flowers. Ibrahim had known the Earth Stewards when he lived in Holland in the 1990s and he had organised PeaceTrees as a joint project with them in Bethlehem, not just as an ecological but also as a social empowerment project. The trees' continued existence showed that something had worked – the locals had got the message.

During the *intifada* people had lost hope. It had followed a period in the 1990s when peace and progress came close and then ebbed away, prompting the uprising, a mass expression of sheer frustration. Israeli measures taken against Palestinians were terrible and Bethlehem had been an epicentre of conflict – remember the shoot-out at the Church of the Nativity in 2002? By 2005, when the *intifada* had subsided, the locals needed jump-starting with initiatives to help them improve their lives and encourage them to invest energy in the future. The regular experience of seeing houses demolished, parts of town wrecked, buildings shelled and people carted off had given Bethlehemites a feeling of futility and pointlessness.

By planting a large number of trees in a very visible place – the main road's central reservation – we caused mild fascination at first, followed by interest and questions. Then people joined in, then energy and enthusiasm grew. We wrapped up the project by saying,

Manger Square and the Church of the Nativity

"If you don't look after these trees, they will die, so it's up to you" –
and we left. The trees survived: someone had made sure they were
watered and cared for. PeaceTrees had worked.

As the young taxi-driver and I returned to central Bethlehem, he
told me that he was a student of accountancy in Hebron and drove
his uncle's taxi to pay his way. He wanted to be my friend and I
promised I would find him again. Subsequently I had a number of
lifts with him, and only half the time did he charge me. He dropped
me off and I headed up to Manger Square, standing there awhile,
taking it all in. A wide, large square, milling with people.

A man approached, asking in quite good English whether he
could help me. Adnan took me to his shop near the square, where
he sold souvenirs – olive-wood religious objects, Arabic dresses,
Bedouin rugs, decorative inlaid boxes and allsorts. Some of the
woodwork was exquisitely carved and the rugs and clothing came
in lovely colours, all with a very hand-made feel to them. Mint tea
appeared and people came and went as we talked. Adnan discovered

Pictures of Palestine

I was a webmaster and asked if I would help him make a website – I said I would consider it. He rang a friend who knew Ibrahim – an answer would come soon about where to find him.

I got out my computer and skyped my cousin, then my son and then my ladyfriend back in England, to tell them I'd got here. I wanted to share it with them. A small crowd gathered round, goggling at this visitor's neat technology, and they said hello on Skype, all very thrilled. My son just said, "Cool", and carried on tapping on his computer. Then he looked up and suddenly saw several faces looking at him through the screen.

"Who're they?"

"I've finally got to Bethlehem, and these are some of the kids here".

"Cool", he repeated, in his perpetually unfazed way, still tapping keys.

My ladyfriend was dumbstruck at talking live to some real Palestinians. Palestinians are people you hear about on the news, you don't expect to talk personally with them on Skype. Everyone helloed, and she helloed back. While I was talking to her, the calling to prayers started up – really loud, since we were right next to the Omar Mosque. She was visibly moved at the sound, as it hit her that I was *really there*. She and my cousin were serving as 'ground control' back in England, and it was fitting to share with them my first taste of returning.

Eventually the grapevine worked and Ibrahim Issa came to fetch me. I'd last seen him five months earlier in England during one of his speaking tours. He had looked tired, not really wanting to stand on stages giving speeches, and I was concerned about him, wondering whether he was burning out. But today he was his sprightly self, at ease, smiling. He's rotund, like a cuddly bear, with a character-filled face and a bright countenance.

I feel brotherly toward him, as if we had made some mutual contract way back in the mists of time, yet I'm old enough to be his father. We hugged in the middle of the street – much to the interest of onlookers – and looked at each other for a long moment. I knew he felt some relief that I was back and had probably wondered whether he would see me here again. Foreigners come and go, saying they will return, but only a few reappear.

Hope Flowers had started as a kindergarten in 1984 and by the late 1990s it was a school with 500 pupils. It shrank after 2000 during the second *intifada*, as the Palestinian economy tanked and hardship set in, but now the school is growing again and a community development centre was started in 2004. I'd been working with the school from Britain, running its website, writing and editing grant proposals, newsletters and outreach material. Now, one aim of my trip to the school was to re-work the website, then perhaps to edit some teacher-training manuals, possibly even help Ibrahim start writing a book about peace education. That was the idea.

The story of the Issa family and Hope Flowers is poignant. Ibrahim's father Hussein, an advocate of non-violence, found himself in a dilemma some years ago when Ibrahim narrowly escaped paralysis, shot through the back by Israeli soldiers. Later, Ibrahim saw Palestinian radicals accuse his father of treason because of his commitment to reconciliation. The family was under attack from both Israeli troops and Palestinian radicals. Ibrahim knew the situation was complex but, to quote him, "The most painful thing for me as a child was that I couldn't recognise the difference between a peace activist and a collaborator – it took years until I did. Palestinian radical groups also couldn't recognise it. When I grew up I started to see the difference". But some Palestinian radicals and Israeli Zionists still don't see that difference, and this makes life risky for people who work for reconciliation.

In 1991 Ibrahim moved to Holland to get out of harm's way. He studied engineering, got a job and became a permanent émigré. He attended courses on ecology, non-violence, community-building and psychotherapy too, mixing with interesting people, some of whom later came to do stints as volunteers at the school in Palestine. Then his father died unexpectedly in 1999 and Ibrahim was asked to return. This involved leaving a secure, promising Dutch life to jump back into the Palestinian frying pan, taking on a burden most sane people would turn down flat. I greatly admire his steadfastness.

Returning to Bethlehem in the midst of the second *intifada*, Ibrahim joined his sister Ghada and his mother Hind in running the school. Later another sister, Hala, a teacher, joined them, as did Ibrahim's new wife, Maram, once a kid at the kindergarten. They ran the school with a remarkable team of teachers, managers and supporters. It felt right to work with these people – I like them all very much.

Now Ibrahim and I went to a café, had a drink and munched nuts, smoking apple-flavoured hubble-bubble from an ornate water pipe. We discussed what I would do during my three months' stay. There was certainly a lot to be done and three months might not be long enough.

Ibrahim told me of difficulties he currently had with a faction in the Palestine Authority (PA). It was the product of an awkward public debate concerning the value of negotiating with the Israelis. Ibrahim, a committed peacemaker and bridge-builder who had had regular contact with peace-oriented Israelis, was under suspicion as a collaborator, and this was complex. The PA, seeking to establish control over an ungoverned non-country, had applied a mixture of Western regulations and Arabic bureaucracy, with not a few personal fiefdom issues thrown in, making life difficult for ordinary people. A peacemaker in a conflict-polarised society is susceptible to accusations of collaboration.

The discussion in Palestine about how to relate to the Israelis was heated and ongoing. Palestinians had bent over backwards to comply with international agreements as part of the 1990s peace process, and yet in Palestinians' perception the Israelis hadn't budged an inch on crucial issues such as settlement-building, land-seizures, Jerusalem or refugees. The result had been continued losses for Palestinians and a growing number of them were now convinced that negotiation and accommodation were pointless, even though very few wanted any return to conflict. Negotiation had been worth trying in the 1990s, but it had not delivered. It's a tragic predicament: if you neither want to negotiate nor to fight, what do you do?

Hope Flowers had been teaching the kids Hebrew to help them understand the Israeli mindset. When the kids were older, this would help them deal with Israeli people and officials. The school set out to help the kids understand the perspectives of the very people who had killed or jailed their own fathers, uncles and relatives. This was not a matter of agreeing with or sucking up to the Israelis, as some suspected. It was a matter of following the old military adage, 'know your enemy'. It was a key issue in preparing Palestinian children for a time when the nightmare of conflict ends – which it shall and must do one day. But in 2009 that day was receding and there was simmering frustration in the air.

Some Palestinian officials didn't like what the school was doing and didn't want Palestinians having connections with Israelis. Ibrahim, who had learned to be patient with Israeli arbitrariness and obstructionism, even having been arrested by them for allegedly harbouring terrorists, understood this viewpoint well. But as an educationalist and peace-builder, he stood up for dialogue with people on the other side just as his father had done.

Westerners, with a tendency to see things in black-and-white terms, oversimplify the intricacies of this situation, failing to understand such sharp dilemmas. "Why don't Israelis and Palestinians just make peace?" Well, as Rabbi Lerner, a Jewish-American thinker, once pointed out, both sides suffer from PTSD, post-traumatic stress disorder – they're super-touchy, super-reactive and suspicious – and untangling this mess isn't as simple as outsiders would like it to be.

It had taken me some 20 years to understand the intricacies of the Israel-Palestine situation, and only visiting the place had brought better comprehension. I started as a peacemaker working on both sides, with the best of neutral intents, but found myself gravitating to the Palestinian cause. I was not turning against Israel, but I felt that they shot themselves in the foot by the hostile attitude they took toward Palestinians. I work where I can most assist, and while Palestinians seemed to appreciate my input many Israelis didn't seem to think there was a need for me to be there. So I ended up working with Hope Flowers.

That's also why I had sobbed from the soul when I arrived in Jericho earlier that day – there was something personal and emotional about all this. As a British dissident, I had had nonsensical and painful experiences that would shock many people, so I could empathise with the Palestinians' dilemma. I saw Ibrahim's dilemma too – that of a peace-bringer whose work is regularly screwed up, not just by Israelis but also by the double-standards of Westerners and the militancy of some Palestinians.

Perhaps Palestinians embody something that exists within many of us when we are repeatedly let down by forces beyond our control, when Murphy's Law applies itself over and over, or when the narrow interests of the powerful few prevail incessantly over the needs of the majority. It's a futile feeling that, whatever one does, nothing will really progress. This kind of thing happens everywhere but, in Palestine, people have internalised it and adapted to it more than is healthy for them.

I stayed at the Issa family's place that night and next day Ibrahim took me to the school, where I was to stay in the volunteers' accommodation on the top floor. Back again – and now to work.

7 Palestine's Situation
the lowdown on a country that isn't

Let me tell you more about Palestine.

Palestine feels like a distinct country when you're there, but it isn't one. It might one day gain independence, in connection with a 'two-state solution' with Israel, but only some people believe this will happen. Personally, I'd give it a 30% chance – sounds pessimistic, but the two-state idea is more a foreign idea than a local likelihood. Some believe in a one-state solution, since Israel is unlikely to give up anything that it considers important, though it might one day start to treat Palestinians better. Pessimists believe that the current unresolved situation could go on forever – and they have a case because some Israelis see dogged non-resolution as the main solution, since it allows them free rein to do what they want. There are other possibilities, but these are the main ones.

The much-vaunted two-state solution won't work because the current Palestinian-ruled areas which would make up a state are too small. They're not joined together, with no external border and the Israelis are very unlikely to allow a change to this. Gaza has a border with Egypt, but even this has been subjected to hyper-control, often closed or restricted.

Israel repeatedly disputes the amount of territory Palestine should have – in particular the 'eternal' Palestinian capital, East Jerusalem. It wants to retain overall control, denying Palestinians full sovereignty. So a viable state is not very visible as a possibility. To make it viable would require Israel to give up more land and control than it is willing to release – the pattern of its settlements, land-appropriations, road-building and the separation wall in the West Bank demonstrates this unwillingness in very concrete terms. But then, in a changing world, all change is possible.

The administrative capital of OPT, the Occupied Palestinian Territories, is Ramallah, north of Jerusalem. Not an ancient city (it was founded in the 1600s), during the 1990s it grew as the capital of the Palestine Authority (PA), the governing body for OPT.

There's a recent complication because, since 2007, Gaza and the West Bank have lived under separate governments. Ramallah is now the capital of the West Bank only. Also, since 2005, Gaza has not been Israeli-occupied, though it has been blockaded, under siege. Both Gaza and the West Bank are still called 'OPT' in international diplomatic circles. Palestinian jurisdiction in the West Bank is complex: Palestinian-majority areas are classified into Areas A, B and C, giving them different amounts of control – about which, more later.

The West Bank is split into parts, called by some observers 'bantustans', harking back to *apartheid* times in South Africa. These are centred around bigger Palestinian towns, themselves separated from each other by Israeli settlements and settler roads, occupied land and separation walls. West Bank towns are thus like islands, capable of being put under military control by the Israelis at any time. Water, fuel, communications and supplies can all be controlled if the Israelis so choose. Road closures and checkpoints have eased since 2008, following international pressure, but the infrastructure of control remains. The changing political climate in Israel impacts hard on Palestinians and their daily lives, and so the situation is constantly variable.

Getting from the south to the north of the West Bank is a longer journey than it ought to be. To avoid Israeli territory and checkpoints one must drive along the circuitous switchback mountain road described in chapter six. It is indeed scenic, but it isn't a 'Route 1' at all, just a joined up series of desert and mountain roads. Its great virtue is that there are few active checkpoints on it, giving relatively free movement.

Pictures of Palestine

In Gaza, access and trade are controlled by Israel and Egypt, but at least there are definite borders and the Gaza government has a more clearly-defined jurisdiction than that of the West Bank. Gaza and the West Bank are not even joined by road; although a link road was proposed by the UN in 1948 and in subsequent treaty proposals, it has never been permitted by Israel.

There is *Palestine*, the state which isn't, and there are the *Palestinians*. Roughly ten million Palestinians, in fact. About 30% of them live in places where their ancestors have lived for generations and the rest are either internal refugees living in the West Bank and Gaza or they are exiles living in other countries.

About 30% of the refugees live in refugee camps in the West Bank, Gaza or neighbouring Lebanon, Syria and Jordan. As a result of population growth, the refugee population has increased since the two main periods of exodus in 1948 and 1967 – from 711,000 in 1950 to four million in 2002. Not all are classified by the UN as refugees. During the 1948 exodus when Israel was established, 750,000 out of 900,000 Palestinians fled or were ethnically cleansed. During the 1967 exodus when Israel occupied Gaza and the West Bank, another 300,000 refugees fled or were 'transferred' abroad. Many Israelis sincerely believe they just chose to leave, or they never even lived in Palestine and UN policy tends to reflect this belief.

About half of the total Palestinian population lives abroad, most of them leading ordinary lives rather than languishing in refugee camps. They live in Jordan (2.7m), Syria (600,000), Chile (500,000), Lebanon (400,000), Saudi Arabia (250,000), the Gulf

Emirates (200,000), other Middle Eastern states (200,000), Europe (250,000) and North America (220,000).

The other half live in the area now comprising Israel and Palestine, often called 'historic Palestine'. Of these, about 2.3m live in the West Bank, 1.4m in Gaza and 1.3m in the state of Israel – five million in all. Palestinians living in Israel proper, labelled 'Israeli Arabs', make up 20% of the population of Israel. The word 'Palestinians' tends to apply more to people living in the West Bank and Gaza. If the total population of both Israel and Palestine were added together, Israelis would slightly outnumber Palestinians, but the Palestinian population is growing faster. There is a demographic problem ahead for Israelis, who will gradually become a minority. This troubles them, but mostly they don't discuss it.

Up to WW1, the whole of the Middle East was part of the Turkish Ottoman empire. Then it was divided up under French and British rule from around 1920. France took what became Lebanon and Syria and Britain took Palestine, Transjordan, Iraq, Kuwait and Egypt, by mandate of the League of Nations.

In 1948 the British gave up their mandate over Palestine and it was partitioned by the UN into a proposed Palestine and Israel. The British had pursued confused, divisive and contradictory policies in 'Mandate Palestine', contributing greatly to the mess that followed. In the ensuing war of 1948 the Israelis took more land than the UN allocated, and kept it. An independent Palestine never came to pass – it was occupied by Jordan (in the West Bank) and Egypt (in Gaza), mainly to stop further Israeli expansion. So Palestine never became a state.

Twenty years later, in the 1967 Six Day War, Israel occupied the Palestinian Territories, expelling Jordan and Egypt, thus controlling the whole of former Mandate Palestine. For twenty further years the Palestinian people lived under direct occupation and Israelis started colonising the West Bank and Gaza, building settlements and military bases there – though they left Gaza in 2005 to concentrate on the West Bank.

Pictures of Palestine

After the first Palestinian uprising or *intifada* from 1987 to 1993, the Oslo Accords of 1993-94 formalised the shape of Palestinian-majority areas to be governed by the Palestine Authority in Ramallah. The PA was founded out of the former PLO (Palestine Liberation Organisation) in 1988 – a fighting movement that became a government, of sorts.

These Palestinian-run areas were to be the start of a larger, incremental handover of land to the Palestinians which was to form a new Palestinian state by 2001 or soon after. That was the plan. But they were islands surrounded by Israeli settlements and settler roads, islands easily isolated and controlled by the Israelis. The negotiation and handover process ground to a halt in the late 1990s and no recognised Palestinian state was declared.

During the first *intifada*, Yasser Arafat's PLO symbolically declared an independent Palestine in 1988, and a form of recognition of Palestine as a state-to-be was built into the Oslo Accords. But this was a provisional independence, contingent on Israel's own decisions. The PA doesn't have sovereignty since its lands and many of its affairs are controlled by Israel as a military occupying power. Some sceptics regard the PA as an overgrown municipality, in charge of policing, social and some economic issues only, handling things the Israelis don't want to take responsibility for, and subsidised from abroad so that other countries can avoid fulfilling their international obligations to bear down on Israel to fulfil its promises.

The signing of the Oslo Accords was supposed to bring sovereign independence within a decade or so. The lack of progress, plus continued Israeli land-seizures, settlement building, roadblocks, checkpoints and military control gave rise to the second *intifada* of 2000-04. The building of the separation wall was started by Israel, preventing contact between Palestinians and Israelis – its rationale was to stop terrorists getting into Israeli territory, but really it created an Israeli-determined concrete and barbed-wire border which would lay down permanent 'facts on the ground'. The matter of independence remains unresolved today – Palestine is a *de facto* nation without legal and political status.

Pictures of Palestine

Palestinian national unity was complicated by the civil conflict in 2007 between Fateh (a nationalist, secular party) and Hamas (an Islamic social reform party). This followed an election in 2006 when, to everyone's surprise, Hamas gained 60% of the vote, to become the governing party of the Palestine Authority. The result was accepted by neither Israel nor the international community – then dominated by the Americans – since Hamas was deemed a terrorist organisation. An economic blockade was enforced on Palestine by Israel and the West, aiming to squeeze Hamas out of office. Development grants, projects and subsidies were withdrawn, causing great hardship to ordinary Palestinians, though these funds were later diverted to Fateh to be disbursed by them.

Political affairs were manoeuvred to shift powers from the Hamas government to the Fateh president. Hamas parliamentarians were arrested and the organisation was hobbled. This was a foreign-inspired *coup d'état* aiming to divide Palestinians, and generally it succeeded. Tensions escalated between Hamas and Fateh and when, in 2007, Fateh vied for military dominance of Gaza, Hamas took control there, whereupon Fateh took control of the West Bank. Gaza and the West Bank were thus no longer united. This situation persists today, though since the Arab revolutions of early 2011, young Palestinians have been agitating for reunification.

Jurisdiction over Palestinian-majority territory in the West Bank is complicated. Under the Oslo Accords, three areas of influence were established: Area A (the main West Bank cities except East Jerusalem), with complete Palestinian control; Area B (mainly urban hinterlands) with Palestinian control and Israeli military precedence; and Area C, with complete Israeli control of Palestinian-majority land. All conveniently split up into little areas.

So now Palestinians exist within these tangled webs. They have limited choice in the matter but they're also tired of fighting. They just want to get on with their lives and yet they can do so only on a day-by-day basis. That's the reality of Palestine.

8 Hark, Your Majesty

amongst all this,
Hope Flowers

Hope Flowers School stands atop a hill, an L-shaped, four-storey concrete building constructed in the 1990s. Here in the West Bank highlands, strong winds occasionally blow in from the desert and when the school is empty at night, there's an eerie whistling and whining as the winds howl through the gaps and open windows.

But when the building is alive with kids, teachers and staff, there's a different spirit – a feeling of vibrancy, the hullabaloo of a busy school. Not just any school, but one where something special is happening. To a visitor it's very noticeable. To the regular school users, it's just another day unfolding in the normal way.

A few years earlier, Pam Perry and I had applied to the UK Foreign Office for a grant to support a course training teachers from other schools around the West Bank. They were to learn and implement in their own schools the trauma-recovery methods used at Hope Flowers. The application failed as the UK government decided, during the time we were applying, to divert aid funds from education to security and the media.

So I wrote to another department in the Foreign Office simply requesting that they observe Hope Flowers' progress, suggesting that the school demonstrated a key approach to conflict prevention. Now, a few years later, I wrote again to jog their memories, and what I wrote sums up what Hope Flowers is all about.

Pictures of Palestine

I'm a Brit doing voluntary work out here with the school. They rely on international funding and they've reached a stage where their educational and conflict-prevention work is increasing in its global significance. I'm here not just to help people in Bethlehem but also because, I believe, Hope Flowers holds some ace cards regarding the rebuilding of societies and dealing with the social causes of conflict worldwide.

The school started as a kindergarten in 1984, becoming a secondary school by 1994, in Oslo days. Then, in 2004, after the second intifada, they started an adult-oriented Centre for Education and Community Development. The centre does teacher training, professional training

Pictures of Palestine

for people working with the effects of conflict, empowerment courses for disadvantaged women and youth and micro-business training. With women's empowerment, they do personal counselling and psychological groupwork, they help them develop cooperative businesses, teach them computer use and business practice and help them get to a level where they can take charge of their lives. This indicates the all-round approach Hope Flowers takes.

The school has over the years developed tried-and-tested ways of dealing with the effects of trauma and the learning difficulties associated with it. As well as providing normal curriculum-based education, it trains children in managing tricky situations in their lives, in democratic practice (discussion, meetings, voting, self-expression) and human rights (good behaviour, negotiating skills, making something of one's life). It trains teachers to deal with their own stress and burn-out too, and to handle wider social and educational problems arising from conflict and hardship.

The school started out in the 1980s with Muslim, Christian and Jewish children. Most Christians have emigrated and the Jews were withdrawn by Israeli government decree and as a result of building the separation wall, blocking their access to the school. The school teaches spirituality and human values more than religious traditions – it highlights what unites rather than what divides people of faith.

The school has in recent years been engaged by UNRWA, the UN Palestine agency, to train teachers from their West Bank schools. Teacher training is a growing priority. In due course we shall compile training manuals for export to other conflict zones.

The school is a low-budget entity, and keeping things going is always a challenge. The teachers and staff, remarkable people, pull off miracles on a shoestring. The school carries on despite everything, and many good outcomes are achieved.

As a volunteer, I work here because I respect the school's integrity, dedication, methods and philosophy. I see the results in the children and their families and in the adults helped by the centre. It's enough to gladden the heart of anyone with a feeling for humanity, a sense of history and of concern for the future.

Pictures of Palestine

In most conflicts, shorter-lived than the Palestinian conflict, people forget what they have learned when peace comes. Not so here, since peace remains elusive: the knowledge and experience these people have accumulated, pulled by a genuine need to solve serious problems in their own backyard, is invaluable to the world. That's why Hope Flowers is worth watching.

That was what I wrote. As a veteran in peace and community-building, I see Palestine as an unwitting incubator of new possibilities. Hope Flowers is a centre of excellence in social reconstruction and the healing of social nightmares.

Pictures of Palestine

We might believe that the biggest challenges of the future are climate change, environmental degradation and economics, and I agree, but we won't get far with these unless humanity goes through a fundamental social change. The cessation of conflict is a key ingredient in meeting these challenges since international cooperation is much needed, and wars create too much destruction, hurt and waste, placing necessary global developments on hold.

As long as violence and devastation are permitted to continue by not being stopped, the saving of species, ecosystems and humanity are condemned to the sidelines. War prevents too many positive things from happening. If, by the end of the 21st century, humanity has a smile on its face and nature is on the mend, this will have arisen because we learned to cooperate, we made peace – or at least we agreed to differ in a peaceful way.

A few vital clues to this cooperative approach are to be found in the benighted land of Palestine and that little town of Bethlehem, a place that billions of people know of but few nowadays visit. Throughout history, in most walled towns the walls were built by the inhabitants to keep others out, but the walls around this town were built by others to keep its people in.

Yet the tragic payoff arising from this situation is that it keeps conflict-prevention knowhow alive and developing at places such as Hope Flowers. This is one of the cruel ironies that face Palestine and Israel today.

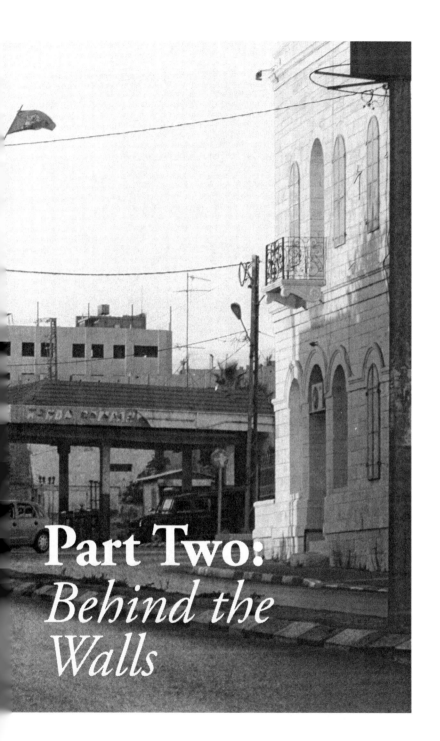

Part Two:
*Behind the
Walls*

9 All Along the Watchtower
a busy day in Bethlehem

I was walking along the Hebron Road into Bethlehem under the hot sun, taking the occasional picture, mainly of architecture, and I heard hollering behind me. Two guys were chasing me! You can always tell PA men – they have a clean-shaven, tight, smart, short-haired look. They hauled me into the Security Ministry compound, which I had just unwittingly passed, and into what clearly was the head honcho's office.

Seven men surrounded me, stern but decent, on alert. Another two outside the door pointed sub-machine guns at me, though not too convincingly. *Ah, I seem to be in a situation.* The usual questions – name, country, where I'm staying, why I'm here – and they examined my passport closely. Then came questions about what I had been doing out there in the street. Actually I had been photographing a lovely arch at the entrance to a mosque.

But before we go further, let me explain the background to their anxiety. The security guys in the PA are important not only because the PA was born out of a fighting organisation, the PLO, but also because, in the peace process of the 1990s, security, law and order were seen as key elements in Palestinian state-building, and there was a lot of money pumped into it from abroad. So they are accountable not just to the PA but also to foreigners.

A key requirement in the 1990s Oslo Accords was that the PA should gain control of wayward terrorist elements, particularly to stop suicide attacks on Israelis. This went slowly because it was difficult. Palestinian fighters were an independent lot, uninterested in being controlled by a single command since this could then be shut down or undermined by the Israelis. The PA also needed to gain the consent and acquiescence of the Palestinian people, who had a tactical aversion to centralising the resistance.

It was a touchy matter. Yasser Arafat, leading the PA at the time, had himself been a dedicated fighter who refused to accept foreign powers leaning on him and spouting catchphrases like 'the rule of law', a notion which they applied differently to themselves than to the freedom fighters they frequently called terrorists. In the Middle East one quickly discovers that Israel and the West are far more violent and destructive than Muslims, and that Western harping about peace is thoroughly hypocritical since much of the conflict in the Muslim world has both its roots and its arms sources in the West.

In the late 1990s the Israelis made a big fuss about Palestinian tardiness in dealing with 'terrorists', thereby conveniently concealing their failure to fulfil their own side of the Oslo agreements, such as ending settlement building and easing their hypercontrol of Palestinians' lives. Israel gained international sympathy thanks to the blanket disapproval of terrorism going on at the time. Also, until the 2006 war against Hezbollah, which devastated Lebanon, the Israelis generally hoovered up most of the available international sympathy by having better PR, lobbying and diplomatic leverage than others. The distinction between freedom fighters and terrorists was fuzzied in the late 1990s by a general suspicion of anyone Muslim perceived to be anti-Western.

After the second *intifada* starting in 2000 and following Arafat's death in 2004, the PA was pressured into getting a grip on Palestinian fighters. The Americans and British gave training, equipment and arms to support these fighters' incorporation under a central command and to build the necessary security structures to satisfy the Israelis. But the Israelis are rarely satisfied, often raising the bar to keep the heat off themselves and make the Palestinians look inadequate and uncooperative.

Pictures of Palestine

The PA gave respectable, well-paid security jobs to former fighters, to pacify them. Advised by the American General Dayton, they also imported exiled Palestinian security men who would have less emotional connection with people on the West Bank, having been born and raised abroad. As a result, Palestine now crawls with armed men in a variety of smart uniforms, busy taming Palestinians and keeping the peace. These men are forbidden from resisting the Israelis. Their wings are clipped, and they hate people knowing that.

Another big issue for the security men is informers and collaborators working for the Israelis and they clearly suspected that I might be some sort of spy. So I showed them the pictures in my camera and talked with my usual reassuring, relaxed, friendly tone. Most photos were of children and street scenes and the men seemed to decide that I was not only harmless but also rather an interesting chap and a solid Palestine friend. They quickly recognise whether or not you understand and support their people.

Their dilemma is genuine because Palestine is just two notches below a war footing and they do have a genuine problem with informants and spies. The Israelis offer decent rewards to hard-up Palestinians in return for useful information or tasks carried out. If you're in trouble with them, one way to escape jail or death is to become an informer. This is how the IDF (Israel Defence Force) targets its missiles and assassinations: all they need is a Palestinian in place with a specially-fixed mobile phone, and a missile can be targeted accurately from an Apache helicopter. If twelve people are killed in the process, well, that's collateral damage, ends justify means and these terrible terrorists must be destroyed at all costs. The Israeli secret service appeals to the despair of Palestinians in trouble, using bribery and reprieves to get very useful results. Palestinians hate the penetration that Mossad, Shin Bet and IDF achieve through informers.

The officer in charge of my questioning clearly didn't want me getting too friendly with his men and quickly reasserted his authority. His solution was to put me back on the street – and fast. Good. Mission accomplished.

Pictures of Palestine

I set off again, eventually reaching Bab al-Zqaq (pronounced *Babiskak*), a crossroad where the Beit Jala road crosses the Hebron road. I headed uphill to a taxi-clogged junction they call Cinema then wandered down Al-Faraheih Street, which led through the Old Town toward Manger Square, catching shots of people in this busy shopping street.

Palestinian streets are wonderful for photography since people are full of character and expression, with a rich variety of dress, manner and type. There are plenty of conversations and human antics to home in on through a telephoto discreetly aimed from a distance. I placed myself in corners and doorways, waiting for good shots to appear in the street. But inevitably I was spotted by perceptive boys who wanted to examine my camera or get in front of the lens, waving arms and making faces – it's a photographer's occupational hazard here.

One thing I couldn't photograph was smells. There is no rain in summer, so aromas build up in the dry heat – the fine fragrances of Arabic perfume, bundles of herbs sold by old ladies who transport them into town on the back of a donkey, the honking stench of

rubbish cooking in metal skips in the afternoon heat, the smell of meat at the busy market halfway down Al-Faraheih Street. They all add an olfactory timbre to the already colourful Old Town environment, where shops spill out their wares onto the street, religiously taken out and back by the shopkeepers every day. Some Israelis see streets like these as the dangerous haunt of terrorists but, unlike Israeli streets, they are free of visible weaponry. Except perhaps for the claws of scraggy street cats.

I ended up sitting and talking with John, a Christian shop-owner, and his friends down near Manger Square. It started as a good conversation but steadily got stuck in a circuit of despond as they talked about conditions in Bethlehem. There's a mental loop where hardship justifies despair and despair tends not to help facing hardship. I butted in to mention my father, at the time 92 years old, who, around 1940, had lived in a time in Britain when many believed that 'the only good German is a dead German'. Yet, by the 1980s he happily drove a Volkswagen and drank German wines. My point was that things change.

I mentioned how Europe started becoming a union of nations just seven years after WW2, and how the EU was founded out of a profound resolve to avoid further war in Europe. Someday, something like this will happen in Palestine too. Peace and mutual tolerance between Israelis and Palestinians currently looks like a pipedream but things will change. It's just a matter of when and how. There was some nodding and brightening up over this. It made me aware that people can be so sunk in the drudgerous facts of their reality that gaining detached perspective becomes very difficult. Holidays and foreign travel, which might give some relief and broaden horizons, are not available options to most Palestinians.

The conversation moved on to the Middle East peace process, such as it was. It was agreed that it was futile – the possibility of success in negotiations had evaporated in the 1990s in these people's view. The conversation stopped there, since my friends could see nothing positive to replace the peace process. Neither negotiation

71

nor fighting had achieved results – so what next? One problem here is that people get stuck in a feeling that what's been happening in recent decades is the only reality which *can* happen. Yet, globally, a bigger agenda and a new reality is dawning, and I raised this.

It concerns the relative fall of the West and the rise of the Rest (Palestine with it). The West has lost much of its purpose and direction, but the Rest have a clear agenda: things just have to get better. That's a motivator, a driver of change. It's causing the Rest to overtake the West.

It also concerns the multiple macro-scale crises that are nowadays escalating worldwide. Global issues are increasingly overriding local and national issues and, unless we act globally, we all suffer locally anyway. This will cause Palestine's scenario to shift, since global challenges threaten Israelis, Palestinians and their neighbours together. There was some nodding at this. My friends knew about the global situation, but they didn't really connect it with Palestine – global issues happen *out there* beyond the walls, in the wider world, not here.

Something quickened in the conversation. Selim, thus far silent, suddenly piped up. He had worked on oil rigs in the Gulf and he explained that, while the Gulf States were at the time peaceful and wealthy, he hadn't been happy there because it was so materialistic and he missed his family and friends in Palestine. Hence he had come back. He said Europeans were lucky because we could move easily from country to country in the EU, but he had also been interested when I had said that the EU arose out of World War Two. Back in the Gulf, they had recently started the Gulf Cooperation Council, a common market of Saudi Arabia and the Gulf States, and he reckoned this could grow to encompass other Arab states.

There was a pensive silence. Then John said, "That means that Jordan, Syria, Lebanon and Egypt would be part of it, and we'd be on our own, stuck with the Israelis".

"Yes", said Selim. "But if America has no more money to support Israel, Israel will be on its own. And the best thing for Palestine would be to join a union of Arabs. The two-state solution hasn't worked because Israel and Palestine are not equal, but a union of Arabs would make us equal." I could see brains whirring. This was interesting.

"That would never happen", said John.

"But you are of my father's generation, and you've always lived here in Beit Lahem", said Selim. "I have friends in India, Germany, the Philippines and Iraq, and their numbers are in my mobile phone. It's different now. Here's my phone: do you want to speak to my friend in Mumbai? He's a Christian like you."

He had a point. Young Palestinians respect their elders but they also see them to be stuck, resigned, regretful and jaded. Meanwhile, the youngsters have global perspectives and social networks. To them, the future will not resemble the past – other possibilities are unfolding. There's a kind of pragmatic vision behind this youthful perspective. The big variable here is the amount of time and hardship that is needed before a new society can take shape.

An Irish chap rolled up. He'd been here six months working for ICAHD, the Israeli Committee Against House Demolitions. They document Israeli demolitions and land-grabs, pressuring their government to stop them. Unsung heroes, organisations like this are now under threat, regarded by Israeli right-wingers as a traitorous security risk. But ICAHD doesn't side with the enemy so much as support Israel's best longterm interests, as they see them – there is, after all, a strong streak of justice and fairness in Jewish tradition. ICAHD believes the occupation is against Israel's best interests.

The Irishman was nervous because he was due to go to Tel Aviv to seek a visa extension to stay longer. Spending all your time in the West Bank is definitely taboo in the Israeli authorities' eyes – you could be chucked out and blacklisted, blocked from ever returning. Working for an organisation like ICAHD is even more of a taboo.

The story he was going to spin was pretty good and he had corralled some Israelis into backing it up. His political roots lay in Northern Ireland at the time of its own 1990s peace process. This guy was determined to stay in Palestine and he had that sincere dedication (or uncompromising foolishness, depending on your perspective) that marks a true peace-warrior. We connected immediately and later I advised him that, if indeed he did get chucked out, he should not lose hope but go home, take stock, give it time and start again, never giving up. Peacework is a lifelong work. As a veteran, this dollop of wisdom I could legitimately share. I don't know whether he remembered what I said: a few weeks later I discovered he had been thrown out.

I went along the road to see Adnan. He was a Bedouin, fortyish, with four children, living in a village outside town. I had decided to make him a website to help sell his goods abroad, and he would give me gifts to take home. A good exchange, I thought. After spending time with him I went to find something to eat – a falafel sandwich, local standard fare for a vegetarian like me. It's a pitta bread with hummus stuffed inside, four or five falafels dropped in, then fine-chopped salad and a spicy relish, mine for six shekels, washed down with fresh carrot and orange juice for four. Wholesome fast food.

I wandered back to Cinema through the old Christian Quarter, which is quieter than much of Bethlehem since many of its residents have emigrated. After dropping into a supermarket for supplies – the shops here are quite well-stocked – I sat with relief, rather tired, in a service taxi waiting for customers, bound for Al Khader.

A woman in the back studiously watched me. People here are always fascinated to find a Westerner among them so you're either asked questions or observed quietly. There's no privacy here: you're public property, attracting eyes, enquiries and generosity of heart. When first you arrive this can be a shock – anonymity and isolation hardly exist.

We headed along the Hebron road through Duha and Deheisheh. These urban areas have filled the gaps between the older towns of Bethlehem, Beit Jala and Al Khader, joined together when Palestinian refugees swelled the local population in 1948 and 1967. I disembarked at The Gate, an archway monument at Al Khader crossroads, and started back to the school. It's a wearing walk if you're tired and carrying shopping, but manageable and cheaper than taking a taxi from town to the door. There are two walking routes from Khader Gate to the school and I took the shorter and harder one.

It goes through some tenement housing where kids play out in the street, shouting hello and demanding a personal response, as if a hello from a foreigner validated their existence. Then it goes past the modern, empty Convention Palace built in the 1990s when Europeans, investing in peace, shelled out vast sums for impressive building projects, many of which were later rendered redundant by the second *intifada*. After the uprising subsided around 2004, the building of the Israeli security wall isolated Bethlehem, shutting off the town as a destination for visitors attending conferences, events and pilgrimages. The Convention Palace, a lovely building, is thus hardly known and hardly used; awaiting better times, it plays host only to geckos and security guards.

Crossing the Irtas road you come to Solomon's Pools, three enormous water cisterns originally fed by five springs to the north and built from Roman times onwards to provide water to Bethlehem and Jerusalem. The name is derived from Suleiman the

Pictures of Palestine

Magnificent, a great Ottoman sultan of the 1500s who invaded the region and built great works to glorify Allah and the Ottoman regime. The stone-lined open tanks, seven acres in area, can contain vast quantities of water but now they are bone dry. The water has been diverted by the Israelis to newbuilt settlements such as Efrat and Gilo. After a while you get used to outrages like this.

Around the pools are the remains of a park with pine trees, which Bethlehemites resort to for family picnics. Around Bethlehem there are few open spaces left, thanks to loss of land to the Israelis and to population growth in the Bethlehem conurbation. Then there's a final heave up the hill on a rough, stony track leading up to Waad Rahal Road, which runs along the hilltop ridge on which the school sits. More kids hollering hello. Once at the school, there is a big gate to unlock, then there's a door, then four flights of stairs up to the volunteers' apartment. To give it a positive spin, it's good exercise!

Once home, I had to sit down for a while, but only after I'd made a cup of tea, in sickeningly British fashion. I sank into a sofa with a wonderful view over the now-dusky valley. After I switched on the lights, I could sense binoculars trained on me from the Israeli watchtower. But that's their problem – after all, an Anglo drinking tea doesn't constitute a serious security risk.

The next task was to plan my work, so the soldiers' next half hour was spent observing me jotting in my notebook. Earlier that day I had brainstormed with Ibrahim, discussing the Hope Flowers website and other tasks. The site needed a complete change of look and content. I was to take new photos and the material was to become a web-resource in trauma-recovery and special needs education. This excited me. Palestine has a lot of experience in living with adversity, and sharing this globally will be important.

Hope Flowers knows its business. No theory, just seat-of-the-pants innovation and experimentation, prompted by sheer need, honed and tested through two dreadful *intifadas* and the consequences left behind. In Geneva two months earlier, while visiting a Jordanian friend who worked in the UN, I met an exiled

Pictures of Palestine

Palestinian academic who told me that the school should send teachers to Oxford University, where she had done her doctorate, to learn peace-building. That was good of her, but no, I beg to differ – Oxford might do better sending people to Hope Flowers, to plug into its real-life experience in on-site peace-building.

Darkness pulled in. I was alone at the school, on the top floor in a spacious apartment built in the days when far more volunteers were expected than actually came. The building was one of those put up in the 1990s when things looked promising in Palestine. It was a little lonely here but that allowed me to get on with work undisturbed. The only sounds were the howling of feral dogs in the hills and the yelling of kids playing football outside in the darkness. Kids here don't get sent to bed at eight o'clock – they disappear off around the neighbourhood and only stagger home when worn out and ready to drop – yet they're remarkably safe in the streets all the same, and the community as a whole protects them.

I sat looking out of the large windows at the dusky vista. Over the valley on the opposite ridge was the watchtower and to the right of it was an outpost of the expanding Israeli settlement of Efrat. The separation wall had been built 350 metres away along the near side of the ridge – though bizarrely it was incomplete and thus useless as a barrier to terrorists. When first planned it was going to cut right across school property and the school cafeteria was to be demolished. The wall would stand humiliatingly close, right in the faces of the kids, but the school activated international supporters who duly pressurised senators, MPs and newspapers who made a fuss and, luckily, the wall was relocated – saving quite a few neighbouring Palestinian houses and farms in the process.

Time for bed; Ibrahim was to come for me at nine the next day. Well, that's nine o'clock Palestine Time, give or take an hour or so, *inshallah*. To you Israeli soldiers in the watchtower, watching over your walled-in Palestinian flock by night, do have a pleasantly peaceful night, won't you? I'm watching you too, remember. Or is the madness of this schizoid country beginning to get to me?

10 **Land of Opportunity**
with a few rough edges

Sometimes Palestinians are too anxious to please and complications ensue. You ask a passer-by for help with something and they try sorting it out themselves rather than just telling you where to go or what to do. You ask for a bus and they fix you a taxi – their brother-in-law's of course. They give an incorrect answer rather than admitting they don't know – all because they so want to be helpful. So a simple question or request can lead to a convoluted process.

Some of course don't fully comprehend you – they might have only a 100-word English vocabulary. Fair enough, except they go haring off trying to resolve the question or request, misunderstanding what the question was, coming back with a not-quite-right solution or a complete mismatch. Then they're disappointed if you're not pleased – *but I was trying to help, wasn't I?* Well yes, but I just wanted to find out where to buy clothes pegs.

I was walking down the street and fell upon two men sitting outside on chairs, locked in discussion. I asked where I might find a café. One invited me inside, sat me down, went off and came back with the remains of the dinner they had just eaten. Now this gets tricky because it's not cool to turn down someone's generosity. He gave me a meat stick with Sprite. Now I, a stroppy purist, am a vegetarian who doesn't drink canned fizz.

Explaining vegetarianism is a non-starter with many Palestinians. I resolved the problem by looking delighted then waited furtively until he went outside, stuffing the meat stick in my bag, drinking a sip of the Sprite and sharing the remains with a pot plant, wandering out looking satisfied and saying *shukran* (thank you), then disappearing down the street, only to give a rather pleased, scraggy cat its dinner when I rounded the corner. Then, where was I? Oh yes... I resumed my search for food, fifteen minutesworth hungrier than before.

There were other situations where explaining my vegetarian habits was problematic. One day I struck on the perfect answer at a café: *humans treat animals just like Israelis treat Palestinians.* That analogy was immediately understood. The café-owners looked at each other, looked at me, realised I'd cornered them, served me falafel and treated me as an honoured guest thereafter. Later, I pointed out that vegetarianism isn't just a Western eccentricity since, further east, there are half a billion Hindu dhal-eating vegetarians in India, more than the total number of Arabs in the Middle East. *Ah, but they're pantheistic Hindus*, came the response, as if this answered everything, *and God made animals for us to eat.* Well, I couldn't agree with that, but I wasn't in the mood for advanced metaphysical discourse and I didn't know enough of the *Qur'an* to field a theological counterattack. So I left it at that. Sometimes, in the furtherance of peace, it's best just to stay quiet.

Pictures of Palestine

In the weeks that followed they welcomed me back, treating me as their pet Englishman with his strange deficiency. They observed, when they asked me my age, that I seemed to do quite well on it. Charitably, one remarked that at least I had no fat belly getting in the way when lying on top of a woman. Many middle-aged Palestinians can be rather, shall we say, substantial in girth and, as a nation facing many frustrations, eating is one way of keeping these frustrations subdued.

To return to where we started, there's another issue. Many Palestinians want to support their family and give their uncle or brother some business or kudos – and that can be more important than providing what you actually need. You ask for a taxi and they phone their relative, who happens to be busy, so you politely wait until he is available while watching other taxis cruise past looking for customers. You find yourself unwittingly helping someone you've never met resolve an issue that has little to do with you. This tendency to get diverted can be frustrating at times, but that's what living in a mutually-supportive society is all about: the way they see it, it's a privilege to assist a visitor, and for a visitor, it's bad manners to refuse help.

I had been trying to borrow a mobile phone for days, and still didn't have one. I asked Adnan, in case his extended family had one lying around, and that took ages but got nowhere. I wished he had just said, "No, I can't help". I asked Ibrahim and he came up with an old Motorola which I couldn't get to work. Who knows, they'd probably both moved mountains trying to help me. So the process took days, and I needed to get a phone, quickly. In the end, a few days later I bought one for 170 shekels in Ramallah, which I should have done from the start.

Then there's the matter of Palestinian sales technique. If I could teach them a new marketing method, it would simply be *let the customer make up their own mind.* Many Palestinian traders agitate for business, suggesting this, wanting you to buy that. As you walk past they holler, "You want taxi?", "You want eat falafel?", "You buy souvenir?" *Go away! I just want to walk along the street, thanks, I've eaten enough, and I'm not a tourist!* You don't *say* this, of course, but that's the reaction that comes up. They'd get far more business if they just let visitors stooge around and take a look!

This marketing strategy is influenced by two adverse factors. The first is the separation wall and the discouragement Christian pilgrims receive from Israelis, who tell them it's dangerous to walk around the streets of Bethlehem or even to visit the place. Visitors who venture through the checkpoints usually come in Israeli coaches, shepherded around to avoid contact with the locals, spending an hour in the Church of the Nativity and then disappearing back to Jerusalem, while the shekels, euros and dollars go to Israeli travel companies and Israeli-certified guides and giftshops. The guides and shops are beholden for business to the Israeli tour operators, who get a 30% cut on the take by supplying tourists. This has led to much loss of trade in Bethlehem, where the tourist sector is centuries old, now much declined. Mary and Joseph found no room at the inn, but nowadays there are plenty of empty beds and they would get princely treatment.

The second factor is the attitude that many Christians worldwide have to the conflict in the Holy Land. They don't want to get involved, preferring to rescue Palestinian Christians and settle them in Europe or America rather than come here to help them or provide business. There are wonderful, charitable and brave Christians who indeed do noble deeds. The Christian Peacemaker Teams, for instance, escort Palestinians past remonstrative Israeli settlers or through checkpoints, at some risk to themselves, but the churches as a whole have tended to assist their Palestinian congregants in abandoning ship. Emigrating Christians have created a changed Palestinian society and a dwindling Christian tradition, together with a significant sense of abandonment amongst those left behind.

The net effect is that traders and taxi-drivers try too hard to attract whatever business remains. In doing so, they often scare off the visitors who do come. Additionally, many visitors are not as prosperous as once they were, thanks to the economic downturn, and newly wealthy Arab and Iranian visitors are not permitted to enter Palestine to replace the dwindling Westerners who ventured there in the past. So incomers resist pressure to buy and, instead of being given space to find gifts they can afford for the folks back home, they buy little or nothing. The losers are the small traders of Bethlehem.

There aren't many issues in the Holy Land that irritate me, but this Christian issue does. Christians could act as a third, mediating force in this benighted land, and not enough of them do so. Internationally, Christians seem divided between those who are charitably big-hearted and those who are hard-line 'tough love' types – and the latter have the political clout. Only a minority of valiant Jesus-freaks take a principled and consistent stand on peace, while many seem to accept war as a fact of life, with some American neocons seeing conflict in crusading terms or even as a prelude to a return of Christ to Earth, a biblical burn-up of human depredation.

Occasionally, trouble accompanies fervent evangelists on their flying visits to Bethlehem. In 2005 I was at the school watering trees for the PeaceTrees project. There were hundreds of trees, water was scarce and I worked hard to get it done as best I could. Along came a group of Americans, visiting the school because in their minds it somehow represented the Bethlehem of Jesus and of Christian peace and goodwill. They were on an evangelical razzle in God's Holy Land, acting as if they owned the place, without realising the school was mainly Muslim.

The leader saw me watering trees and commanded me to yield up my watering can, a spade and a tree, as he led his flock, together with camera crew, to a piece of land where holes had been dug for tree-planting the following day. The holes awaited the attentions of my watering can so that the moisture would soak into the dry ground overnight. The visitors trampled all over them. The leader started preaching at length about olive branches, doves and Deuteronomy as I stood there, wondering how long this would go on.

Finally he instructed his camera crew how to shoot the next take, then started planting the tree, using up a whole can of water, drowning the poor tree and getting one of his followers' feet wet in the process. Raising the spade like a sword, nearly hitting another follower, he faced the camera and cried out "This is for Calvary!" Well, perhaps. To crown it all, he hollered at me to fetch soil to fill the hole. I responded, "It's under your feet – you're standing on the pile". He didn't like such insubordination. I stepped up, firmly took the watering can and spade and said, "Now you can go". To my surprise, they went.

There's another question. If Palestinians love this land so much, why wreck the place with junk, plastic bags, scrap metal, rubble and all manner of garbage? Palestinians just love contemporary appurtenances such as plastic bags. Like Westerners until recent times, they probably don't think about the effect of a billion plastic bags blowing around Allah's good Earth.

To a European tree-hugger like me, the most alarming thing is this: household waste is collected in rusty skips out on the street, which the local authority then fails to empty, so some public-spirited person thoughtfully sets fire to it. The rubbish, including plastic and all manner of nasties, then smoulders smokily for a whole day, blowing toxins everywhere. It makes room for further rubbish, to be sure, but it's catastrophic for the environment and public health.

True, people don't like Westerners preaching at them to clean up their act, when all they're doing is what we ourselves have done for the last few centuries. But this is an urgent issue today, and Planet Earth cannot wait another 200 years. If only Westerners, in the days of our dark, satanic mills of yesteryear, had realised that wrecking the Earth wasn't cool, we wouldn't have this problem.

I'd been talking to a few Bethlehemites about 'transforming resistance'. Standing up for Palestine is fine, but 'resistance' is not just about hating Israelis and fighting them. It's about strengthening your own culture from within so that it becomes more vibrant in itself, and it involves building up a nation's natural resistance to the degenerative ills of the wider world. A content, confident, united and motivated nation is difficult to subdue.

This is also an ecological issue: if you fight for your country while letting the land and ecosystem deteriorate then, win or lose, you make your land less fruitful for survival. If you lose, the invaders can claim they're rescuing you from yourself and, if you win, you have to resort to imports or international aid to feed your people. In Palestine's case, insufficient care for the environment gives Israelis the argument that Palestinians are medievally negligent and that taking land from them for Jewish settlements is thus justifiable. Palestinians do indeed care deeply for the land, but they suffer water shortages and the insecurity arising from conflict, which makes them feel hopeless about investing effort in the long term future.

But for so many reasons it is vital to give more care to the land and the environment.

When it comes to violence, Palestinians cannot beat the Israelis – instead they survive by outlasting Israeli attacks on them. This *sumud*, or steadfastness, does work, but painfully so. Palestinians take the hit and don't budge an inch so the Israelis impose curfews, power-cuts and blockades and then the Palestinians retreat to their beds. Lo and behold, a baby boom follows next year. This is strategically self-defeating for the Israelis, who would prefer Palestinians to dwindle, not multiply, in number. Palestinians are pretty good at depriving the Israelis of a clear sense of victory, eating away at their feeling of superiority and their need to win at all costs. It vaguely works as a strategy, but is the pain incurred really worth it?

There's yet another aspect of this idea of transforming resistance. To an outsider, West Bank society seems to be strangely happier than Israeli society. Yes, *happier*. Just catch the 21 bus from Jerusalem to Bethlehem – a short journey – and you'll see the difference. Paradoxically, the losers, the Palestinians, seem to be winning this conflict in real human terms. Israelis have undermined their own society and culture by subsuming it to military and capitalist priorities, while Palestinians are getting on with being alive, taking each day as it comes. This makes for a very different kind of community feeling – it's a philosophical, even a spiritual attitude. Westerners pay large amounts to go on trainings teaching them how to 'live for the moment' and 'count their blessings' while it's available for free here in Bethlehem!

Palestinians could also help the resistance by focusing on their social strengths, music and literature, national self-confidence, women's rights, their children's happiness and the richness and fertility of their land. They already do quite well on these fronts, especially considering that their country has not experienced much in the way of proper governance in the last few generations – and perhaps this is one reason why Palestinian society is quite vibrant. Western conservatives moan about 'big government' and its ills.

Pictures of Palestine

Well, Palestinians have until recently had nearly no government. They achieved this without being right-wing: the capacity to govern themselves was taken away from them in 1967 and they adapted by strengthening their families, clans, neighbourhoods and community values. To win this conflict without fighting, the human factor in Palestinian society is the chief weapon.

This is what Hope Flowers is all about. Arguably, it's doing far more for the resistance than any gunmen can – but don't tell the Israelis because they might try to close the place down. Hope Flowers seeks to strengthen society, to empower 'us, here', discouraging use of weapons against 'them, there'. This is a weapon the Israelis cannot easily hit back against. If only the PA understood this, seeing Ibrahim Issa as a patriot rather than a suspected collaborator. The mindset of 'with us or against us' which thrives in conflict situations doesn't do much good for the Palestinian cause. Strangely, reconciliation goes hand-in-hand with cultural resistance.

This brings me back to the litter and junk. Palestinians could, without much cost and effort, make their living environment so much better. They do well on architecture, and much of the landscape is quite beautiful, but let's do something about the crap and wasteland, let's stop burning plastic rubbish, dumping litter and rubble and poisoning the land and people, let's get people working together on levelling out the tips and planting trees. It doesn't take a PhD to work this out or even for foreigners like me to nag about it. It's simply an act of love for the land and people, an act of resistance far more effective than rockets or suicide bombing.

It could also help young Palestinians decide to stay home rather than escaping to Sweden, Dubai or North Carolina. They would more genuinely love this land and feel happier here, whatever their prospects and whatever the Israelis do to make life miserable. In a strange way, Palestine is a potential land of opportunity; it has an opportunity to make a really good solution out of a bad situation. But I can understand how many Palestinians find this difficult to see. It is difficult to see when you're up against the obstacles of occupation, day after day.

11 Sheqalim
ATMs and a Clash of Incantations

I shared my top floor accommodation in the school with only a few mosquitoes and a visiting gecko. The gecko spent his time watching me intently, though mozzies were his main interest. The apartment was spacious, with three bedrooms, a kitchen, a sitting area and work place with big, wide windows and a poignant view over the sharp-edged border between Palestinian and Israeli territory – the separation wall was a few hundred yards away, in full view. Sometimes it was a welcome retreat from the busy and periodically hyperactive atmosphere in Bethlehem, and at times it was lonesome out there on the edge of town, looking over the great divide. I worked here on web-pages, grant applications, letters, PR and other things as they came up.

Five times daily the calling to prayers started up in five different neighbouring mosques – it was a cacophony! I found myself wondering whether Allah sticks His Fingers into His Everlasting Ears. Or perhaps He doesn't have the same problem concentrating on His meditations as a mere mortal such as me. Or maybe again He is too busy with other things to notice the disharmonies of competing *muezzin* in and around Al Khader, praising His ninety-nine holy names, all out of time with each other – I mean, can't they devise a way of singing *together*? But then, at that time Allah was dealing with bomb-blasts in Iraq, riots in Iran and a host of other problems – and that was just in the Muslim sphere. I hope He's better than me at multitasking because, if not, we're in trouble.

Pictures of Palestine

The soldier-children of the Jewish G-d, doing long shifts in the watchtower on the hill behind the insecurity wall, faithfully keep watch over this source of holy cacophony, keeping us all 'safe', with machine guns at the ready. I appreciate their protection. Question is, protection from what? Mozzies? Oh, and by the way, the word 'God' should only be *alluded to* by Jews, which is why they write his name, in English at least, as G-d, since G-d is ineffable, too big to be enc-mpassed in a mere word. I get the point, but surely, since G-d is beyond words and concepts, would it not be better, like Buddhists, to have no word at all?

Meanwhile, the bell-ringers of Jesus' lot have an age-old arrangement with the *muezzin* in the mosques. I have no idea how old the arrangement is – could be more than a millennium – but the Christian church bells and the Muslim calling of the faithful do not clash. All is well in God's Holy Land between Muslims and Christians, but not with Jews, who seem to want the Muslims and Christians to go. This is problematic. From a God's-eye viewpoint, there must be something strangely tragi-comic about watching humans fight each other to create their own version of Heaven on Earth, busily ignoring God in the process.

Pictures of Palestine

I coined a neat title, *Sheqalim* or 'shekels', to this chapter, but then got diverted onto writing about *muezzin*. My original intention was to write about ATMs – Mammon's wee streetside altars where you make a temporary sacrifice of plastic to be given the divinely fiduciary blessing of banknotes, kindly distributed to us by the Bank of Israel. Yes, Palestinians have to use Israeli shekels, for their sins.

Now I studied economics when I was young, and my observation of Palestinian ATMs gives me the distinct impression that most transactions in Palestine are cash-based, not banking-based. How did I figure that out? Well, many ATMs cough up Jordanian dinars, not Israeli shekels. Jordan used to rule the West Bank until the Israelis forcibly relieved them of it in 1967, and Palestinians still hold a certain allegiance to the Jordanian dinar, the 'JD'. But the daily-life currency is shekels. So why would ATMs disgorge dinars? Well, Palestinians use shekels in their daily lives and dinars for going abroad, since the first stop when going abroad, for those who can, is Jordan. Palestinians can't go to the nearest airport, Ben Gurion near Tel Aviv, since as we know they're all terrorists, so they're not permitted transit through Israel to the airport, and neither are they permitted their own airport.

So in daily life they use simple cash-dispensing devices called pockets and purses, only using ATMs when they need money for going abroad. They save their money in banks for periodic trips made over the King Hussein Bridge to Jordan, the land of the relatively free – assuming they're permitted to leave, of course. That's why ATMs stock mainly dinars, methinks.

Yet the everyday currency is shekels and one of the mild humiliations Palestinians live with is the dubious honour of using *sheqalim* with a picture of a serious-looking Jew on the back. I have no idea who he is – his name is written in Hebrew characters. But then, in Britain we have Adam Smith on our banknotes – typical mercantilist Brits, making a deity out of the author of *The Wealth of Nations*. Then we have our great mother-goddess Queen Elizabeth II on the other side: I wonder what the Grand Ayatollah of Iran thinks of that? People looking to a *woman* as their supreme leader? How depraved.

Talking about goddesses, Bethlehem was a goddess centre once, an ancient Canaanite hilltop holy place, for a far longer time than the Christian and Muslim periods combined. This is where 'lahem' comes from – 'beit' meaning house or home. The Hebrew name for Bethlehem means 'house of bread' and the Arabic version means 'house of meat' (a place of food offerings), but the place-name was in use before either Hebrews or Muslims came along. In the ancient Egyptian Amarna Texts of around 1400BCE, it was called *Bit Lahmi*, so they can't claim proprietorship over the name since it preceded them. 'La' relates to a deity – as in *Al-Lah*, meaning 'The God' or perhaps, before monotheism came along, the chief god of all gods. So, I suggest, Beit Lahem refers more probably to a holy place of deity, possibly a feminine one, since there are ancient hilltop wells here – nowadays called King David's Wells, surely formerly known as something else. Wells and springs are usually associated with feminine deities.

Bethlehem was the birthplace not only of Jesus but also of King David, reputedly the founder of the first unified Jewish state, so there's something special about getting born in Bethlehem. There's hardly any information about Bethlehem in David's time, or any time up to the arrival of the Greeks. The Greek conqueror Alexander the Great and his gang came to Beit Lahem and sent the local gods and goddesses packing, building a temple of Apollo. Thus it more or less remained until the Christians did another takeover in the Byzantine era, building the Church of the Nativity on poor old Apollo's temple – holy spots were, after all, premium property in ancient times.

Christians might not like me saying this, but it's likely that the story of Joseph and Mary travelling to Bethlehem for the sake of a census could be spin. The reason they came here was surely that it was a special place, an astute location for giving birth to God's only Son, with a lovely hilltop aspect and a suitably wide-open firmament for the Star of Bethlehem to hover in. It's that kind of place, 2,300ft or 770m up in an impressive highland area. Even today Bethlehem is pretty friendly, inclusive and positive in its atmosphere, despite its traumas. So, if you're about to give birth, try Bethlehem. There's plenty of mother power around here – not just from the Blessed Virgin Mary but also from all the veritable matriarchs in the streets and houses who, if truth be known, secretly run the place.

The Mary and Jesus statues dotted around town embody an upgrade of the local goddess imagery – the nurturing mother with child. It's a local archetype which, together with the Star of Bethlehem, is the town's main emblem. The Muslims are fine with this since they appreciate living in a place with global name-recognition and Mary and Jesus figure in their tradition too, Jesus being one of the great prophets of Islam. Say the name 'Qalqilya', and everyone says "Where?". But *Bethlehem*, everyone worldwide has heard of it – though some Westerners erroneously believe it's in Israel.

It was those Greeks, reincarnating as Byzantines, who really made this an institutionally Christian town – especially through the Empress Helena, who endowed churches and staked out Palestine for the Greek Orthodox church. In a still later upgrade to the

Byzantine Christian one, the Muslims were pretty astute during their invasion in the 600s by Caliph Omar and his gang: they honoured the Christians and built the Mosque of Omar over the other side of Manger Square, instead of demolishing the Nativity Church and driving out the Christians. So the church and the mosque face each other quite happily across the square.

Mercifully, in Caliph Omar's days they didn't use loudspeakers for the calling to prayers like they do nowadays. Today, the poor old Church of the Nativity rattles and vibrates to the booming sound from the Omar Mosque's minaret – the sound system no doubt financed by sheikhs in Saudi Arabia who are big on installing amplified *muezzin* everywhere they can. Meanwhile, the Christian bells of the Nativity Church are relatively muted, rather tinkly: frankly, a peal of English parish church bells knocks spots off them anytime.

Then along came the Crusaders around 1100, kicking out the Muslims, taking over Bethlehem and allowing Europeans to flood in on pilgrimages – though not yet in Israeli luxury coaches. The indigenous Christians had quietly been here since Jesus' time, but many Crusader Catholics thought that they themselves were the true Christians and these locals were imposters. The Crusaders ran Bethlehem and Jerusalem for nearly a century, whereupon Saladin, the Muslim ruler of Syria and Egypt, decided that they had to go.

He did his damnedest to kick out these badly behaved tin-can wearing, stallion-riding Crusader hypocrites. They wouldn't make a treaty with him to share the Holy Land, even though he offered a sharing plan through his brother Al-Adil, who acted as a go-between. Richard the Lionheart, the Crusader leader at the time, at first responded positively, proposing marriage between Al-Adil and Joanna of England to seal the deal, but neither prospective spouse would have it. Besides, many Papists from Europe wanted complete control of Palestine, opposing such reconciliatory treason, so a deal was never made. Salah-ad-Din realised the only way to deal with these smelly, oversized marauders was to get rid of them – a task in which he nearly succeeded. He eventually got them out of Bethlehem and Jerusalem, penning them up on the coast.

What a precedent that was – offering to *share* the Holy Land. Though Saladin felt duty-bound to kick out these bloodthirsty, territorial Crusaders, as a good Muslim he respected *all* people of faith. Well, sort of. The Crusaders had two conflicting camps. Salah-ad-Din had a problem with one camp, the arrogant European incomers, a bunch of booty-seeking, power-mad fundamentalists, but not with the resident Crusaders who had lived in Palestine for generations – they were acculturalised to the Holy Land and generally behaved themselves. The incomers out-voted the resident Crusaders and had their way. So Salah-ad-Din had to do something.

Permit me to interject a brief aside. The Crusaders loved big stallions. They'd get kitted up in armour, mount their enormous steeds, form a column and charge, breaking a hole in the enemy line, wheeling round and attacking from behind. Classic Western tactics: apply overwhelming force, mercilessly decimating the enemy – now done with bombers and drones. But Salah-ad-Din rumbled this. He used fillies, which are agile and manoeuvrable. He had a secret weapon too: he got fillies that were on heat. The Crusaders couldn't figure out why their trusty steeds suddenly disobeyed orders in a most unchristian fashion. Good tactics, huh?

Or, try this. Salah-ad-Din didn't favour bloodshed, which is unusual for a general. Before re-taking Jerusalem, he drew the Crusader knights out of town and set a trap. Knowing that they used metal armour (his own men wore felt and leather) he drew them into the hills above Galilee, taunting them forward. The Crusaders charged along, only to find themselves standing atop a hill, surrounded by Muslim warriors. Salah-ad-Din let them stand there under the hot sun, roasting in their armour. He held them there until they wilted and surrendered. That's *strategy*. The Crusaders were foiled at the Battle of Hattin, and before long Salah-ad-Din had Jerusalem surrounded and retook the city.

Later he had the Crusaders penned up in a double-siege of the town of Acre, just above today's Haifa, in which the

Pictures of Palestine

Crusaders besieged the Muslims in the town and Saladin besieged the Crusaders. This became a long, sad story. Salah-ad-Din was reluctant to go in and finish the job because he rightly believed that every drop of blood spilled charges its price. He wanted the Crusaders just to get in their ships and buzz off. Of course, they didn't.

Meanwhile disease broke out among the townspeople and the Crusaders catapulted diseased bodies at Salah-ad-Din's men who, as Muslims, dutifully went about burying them. They were infected, and many Muslims died of a kind of medieval biological warfare. A few years later Salah-ad-Din died too, of a broken heart. He couldn't stand the mess he had got into.

Why tell you this? To point out that the intractable conflict in this area has its precedents. Bad precedents make subsequent misdeeds easier. In the end the Crusaders were finally kicked out by an Egyptian Mamluk sultan called Baibars and Christians and Jews were allowed to carry on here as long as they paid their taxes. But this story has a sad ending.

In the 20th century, Europeans gave the Jews in Europe such a hard time, ultimately leading to the Nazi Holocaust, that the Jews became deeply hurt and damaged. Such was the level of cruelty meted out to them, they caught this virus called 'cruelty'. It's common in history that warrior peoples become warriors because they have themselves been kicked around. Classic examples are the Mongols, hit by the Chinese; the Romans, assaulted by the Celts, and the British, invaded by the Saxons, Vikings and Normans. Violence is a virus, infecting populations which lack immunity to it. The consequences of this infection have been tragic in Palestine. When Jews immigrated into the Holy Land in the 1930s-40s they were desperate and were told by their leaders that this was a 'land without people waiting for a people without a land'. They took more land in the 1948 war than the UN had given them, killing Palestinians, occupying their villages and driving people out in classic European style.

Pictures of Palestine

When I was there in 2005 I saw a house-demolition going on close to the school – the Israelis were clearing Palestinians away to expand the settlement of Efrat. It was distressing to watch. The Israelis had given the Palestinian house-owners three days' notice to get out, knowing that a court appeal would take months and get nowhere. Then they came in, with the backing of the army and reinforced bulldozers, immediately embarking on demolition.

But then we Brits have taken over lands great and small, booting people around, robbing, enslaving and colonising, thinking we knew best. We set many colonial precedents in Palestine and even trained Jewish fighters in our own techniques of warfare and oppression, to deal both with Arabs and the possibility of a German invasion of the Middle East in WW2. Then, weakened after WW2 and abandoning our precious empire, we left dire messes in places such as India-Pakistan, Nigeria, Iraq, Iran and South Africa, as well as Palestine, the effects of which have continued for decades.

Every drop of blood spilled charges its price. This is why I say to militant Arabs that, if indeed they did drive the Israelis into the sea – unlikely, but still a potent idea that some cling to – the result would not be good for Arabs themselves. Once they'd forced the Jews out they too would be infected with the cruelty virus. They would probably turn their guns on each other or give their society a problem just as bad as the problem the Israelis give them today. That would start a new nightmare, not a healing, which is why peace must come by agreement between peoples, by a calming of conflict and its supporting psychology, by stepping back from the brink. Justice is the necessary precondition. It has to be a fair deal and everyone is part of the solution.

12 Volunteers and Prisoners
Israeli land-grabbers
and other tales

Mark is an Irishman who has visited Bethlehem several times. He's a good-hearted chap, smitten with the Palestinian allure. He comes to paint murals and join humanitarian activities and he told me of a demo organised by Israeli peace activists, protesting against Israeli settler land-appropriations at the village of Tuwani, south of Hebron. The settlers, with the tacit support of the army, were forcibly encroaching on Palestinian farmland.

There's more to this. The Israeli Defence Force exists to protect Israelis. Fair enough. In doing so, it calmly overlooks the fact that many settlers deliberately put themselves in danger, thus manipulating the army into protecting them, often treading into Palestinian land. That's a neat trick – and a convoluted process. Some rabbis encourage young Orthodox Israelis and settlers to join the army and choose units that operate on the land-appropriation frontline, so that these army units back up settler encroachments. Extremist settlers thus have become a law unto themselves, an invasion force with army backing.

The saddest thing in this instance is that the protesters at Tuwani had obtained a court order preventing this illegal encroachment – difficult in itself – but the local army unit refused to accept the judgement and were going to do it anyway.

This situation highlights the Israeli system, which is very nicely complex, considering it's a small nation. For example, when the government publicly protests that it cannot stop settlement building, it is *partially* correct, technically. Some Israeli settlers accept the rule of law and government only when it suits them. They take their guidance from the Torah, not from the government. Since there is no institutional 'church' for Jews, divided as they are into different camps and traditions or following a variety of independent-thinking rabbis, the holy books and traditions can be interpreted in a multiplicity of ways.

   Israelis spend a lot of time arguing over land-appropriation. Some Jewish settlers, an insistent and wilful bunch, invoke God and history to justify their refusal to consider anyone else and in response, many reasonable, mainstream Israelis shrug their shoulders and leave them to it, feeling helpless, at times even scared. Settlers' loud arguments and bold initiatives drive the political centre of gravity in Israel stridently rightwards. Added to this, in recent decades many liberal-thinkers have left the country, and many right-tending immigrants have arrived, moving straight to West Bank settlements. Since the 1980s Israeli society has changed quite fundamentally.

Pictures of Palestine

But there's another factor too. The Israeli military was founded on a cellular basis back in the 1940s, before an Israeli state existed. Jewish militias organised themselves into individual cells so that no one knew exactly who everyone else was or what they were doing – thus they insulated themselves from penetration and defeat by the British authorities. They also reflected differences of opinion and approach between different immigrant Jews of the time. When Israel declared independence in 1948, competing groups of Jews argued over the aims of the new state and these aims were never properly clarified in a constitution or unified system of basic law – a situation persisting to this day.

It means that various arms of government and the military tend nowadays to act by their own rules and preferences. These actions can be retroactively incorporated into official policy, or officially denied but accommodated anyway, not least because the arguments and stalemates which would arise if this were not done would be ruinous. Added to this, three systems of secular law – Ottoman, British and Israeli – are used and applied as convenient. Then there are religious laws which, in some Orthodox Jews' eyes, override secular laws. As well as all this, in the occupied territories, there is a military-controlled civil administration which is not part of the government of Israel proper, subject only selectively to the Israeli state's laws. Everything is nicely prone to dispute and denial, which makes things wonderfully complex, arbitrary and... quarrelsome.

Culturally, Israelis define themselves by stroppy individualism, disagreeing with each other to the extent that the joke 'two Israelis, three opinions' indeed becomes true. Israeli society operates by a kind of consensual truce and a dogged avoidance of key issues, united by sharing one enemy and by a deep-seated cultural agreement to stick together as Jews. Sometimes a disgruntled group, perhaps reinforced by headstrong immigrants and money from the wilder side of American Jewry, heads out into the West Bank to start illegal outposts and do its own thing regardless of the state, evading control by a variety of neat tricks. Or the army clears them out and they go straight back, then the army shrugs its shoulders saying nothing can be done. Some Orthodox groupings, though many of their members are financially supported by state benefits, do exactly as they please.

Not surprising then that the army unit south of Hebron, stocked with hard-nosed nationalists, decided that the court of law could go hang. The court was stating *an opinion*, and the IDF unit chose not to accept it. By this means, the Israeli government conveniently covers itself, pleading that it cannot control situations that, in truth, it doesn't want to control. After all, extremists achieve things a government cannot be seen to be doing – they're convenient proxies. This leads to ridiculous situations, such as the government's claim that it didn't issue orders to kill innocent civilians during its bombardment of Gaza in early 2009; neither did it order incursions of troublemaking settlers into the Muslim holy places in Jerusalem in early 2010; neither does it fully control the building of some settlements in the West Bank. Yet shouldn't a nation take its lead from its sovereign government?

Pictures of Palestine

If one part of the system doesn't want to do something, another part will. If one organisation is 'too soft', a militant grouping will raise the stakes. Someone takes an initiative which then cannot easily be undone and foreign governments give up trying to impose international law on Israel because they get nowhere, landing up in a tangle over definitions, procedures or other obfuscations. They gain and accept assurances that something isn't happening when in fact it is. They pursue lengthy negotiations while 'facts on the ground' are busily being established, making negotiated agreements impossible to implement. The Israeli government stalls and stonewalls, refusing to accept international judgements and making a big fuss over small issues, while facts on the ground assert a *fait accompli* and progress in negotiations flounders. This controlled chaos is very effective. Henry Kissinger once observed that Israel has no foreign policy, only domestic policy.

Israel must progress and prevail, whatever anyone thinks – this is the philosophical basis of Zionism. The end justifies the means. If the means are unsupported by a majority, then someone does it anyway so that the majority is not responsible. This is how the Israeli body politic works, and the Palestinians suffer the effects. In this case villagers in the south were losing their land and they had the added problem of being too distant from Ramallah or from international attention to gain much support.

Mark was one of many volunteers who come to Palestine. He was staying at a permaculture farm below Beit Sahour, which focuses on constructive initiatives in farming and is run by a Welshman married to a Palestinian. At the farm there were Europeans and Americans as well as a few Palestinians. Apparently the local neighbours worry about this gaggle of unmarried people living together, but Palestinians largely accept Westerners and their strange ways, so they mumble but don't do anything.

The farm develops remarkable composting, crop-growing and water-conservation techniques to demonstrate new land-management methods to Palestinian farmers and smallholders. They recycle water bottles, using them as mini-cloches for seedlings, they cover areas of ground with old rugs to 'weed' the ground, start seed-banks, perform land-shaping for irrigation and play all sorts of eco-tricks with meagre available resources. The system hangs around 'permaculture design', making everything in a farm, garden or landscape reinforce and assist everything else. Permaculture has much to contribute to Palestine since its principles can bevel with indigenous traditions and the imagination of local people, and it costs little except hard work.

Mark wondered out loud to me what good he actually brought to Palestine by coming here, but he and people like him do bring genuine benefit. It's important that foreigners spend time here, chipping away at things and helping projects progress. Without them this place would be isolated, lacking something, not just financially but in terms of ideas and moral encouragement. Talking to foreign visitors gives Palestinians a sense of perspective on their lives – they feel *witnessed*, de-isolated.

After our chat Mark took me down to the permaculture farm. "Not far...", said he breezily. I discovered he was an avid, long-legged speed-walker and by the time we got there I was worn out. But it was mostly downhill – Beit Sahour is below ridge-top Bethlehem, and the farm is in a valley below Beit Sahour.

I sat recuperating and conversing with some of the young volunteers. There was one young hobo from Spain who liked moving around the Middle East making himself useful and reckoned that Palestine was the best place anywhere; there were also some dedicated thirtysomething English permaculture activists with dreadlocks, busying themselves with tasks and keeping half an ear cocked when I was talking. This old geezer seemed a right-on sort.

There was a Jewish Frenchman who lived in Sderot, Israel – the town most affected by rockets from Gaza. He was attending college there. He applied the adjective 'boring' to Sderot, telling us that the locals treated rocket alarms and bomb-shelters as tediously routine. He added that Sderotis were fed up with media exaggeration and government propaganda, saying that more residents died from motor accidents than from rocket attacks. Nevertheless, life there is difficult. His French passport permitted him to enter the West Bank – an Israeli Jew cannot.

There was a bulbous, pleasantly bossy American woman who mothered the house, and an Italian who was an ardent pro-Palestinian activist who had got chucked out of Saudi Arabia for mixing too much with women. He had landed up penniless in Egypt, only to find the competition between beggars to be so intense that he had to get out. How he had got past Israeli border controls I cannot guess. Then there was a hard-working, salt-of-the-earth Hungarian, busying himself with fixing a chicken coop.

All of them were the current floating members of this permaculture community, young enough to be Mark's and my sons and daughters. Later I left, finding a taxi-share to return home to the other end of Bethlehem, with a few diversions *en route* to pick up and drop off extra passengers on the way.

As for Mark, I met him once more and he then returned to Ireland. He's what Palestinians call 'a good man'; each year he goes to a worthy country for a meaningful do-gooding adventure. He *does something* for humanity. I respect people like that.

13 Palestine up to WW1
before modernity broke up the Middle East

The history of Palestine is, as you might have gathered, long and complex. People lived here very early in human history at the crossing-point between Africa, Europe and Asia and a source-region of human life, culture and civilisation. When the 'Out of Africa' migration of the earliest humans took place, they came through Palestine. The earliest human remains come from 1.5m years ago at Ubeidiya, east of Bethlehem. Later, Neanderthals and humans coexisted alongside each other from roughly 250,000 to 40,000 years ago.

In Ramallah and Bethlehem tools and remains have been found from the nomadic Natufian culture of 14,000-12,000 years ago, at the end of what, further north, was the Ice Age. Early horticultural communities grew up from then on and the world's oldest known continually-inhabited town is Jericho in the Jordan valley, founded as a village around 10,500 years ago, next to substantial springs that surface there. Ancient people were mostly nomadic herders and horticulturalists wandering on an annual round, weeding out plants in some places to favour selected species, planting and propagating seeds in other places where, when they returned, they'd glean a harvest.

Life went on in this wooded land of milk and honey, which had a far more equable climate than now. By 3000-2200BCE, the pyramid-building time in Egypt, independent Canaanite city-states had developed in Palestine, trading with Egypt, Sumer (Iraq), Lebanon and Minoan Crete. The Canaanites were a mixed collation

103

of tribes and lineages of descent in this intercontinental crossing place. A long time passed before the Jews came along.

Biblical tradition has it that Abraham came here around 1800BCE with a group of *Habiru* from Sumer, buying land at Hebron, a Hittite town, and living peaceably with the locals. Later they moved to Egypt due to famine. However, this tradition and the biblical narrative of the origins of the Jews, though strong and enduring, is not entirely backed up by archaeology and historical analysis and it's possible that Canaanites and Jews were not as different as we're led to believe today.

Later still, around 1200BCE, various peoples migrated into the area. These included Phoenicians from Bahrain, Hittites from Anatolia, Philistines from the Aegean and Hebrews returning from Egypt in *Exodus* days. This time, according to biblical tradition, the Hebrews, led by Joshua, invaded the area, though archaeological evidence suggests they moved in alongside Canaanites and others, occupying hilltops and unused land. They established themselves around Shechem, today's Nablus, though life was difficult for them for some time to come.

Migration was common around the Middle East – a habit that the Bedouin have retained up to the present day – and while there were zones of influence such as those of the Egyptians and Hittites, countries with boundaries and borders as we know them today didn't exist. For many centuries people lived in fluctuating patchworks of ethnic settlement.

According to Biblical tradition, the first proper Israelite kingdom was founded in the West Bank highlands by King David, leader of the southern tribes of Judah. It was based in Hebron. Later, the northern Israelite tribes of Shechem adopted him as king. To unite them he conquered the Jebusite town of Zion, which became Jerusalem – it stood in between Judah and Israel. He was followed by his son Solomon around 970BCE, who built the first Temple in Jerusalem, extended Israel's reach over neighbouring areas and presided over a prosperous nation, ruling for 40 years. After his death around 930BCE the Israelite kingdom split into two, Israel in the north and Judah in the south, and, despite some religious conflicts and frictions, they survived until around 730BCE. Realms such as the coastal Philistine city-states (Gaza), Moab (southern Jordan), Ammon (northern Jordan) and the Phoenician trading towns of Lebanon surrounded them.

The area has consistently been multi-ethnic, with adjacent villages, areas and quarters of towns all occupied by different tribes and peoples. Kingdoms were run by dominant clans and lineages but the people under them were ethnically mixed, often village by village, each with their own gods, traditions and ways of living. Even the Jews had not yet settled into their later belief in one God – Yahweh was one of several gods. Most of the time people got on with each other, performing different socio-economic roles within a larger society.

Around 720BCE, Assyria (in today's northern Iraq) destroyed the northern kingdom of Israel and its inhabitants were dispersed far and wide. Small groups eventually went as far as India, Turkestan, Afghanistan, Yemen, the Caucasus, south west France and even, reputedly, Wales. The southern kingdom of Judah, including Bethlehem and Hebron, was conquered by the Babylonians over a century later in 586BCE. Its elites were carried off to Babylon, where the Jewish scriptures were laid down during the Babylonian Captivity – and during this period the Jewish faith, its doctrines and rabbinical traditions, took a more solid shape, becoming firmly monotheistic. Some returned after the Persian Cyrus the Great took over Babylon in 538, while others stayed or progressed eastwards into Persia, Afghanistan and Kashmir.

Thereafter the area was largely united under a succession of foreign empires – overlords ruling over ethnically mixed lands. First came the Persians for two centuries, 538-333BCE; next came the Greeks for two centuries, following Alexander the Great's whirlwind invasion of 333BCE; after this, for a century there was an independent Jewish kingdom of the Hasmoneans, 140-37BCE. Then came the Romans for over three centuries until CE330. During the Roman period the Jewish revolts of CE66-73 and 132-135 led to defeat and further Jewish dispersion around the Mediterranean and the Middle East. Some remained in Palestine, gradually losing their ethnic identity and becoming part of the people we now identify as Palestinians. Most 'Romans' in the area actually lived Greek-style lives, and the East Roman empire was culturally Greek.

To Westerners, the big event of the Roman period was the life and death of Jesus. Locally, this had but a small effect, and Jews did not recognise him as the promised Messiah. Jesus was one of several Jewish teachers who came and went, and his teachings spread amongst Mesopotamians, Syrians and gentiles in the Roman world, although not without opposition and repression. After three centuries, Christianity became a Roman state religion with two main branches, Catholicism in the west and Greek Orthodoxy in the east. In Palestine a variety of churches had evolved and, under the Greek Orthodox Byzantines, they thrived.

Pictures of Palestine

As the declining Roman empire divided into western and eastern halves, the eastern Greek Romans reinvented themselves as Byzantines, ruling Palestine from 330-640. Here came the growth of Christianity as an institutional faith: old Christian churches and communities, originating in the decades following Jesus' crucifixion, grew in stature and power and Byzantine Palestine prospered for centuries.

The culture of today's Palestinian Christians has its roots in this time. Many of their ways are Greek in style, though some claim ancestral descent from Yemen, and they are Mediterranean in character. In recent decades a great proportion of them have left for the West.

Over the centuries there was little conflict between Christians and Muslims or, until the 20th century, between them and Jews – they all rubbed along. The Byzantine period was ended by the Arabic Muslim invasion of 630, leading to 1,300 years of Muslim predominance. Christians, Jews and other minorities had rights and protections under Islam and, while not forced to convert, many gradually became Muslims. Islam, with its legal, philosophical and religious codes, was regarded as an upgrade of earlier faiths and cultures – and Muslims paid less tax. Ancient beliefs and mystery schools pervaded the area and Islam had a unifying, modernising influence. There were social advantages to conversion, rather like the advantages conferred on non-Westerners by buying into Western ways during the 20th century. Islam was pluralistic, drawing on Judaism, Christianity and Zoroastrianism, with lineal grandees such as Abraham and Jesus as prophets. Many Byzantine administrative and trading customs were adopted by the Muslims.

In 691 the Dome of the Rock in Jerusalem was built by the Islamic Umayyad dynasty of Damascus, Syria – the rock, a significant site in the story of Abraham and Isaac, was also the site of Muhammad's mystical ascent to heaven. Then the Al Aqsa mosque and the sanctuary of Haram al Sharif were built on the site of the Roman-destroyed Jewish Temple – nowadays a focus of contention between Muslims and Jews. Jerusalem was Sunni Islam's third most holy place after Mecca and Medina in Arabia. Originally Muslims prayed facing Jerusalem, not Mecca. By the 700s and 800s, under the Abbasid caliphs of Baghdad, the area prospered, enjoying an ascendant, cosmopolitan culture and playing a part in a vast Muslim system.

In Europe these were the Dark Ages but in the Middle East – also in West Africa, India, China, SE Asia and Mexico – they were an Age of Light, a zenith of civilisation. The Muslim world was vibrant until the 1200s, a relatively stable culture unified by Muslim law, Arabic language and a commonality that exists today, whatever boundaries and regimes are established to split it up. But trouble came from Asia: around the 1250s the Mongols swept in from the east, ending a golden age. They didn't last long, and the regional vacuum following their disappearance was gradually filled in the 1300s by the Turkic Ottomans. By the mid-1500s the Ottomans ruled much of the Middle East, the Balkans and the east Mediterranean.

But before the Mongols there was a little local difficulty in Palestine. Europe's first colonial adventure, the Crusades, came in the 1090s, driven by a desire to retake Jerusalem for Christianity. This they did murderously in 1099, reputedly killing all of Jerusalem's inhabitants. Here were laid down many precedents for today. They founded the Crusader kingdom of Jerusalem, covering today's Israel and Palestine.

Some Crusaders settled, adopting local ways and intermarrying, while others kept apart, coming and going, asserting distinctly European values and feudal rule. There was rivalry between these two camps and their dissonance became their eventual undoing. Some Muslims today see the state of Israel as a throwback to the Crusades and, arguably, differences between liberal Jews and Zionists of today parallel Crusader times. In both the Crusades and today it was Western money, people and weapons that drove the enterprise, and both saw themselves to be returning home. But these parallels should not be taken too far.

Pictures of Palestine

In medieval Europe, persecutions against Jews started in Crusader times, since Jews were seen as exotic, different and responsible for the death of Christ. Ironically, they were identified with infidel Muslims by Europeans. This set a pattern of oppression of Jews in Europe which by the 20th century was to bounce back on Palestine. Meanwhile Jews in Palestine, living in peace largely around Galilee, played their part in the multi-ethnic Middle East. Neighbouring Muslims coexisted with the Christian Crusader kingdom, but waves of aggressively single-minded Crusaders occasionally sailed in from Europe, gaining the upper hand, behaving badly and upsetting people.

By the time Saladin, sultan of Egypt and Syria, came along, tensions were high. He summoned the Muslims and beat the Crusaders at the Battle of Hattin in 1187, mentioned earlier. Then he took back Jerusalem, bestowing far more mercy on his enemies than the Crusaders had done 88 years before. It was not foreigners with a different faith that troubled him: it was their behaviour. This we see today with Palestinians: most accept Jews and the existence of Israel, at least within its pre-1967 borders, but what troubles them is the *chutzpah* and force of Israeli behaviour, driven by Zionist impulses.

Salah-ad-Din penned up the Crusaders in Acre and later, by 1291, Sultan Baibars finally got rid of them. Some Crusader families stayed, merging with the population, and some Palestinian Christians, such as my friends Albert and John, thus have Crusader ancestors.

The notion of sharing the Holy Land has a string of historic precedents during the time of Joshua, the Assyrians, Babylonians, Romans, Crusaders and Ottomans. It has been a story in which nationalist and religious rivalry has vied with multi-ethnic, multifaith tolerance. Tolerance is a carefully-cultivated social condition, easily broken by hard-nosed, divisive elements and elites. Today, it could be argued that it's not a conflict between Israelis and Palestinians but between divisive and multi-cultural people and beliefs.

Pictures of Palestine

During the Mamluk period, 1270-1516, the Egyptian rulers of Palestine, anticipating another European invasion, destroyed many of its coastal harbours and cities. Life was centred in the inland highlands of the West Bank and Palestine became peripheral, its Mediterranean and Mesopotamian connections largely lost.

Then came four centuries of Ottoman Turkish rule from 1516 to 1917. The Ottomans had taken the rich Byzantine capital of Constantinople in 1453, renaming it Istanbul, expanding their realm from there. The Holy Land was taken by Sultan Suleiman the Magnificent, an empire-building general, engineer and lawgiver. After a good start, Palestine gradually became a relatively neglected area of the Ottoman domain, peripheral to the main hubs of Istanbul, Cairo and Damascus.

Life carried on all the same for centuries, with its ups and downs. The Ottoman world eventually creakingly declined in the 19th century as Europe came to dominate the world, and the empire fell in WW1. Already, in its final decades, an Arabic movement in Palestine had campaigned for self-determination, leading to a revolt against the Ottomans in 1906, but events overtook them, and the trouble only really started for Palestinians during WW1. Westerners, in the form of the British and the French, came and broke up the Middle East, occupying the Ottoman lands. But that story comes later.

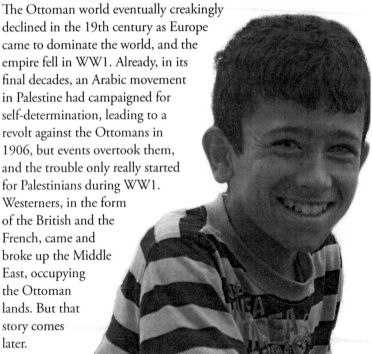

14 **Cultural Resistance**
how wars are truly won

I learned something about cultural resistance when I was a teenager in Liverpool, a million city then with a lot of violence, vandalism, class war, racism and polarisation – particularly between Catholics and Protestants but also affecting Jews, Chinese and blacks. Once the world's greatest port, in the 1960s it was declining. The working class culture of dockers and factory workers was dying and the British empire was gone.

Then came a cultural transformation, gathering pace from about 1964 onwards. It involved musicians, comedians, poets, footballers, plans to rebuild the city and a fizzing liveliness that brought an exciting edge to this depressed urban centre. When, suddenly, Liverpool was *the* place to be, guess what happened? The violence and vandalism subsided. This was not 'economic development' costing billions; it came from the creativity of *people*. Their hardship and imagination drove Liverpool to become world-famous.

This transformation broke a pattern. Up to then, if you had money, education or connections, you'd disappear off to London or America. No longer: the world turned its eyes and ears our way, we set the pace and others followed. Well, at least for a while.

Fortyish years later, I was in Palestine. The place is denied national status, propped up by UNRWA, NGOs and aid agencies, obstructed by Israeli border controls and checkpoints, with no port or airport and imprisoned in high walls. Here, you get nowhere or you get out. I know a team of brainy Palestinian doctors in London who are world-leaders in coronary research, and they 'made it' by becoming exiles.

Pictures of Palestine

To an extent, aid coming in through UNRWA, the EU and other sources weakens this country, giving Palestinians a feeling of dependent uselessness and grateful powerlessness. It corrupts in many different ways, giving great power to those who dispense the funds. To succeed, if you don't leave, you get your snout in the trough, working for the PA, a foreign company or an NGO.

But it doesn't have to be like this. The more that Palestinians take charge of their lives, developing their skills and creativity, healing themselves of psychological damage and defining themselves as a self-determining people, the more Palestine will revive. This is what Hope Flowers specialises in. It focuses on children, women and the disadvantaged, the people whose progress will determine the future.

A culture revives and regenerates out of igniting a spark in people's hearts and spirits. Pain and hope, a cruel pair when combined, are the ignition. Our resolve to be unbeaten by hardship and disadvantage is a source of power and intelligence. Drive and good-heartedness will revive Palestine far more than foreign aid can.

Pictures of Palestine

Palestine doesn't have to measure up to other people's norms to succeed, doesn't have to bend over backwards to comply with conditions and requirements determined by Israelis and foreigners. Palestinians don't have to fight the Israelis: fighting the enemy and answering back with force hasn't achieved the needed results. In the long term, it weakens Palestine's culture and society, bringing death, emigration and suffering – although submission is no solution either. But the experience of conflict has forced Palestinian society to face some important human issues concerning the kind of society they're striving for.

The rich Gulf States have oil, money and shopping malls, but their pride and momentum depend on wealth, which flows where it wants, and on rulers and elites whose power is more precarious than they prefer to believe. Palestine has no oil or significant resources: its wealth lies in its society.

Palestine needs to name the game on its own terms, making use of *what it has*. Back in Liverpool, the Beatles were the first musicians ever to be heard by people of all ages and all cultures, globally. They had no degrees, wealth or status, and they started without good connections in a place that was far from being a known centre of culture. But everyone everywhere ended up singing their songs, even when they didn't understand the words.

The Beatles sang a new kind of song, experimenting with new musical forms, art and behaviour, and this florescence left its mark worldwide. They broke the rules, innovating faster and further than anyone else and they became iconic. They didn't try to bring down the old order, they simply overtook it on the outside, showing that a renaissance emerges not through normal, formal channels but through bypassing and superseding what has gone before. There's a lesson here for Palestinians – and the challenge is to cultivate a cultural upswing that shifts the agenda and changes the landscape. This has recently been proven by the younger generations across the

Middle East, who see things differently from their elders, and their analysis has been determined by looking pragmatically at their current situation rather than by referencing to all that has gone before.

Hamas talks a lot about resistance. They have a point, since the Israelis are, in Palestinians' eyes, unreasonable, unmovable. But the resistance of guns and rockets hasn't succeeded, and the Israelis respond with the hammer, screeching incessantly about terrorism and security. Hamas is at heart more a social than a military organisation, working to improve health, education and welfare, and this is its strong point, which it now risks losing by getting stuck in a pattern of military resistance. True resistance is more than this – it's a cultural and a social-vibrancy matter, *a matter of spirit*, or spiritedness, not just of religion, welling up from the roots of society. There's no standard recipe for igniting it, but when it gushes out, everyone knows.

What great strength does Palestine have? What does it need neither to import nor to imitate? It has the societal power to survive hardship and disappointment and it remains unbeaten, even under extreme duress. In Britain we call this 'World War Two Spirit' – a holding together and survival against the odds, undeterred by adversity.

Meanwhile, globally the world is entering a time of crisis. Its climate is changing, population is ballooning, its ecosystem is deteriorating, its economy is beholden to financial speculation – and we're heading for times of fundamental change. The bottom-line issues of the future, for many of the world's inhabitants, are survival, sufficiency, resilience, cooperation and basic social contentedness.

Palestinians know about hardship, endurance and cooperation. Soldiers have kicked down their doors and tanks have ripped up their streets, people have been killed, made hungry, rejected, ignored, and half of the population is in exile. But they're *still here* and unbeaten. This, in the 21st century, is important knowledge for a society to possess – the art of collective survival.

Pictures of Palestine

In future times, *Palestinians could be advisors to the world*. Aid teams of the future will come from places like Palestine, not with truckloads of food and building materials but with teams of people bearing *knowledge* and *experience* – stuff that costs little. Palestinians are doctors who can work on a shoestring, builders who can construct with what's available, teachers who know how to work with social trauma, communities that know how to stand firm through hardship.

Resistance is a cultural thing. It's about *community resilience*, the ability to adapt to facts and make a bad situation good. It's about being happy with simple things – a song, some bread and hummus, being together with people you love, and even getting on with people you dislike. It's about befriending life, nature and humanity, it's an attitude.

This is what we need to talk about if we're discussing resistance and development. *This is where Palestinians are strong*. The battle is won with attitude, sharing, community, family, goodwill and generosity. Palestinians are qualified to look at the world and say, *"Can we teach this to you too, and send in a team to help you?"*

15 Ramallah
visiting the capital

One day, Ibrahim and I visited Ramallah to see a deputy minister in the PA about a radio station Ibrahim proposed to start. We reckoned that perhaps my presence, as a Westerner, might add some weight, giving an impression Ibrahim was well-connected – this can matter.

Ramallah is due north of Bethlehem and Jerusalem lies between them. But our journey to Ramallah followed a lengthy route around East Jerusalem, throttled as it is by security walls and checkpoints, on the circuitous road linking the southern and northern West Bank. The roadblocks were clear today, so it took an hour and a half to do the 70km road journey to Ramallah – 25 km as the crow flies. The return journey took three tiring and hot hours, thanks to traffic jams at the Qalandia checkpoint outside Ramallah, even though we only had to go past, not through it, staying on the Palestinian side of the separation wall.

From Bethlehem the road weaves northeast through Beit Sahour and Ubeidiya, passing near Abu Dis and Al Azariyah on the eastern edge of East Jerusalem, then around the Israeli settlement of Ma'ale Adumim. From there it heads eastwards down the Israeli trunk road from Jerusalem toward Jericho and the Allenby Bridge, a fast and smooth road that Palestinians are permitted to drive along. Then we turn off northwest along a winding stretch up through the Judean hills, past several Bedouin encampments. Next it turns west and south again, for a while following the separation wall enclosing the northern outskirts of Jerusalem, until the route reaches the big, unsightly Qalandia checkpoint, where it turns north into Ramallah.

The scenery along the road is spectacular, with rounded limestone ridges up to 600m or 2,000ft high and deeply incised valleys. At places it zigzags steeply down into the valleys and snakes tortuously up the other side, passing through hilltop Arab villages hugging the road, some with impressive views over the hills east toward Jordan.

Israel was originally meant to occupy the rich coastal plains alongside the Mediterranean, which it did until its 1967 occupation of the West Bank. For Israelis there were two big problems with Israel's original shape: first, the coastal plain was narrow and strategically vulnerable to attack from the West Bank highlands, ruled from 1948 to 1967 by Jordan; second, the historic Jewish

kingdoms of two millennia ago, Judah and Israel or Samaria, lay in the West Bank, now populated by Arabs. So for Israelis it made both strategic and historic sense to take the West Bank in the Six Day War. For Palestinians it was disastrous.

Though the Israelis caught an infectious disease of persecution and oppression from the Nazis, they didn't take on the 'final solution'. Many Palestinians have died in targeted assassinations, shoot-outs and Israeli trigger-happiness, but systematic elimination of masses of Palestinians has not taken place. Here, the accusation that Israelis are attempting genocide is incorrect and excessive, for whilst there are elements in Israeli society that would like to drive out or otherwise disappear the Palestinians, they have not done it. It could be argued that they have paid a price for that, since those Palestinians just keep on causing trouble, and they still form the majority in the West Bank.

Gaza does not share the same historic and strategic position as the West Bank. In former times Gaza was an important coastal trading place where the main route from Egypt to Syria met the caravan trails coming up from Arabia. It was a centre for slave-trading of Africans and war captives, which somehow casts a shadow today. But nowadays Gaza is of marginal strategic importance to Israel, except for one thing – there's natural gas in Gazan coastal waters which Gazans cannot themselves exploit because of Israeli restriction of their access to the sea. Israel keeps quiet about it because it has no legal jurisdiction over the gasfields, though it is attempting to drill into them sideways from its own undersea territory. It has recently discovered some gasfields of its own too.

Ariel Sharon's withdrawal of Jewish settlers from Gaza in 2005 was a big issue for the 7,000 or so Israeli settlers who were affected, but Sharon was a military strategist and proponent of settlement-building who wanted to focus Israel's attentions on the West Bank. Since 1.5 million Palestinians live in Gaza, a large proportion of them refugees, and since Gaza City is Palestine's second largest city, the Israelis decided to abandon Gaza, quarantining it as if to make Gazans disappear from view. Hence the use of rockets by

Pictures of Palestine

Gazan militants, firing over the military cordon. The irony is that, while Gaza is blockaded, it is internally free of Israel settlements and land appropriation, possessing a distinct, clear border, unlike the West Bank.

But the Israelis shot themselves in the foot because Gaza was a Hamas stronghold, remaining to this day a thorn in the side of Israel and an awkward focus of international attention. This was highlighted during Israel's cruel bombardment of Gaza in late 2008 and by the Freedom Flotilla incident of 2010, which made even some Israelis and international Jews think twice.

It took time for me to find a roadmap of the West Bank and I soon learned why. Palestinians and Israelis know where the effective border lies and which roads they each may drive along – but that is subject to change, so it's unclear on maps. Internationals can drive most places, although what happens at checkpoints depends on your number plates and who you're travelling with. Most tourists stay in Israel proper or are guests of Israelis, who treat Palestinian areas as no-go places, or they follow settler by-pass roads.

Then there's a cartographic issue. Marking a border on a map denotes a fixing and recognition of it and Palestinians don't want to do this – they regard the Green Line, the 1948 armistice line, effective up to 1967, as their official border, and recognition of anything less signifies a surrender of territory. So *checkpoints* are marked on Palestinian maps, since they affect traffic and access, and the Green Line is marked too, but the Israeli-defined *de facto* border stays unmarked. Checkpoints often aren't on the border anyway – they're placed wherever Israelis wish to assert movement control. It's also not clear on West Bank maps which are Palestinian roads, which are Israeli settler roads and what access is permitted where. Nicely complex, yet again.

Meanwhile, Israel pursues its surreptitious 'facts on the ground' approach. The separation wall, eating into the West Bank inside the Green Line, constitutes an Israeli-defined border, yet plenty of Israeli settlements exist on the Palestinian side of the wall too. Israelis are allowed through, and Palestinians must have permission.

Pictures of Palestine

Israeli maps show no border since, to them, all of Israel and Palestine is theirs, though a faint wiggling line sometimes marks the separation wall. It's a 'security fence' to Israelis, initially a 'temporary protective measure', except it isn't, since it's pretty permanent and its demolition will cost billions.

It's all suitably complex, a situation where the Israelis regard Palestinians as squatters on the West Bank, managed by the PA, and surrounded by Israeli settlers, walls and security zones. Meanwhile Palestinians regretfully comply with movement restrictions while counting the whole of the West Bank within the Green Line as theirs – which, according to international law, it is. But international law is not enforced. This means that, as a foreign visitor, you need to have friends and taxi-drivers to advise you, or inside knowledge or good antennae to get around, although transgression usually means annoying delays and questionings rather than mortal danger.

There's more to this. The rules in this land are inconsistently and unsystematically applied. Sometimes it's okay to go somewhere and other times it's not; until recently, movable 'flying checkpoints'

Ramallah

added hidden surprises to any journey. Setting out for another town or going to work, people are never sure that they'll get there, or when. One unintended consequence of this is that Palestine has a high uptake of mobile phones, helping people deal with uncertainty. Even international NGOs complained in 2006 that they had to establish depots and offices in every Palestinian enclave because travel was so difficult – ridiculous when you consider how small Palestine actually is.

But then, the Israeli authorities don't want internationals in Palestine – we are supposed to go to Israel only. Israel doesn't want us seeing things they don't want us to see, or giving the wider world inside information about Palestine.

When Israelis think up a law or regulation pertaining to Palestinians, they frame the details very much from their own blinkered viewpoint, frequently overlooking issues such as practical workability, real life or legality. There is arbitrariness and confusion in the application of laws and regulations for Palestinians, and this is partially deliberate, to undermine all sense of normality or rights. It's not uncommon to see confused Israeli officials fretting, charged with effecting such imperious diktats while being faced with real-world situations where they must make real-life decisions. This arbitrariness has a confusing and disempowering effect. Palestinians are accustomed to it: the trick is to find the gaps and loopholes, or simply to turn up on a good day.

This obstructionism lightened up in 2008-09, with the removal of many roadblocks and checkpoints, after international pressure. But the pattern of control still remains. Arbitrary actions are taken, announcements are made that aren't acted on, actions are taken that aren't announced, one authority says one thing and another says something else, you're bounced from office to office until you give up, laws are interpreted in a great variety of ways, and rights are consistently whittled away. It's a kind of systematic chaoticism with one clear objective: *Israel shall decide and prevail*. But Israelis thoughtlessly undermine even their own best interests: they generate ill feeling by making life difficult, and they get themselves thoroughly confused too.

Pictures of Palestine

Palestinians take it in their stride because this is the shape and nature of their lives, but it still undermines plans and timings and, at times, drives them to despair. It's rarely easy predicting how long anything will take, when it will happen, or how. Even if you're near death's door in the back of an ambulance, that's no guarantee you'll get to hospital. So people develop an elasticity which certainly has its virtues, but it's debilitating. Sure, traffic jams, delays and complications happen worldwide, but they're usually not as deliberate as here.

On our journey to Ramallah, Ibrahim and I had an interesting discussion. We were talking about *apartheid* and its effects and he observed that there are two areas where Israelis and Palestinians have complete cooperation. This arose from my expressing a belief that Palestine has a public health and toxic pollution risk. Palestinians have no lack of doctors, knowhow and educated people but they lack funds and hardware and, as a result, important things get overlooked, creating a crisis just waiting to happen.

The two areas of complete cooperation according to Ibrahim are public health and mafias. For public health they have joint committees and projects and doctors and public health officials from both sides meet regularly. Well, that's good, a sign of rare pragmatism in an otherwise crazy land.

Then there are the *mafiosi* of Israel and Palestine. The most adaptable and flexible business entities in any society are those of organised crime – they innovate and open up possibilities that businessmen and officials avoid. In Israel there is a quiet, comfortable arrangement between crime, business and government which started during the British Mandate when Jewish smuggling of goods, weapons and people under the noses of the Brits became an institution.

The Israelis prefer to supply Palestine with goods and services through monopolies, some above-board, some less so – Israeli outfits are given the contract to supply, say, oil, medical products, food or consumer goods. There's big money in this, and monopoly control also means that they can shut off supplies when they wish or control terms, quantities and prices – this is how the Gaza blockade has operated. It's a convenient system where government and security bodies work alongside organised crime, quietly giving them lucrative tasks and thereby gaining favours or some control, while raking off the occasional disguised cut or mutual back-scratch. Please don't tell anyone – this is, of course, *not happening.*

Israeli monopolies deal with Palestinian monopolies on handshake terms, with everyone officially turning a blind eye. The core of the Palestinian *mafiosi* is 'the Tunisians', the senior elite of the PLO who spent years in exile in Tunisia, returning in the 1990s when Arafat took over the reins in Palestine. They were entrusted with the big contracts that emerged with the new PA dispensation. So the Palestinian 'shadow power structure', shall we call it, interacts co-dependently with that of the Israelis, and the sums and influence involved are huge. There's a cat-and-mouse equilibrium to it which is insidiously large-scale, running alongside the ruling Fateh movement in Palestine and rendering it somewhat beholden to Israeli preferment and arm-twisting.

There's more. One reason why Israel is reluctant to allow Palestinian independence is this: it would lose several million captive consumers, the Palestinians, and there are only six million Israelis. The Israeli economy would shrink enormously, losing cheap labour, a swathe of building land and a military control habit in the process.

Almost anything you can get in the wider world you can get in Palestine, if you have the right money or connections. Much exchange operates under the table, and the Palestinian economy is insufficiently formalised to do much else. Figures and consignment notes are somewhat, shall we say, fictitious or inaccurate, petrol is pumped from a tanker on one side of a roadblock to the other, consignments are inveigled across permeable points in the border, matters are quietly fixed and dealings are nicely overlooked.

It involves not just *mafiosi*, but ordinary people too. A Palestinian charity was donated a photocopier by a Dutch organisation, but this was not permitted. So it went to a Palestine-friendly Israeli organisation, where it sat for a few months. Then, on an agreed day, the staff held a meeting upstairs while the Palestinians came along and 'stole' it, beetling off to the West Bank with it. The theft was reported next day and the case remained mysteriously unsolved. In this land, if you hear of crimes, murders or funny stuff which remain unsolved, it's a sure sign something fishy is going on involving intelligence services, the military, settler networks, resistance groups or *mafiosi*.

There's a lot of half-truth circulating and everyone participates in it. Settlement-building is *not happening*, the Israeli military nuclear facility at Dimona, southeast of Bethlehem, *isn't there*, and many transactions are accounted for by other, unseen means. In Palestine, there are two governments, both unconstitutional, of what might be either one or two countries (Gaza and the West Bank), except neither they nor Palestine as a whole are legitimate countries, instead being blockaded and occupied. All half-realities, half-truths, unresolved issues and outstanding questions, rendered suitably unclear.

Israel is controlled by a number of families and puppet-masters in the military, government and business worlds; its government is a kind of democracy excluding 30% of the population and its economy is a kind of free-market economy except it isn't, being artificially inflated and distorted by foreign subsidy and enormous military spending. Official and *de facto* realities coexist flexibly and interdependently. Palestine is controlled by a closed, unofficial network too, gaggled around the PA, and *that's the way it is* – except it isn't. Believe what you're told, not what you observe. Everyone does it, in the street and the loftiest of international institutions. Even great nations and the UN lie about Palestine.

Ask questions and you'll be ignored, shoulders will be shrugged, you get a strange look or the subject is changed. It's a social compact. This is not exactly *crime* nor even *corruption* – it's, well, a matter of creative business and statecraft. It's worth billions, controlling both countries, holding the world to ransom, and it's a neat arrangement that works at present, at least for its beneficiaries, who have a vested interest in maintaining it. If the Palestinians suddenly got up and voluntarily transferred themselves out of Israel, dissembling this arrangement, as some Israelis naively want, Israel would take a dive, its economy would deflate and its future would be threatened.

Actually, these 'corrupt criminals', are not necessarily bad guys – they just like to be in control and make money. Global capitalism favours them as partners to deal with. Anything that makes a profit is *good*, and this is how the world works, even if it destroys everything in the process – losses can after all be written off in the accounts. Palestine is not as blatantly corrupt as many countries – there is even a certain shared morality to the way things work. Much passes under the counter but people don't rip each other off if they can help it.

I once took three Israeli ladies to a Palestinian shop in an Area C district above Beit Jala – Palestinian majority and Israeli controlled. At first they were scared to enter but, once inside, they were amazed that prices were much lower than those in Israel, even for the very same products – and some goods imported from Middle Eastern countries were unavailable in Israel too. Goods and services in Israel are heavily taxed, and subject to those unstated taxes and rake-offs that Westerners blithely ignore – corporate profits and weighty retail mark-up. Palestine doesn't have stiff taxes, clunky corporate structures and a shareholder class to support, so things are cheaper.

Muslims have a different attitude toward charges, prices and profits to Israelis. Most Palestinians' wages are low. So a taxi-ride in Bethlehem might cost 10 shekels while in Jerusalem a similar ride costs 25. Yet the cost of living is lower in Palestine, and thus the real standard of living is not as low as one would think – and much operates through the grey economy or family networks. The Israeli ladies quietly debated whether any of them dared come back to this shop alone; one said she used to buy in shops like this in the 1990s before the wall was built. I could see the Palestinian shopkeeper quietly smiling – he gets a lot of this, and probably does quite well from it.

Pictures of Palestine

Although there's much talk about *apartheid*, there are also plenty of instances where the lines are not clearly drawn and there are ways around things. There are back roads, places where you can get certain items, people who can fix things – you just need to know where to go or who to ask.

In Palestine there are rich and powerful people, but the trickle-down of money and beneficence is significant. Palestinians rate family, clan and community highly, and those in power gain a certain satisfaction from practising magnanimity, even if mainly within their own clan – but clans are large so that can extend widely. Everyone is somehow related, and rich and poor interact far more than in the West. This arises from traditional, Muslim and Arab-socialist values intermixed, hammered together by shared hardship over several generations.

There is a vague sense of duty and shame amongst rich Palestinians, causing them to invest liberally in Palestine, employ people and spread wealth around – not least because generosity today might save your life tomorrow. Even many secular Palestinians still work on a subconscious basis that Allah sees everything and shame must be avoided. This adds an ethical dimension to life that is not really shared by Israelis.

A factor that exaggerates and pollutes this mutualism is foreign influence – politics, weapons and money – without which the scale of patronage and preferment, funny money and corruption would be much reduced. Western corporations and governments favour existing power-hierarchies if they deliver order, good business and accountability (which means, 'do it *our* way, not yours'). The biggest source of funds in Palestine comes from humanitarian and development aid, particularly from Europe. Those who receive and dispense these funds are selected by Western criteria. The PA prime minister, Salam Fayyad, once a senior official in the World Bank and notably uncorrupt, tops the pile of fairer and more dedicated Palestinian public servants. But they, nevertheless, are beneficiaries of the Western dispensation and are in office because of it and they also hold certain values that are not shared by the Palestinian majority.

Pictures of Palestine

During our visit to Ramallah I met a former 'Tunisian', a deputy minister. He was about my age, a decent chap, definitely in charge of his patch and quite receptive to our proposal. Ibrahim wanted to start a radio station advocating peace, seeking to broadcast unbiased, informative, educational content to counterbalance the commercial rubbish and strident nationalism that comes out on most Palestinian radio channels. Balanced content is crucial when conflict heats up and polarisation rockets. In January 2009 when Gaza was under attack, most radio stations yelled and screamed anti-Israeli rhetoric, depriving Palestinians of decent coverage and debate of the issues.

The deputy minister sat comfortably in his nice leather chair, probably brought in from an IKEA store in Israel. He was competent, obviously knew his stuff and likely occupied that seat because he had been in with the right guys at the right time. He wasn't a bad guy – that's just the way it works. A few weeks later I met another official who, in my judgement, shouldn't have been in high office, being more interested in his own power than the wider good of the Palestinians he serves.

Anyway, the deputy minister explained that Palestine's radio-frequency slots were all taken up and the total number of available slots was determined by the Israelis, which he couldn't do anything about, so he recommended taking over an existing station – an action that he would support and approve, since he believed radio standards needed to rise. Actually, he thought many stations were a pile of crap – stated in Arabic, of course. Our problem was that a takeover would cost around $120,000 before even going on air – a tiny fraction of the price of a helicopter gunship, but a large sum when you're Palestinian trying to raise it on an altruistic basis. Then there would be running and development costs too. Ibrahim wasn't put off by this – he's a real trooper – but it's a steep slope to climb.

Ramallah is a scrappier place than Bethlehem, which is perhaps the finest of Palestinian cities, more loved by its inhabitants than Ramallah. But Ramallah is cosmopolitan, central: here are PA government departments, NGOs and foreign organisations, some quite plush. Many suit-wearing foreigners are here, as well as the PA oligarchy and the educated Palestinian overclass. Yet Ramallah is piecemeal, a town that grew chaotically as the separation of Palestine and Israel took place in the 1990s, while East Jerusalem was progressively ring-fenced by Israel, judaicised and deprived of its status as the Palestinian capital.

Ramallah is business-oriented, even down to its children. A kid came up, trying to sell me a stick of chewing gum for a shekel. He persisted. Foolishly, I eventually yielded, and he affixed himself to me. I was seeking a mobile phone shop and he took me to ask a man who pointed me in the right direction. Then the boy followed me demanding ten shekels for his assistance.

Eventually I got rid of him but, twenty minutes later, having bought a phone, I was standing waiting for Ibrahim and three of his friends came along, obviously tipped off, to hassle for money. They have a whining, emotional, downtrodden tone to them when wheedling cash, trying to give you the feeling that they might die if you don't buy chewing gum or give money. In due course I was rescued by Ibrahim, who ticked them off. I felt like a naive Western fool, which I was.

After a long day and the arduous journey back, including that traffic jam at Qalandia and a clogged checkpoint in the hills near Ma'ale Adumim, I was glad to return to Bethlehem when Ibrahim finally dropped me off in the centre of town. But the day wasn't finished yet.

16 The British Mandate
Palestine in the inter-war years

Here's a bit more history. The Middle East was taken from the expiring Ottomans in WW1 by the British and French, who split the region into small countries and drew lines across the map for borders. In doing so they introduced the very European idea that different ethnic groupings would gain security by living in separate independent nations – except they didn't consider carefully the groupings they threw together or forced apart. Really the new borders reflected colonialist priorities and control agendas more than natural ethnic areas or local need. They aimed to stop a united Arab nation rising from the ashes of the Ottoman empire.

Before WW1 different ethnic groups had coexisted in the provinces of the Ottoman sphere, taking on interlocking social roles and niches within a multi-ethnic society. But the British and French gave power and advantage to certain minorities chosen as middlemen to keep majorities under control – Jews in Palestine, Maronite Christians in Lebanon, Awalites in Syria, Sunnis in Iraq and Bedouin in Jordan. This is where the trouble of subsequent decades was really seeded, setting people against each other and fostering minority elites.

Palestine went through three decades of British rule during which its economy was modernised and trade expanded. It received more attention than under the Turks, but with mixed results. A new influence was arriving, playing a part in that modernisation: European Jews. About 30,000 had come in the 1880s and 1890s, in the first *aliyah* or 'return'. They bought available land and houses, mainly from absentee Ottoman landowners, and local Arabs accepted them, with reservations, since Jews had lived in the region throughout history. Numbers grew by another 40,000 by 1914, many of them business-oriented townspeople and socialist idealists, founders of the communal *kibbutzim* and the *moshav* collectives. Both their impact and Arab reservations grew incrementally at this time.

Then came the Brits in WW1. The Balfour Declaration of 1917 supported the idea of a Jewish homeland in Palestine. It came about as a fluke, a return favour for a valuable military invention made in WW1 by Chaim Weizmann, a chemistry professor in Manchester, England, and an early Zionist. Other Brits had qualms about the Balfour Declaration, and this foreign policy dualism has continued up to the present day – actually a tripartite friction between Jewish, business and Arabist influences in the British diplomatic world.

Even so, the 1920 Mandate

enabling British rule, made by the League of Nations, stated that, with the establishment of a Jewish homeland, "Nothing should be done which might prejudice the civil and religious rights of existing non-Jewish communities in Palestine". That bit was to become problematic: Jewish immigrants were being told by Zionists back in Europe that this was 'a land without people waiting for a people without a land', as if theirs for the taking. Now a disjunction of interests was taking shape.

Zionism, propounded by Theodore Herzl, Chaim Weizmann and others, was a nationalist belief in promoting Jewish rights and identity in Europe which developed into an urge to found a state of Israel. Religious Jews at the time opposed this, since a set of prophetic preconditions had to be fulfilled first, but many Zionists were modern Europeans who saw such ideas as an obstacle and national self-determination as an emerging right. Originally Zionism's advocates had a variety of leftist, secular, humanist and utopian leanings. Many decades later, by the 1980s, Zionism leaned rightwards, by then informed by a mixture of territorial expansionism, business and military agendas and Orthodox Jewish beliefs.

Jewish immigration to Palestine increased in the late 1920s and the 1930s as pressures and persecutions escalated in Russia, Poland and Germany. The Zionist movement, spearheading this migration, grew in momentum, aiding and financing the relocation and buying up land for settlement. European Jews brought with them urban ways, money, lifestyles and values, settling mainly around Haifa and the newly-founded city of Tel Aviv. Jewish economic growth was about 13%, largely urban-centred, while Palestinian growth was around 6%, largely agricultural.

Roads, railways and infrastructure were developed by the British. Palestine was pulled into the Western-dominated 20th century. Palestinian society was by now changing, with some Palestinians joining the 'march of progress', others not. Frustrations and frictions grew and Zionists began discreetly planning the founding of a Jewish state. Jews elbowed Arabs aside, Arabs started attacking

Jews, and Jews started fighting back. Arabic unease over social issues, colonial injustices and the scale of Jewish immigration caused the British to increase repression of Palestinians – which naturally favoured the Jews.

This led eventually to an Arab Revolt in 1936. Palestinians were upset over loss of land and influence and the inadequacies and cruelties of British rule. Increasingly they sought self-determination. The British used repressive measures, effectively decapitating Palestinian society by removing its leaders by killing or exile and by using 'divide and rule' methods.

Meanwhile, by 1938, Jews formed militias such as Haganah, Lehi and Irgun, nominally in self-defence, supporting British rule and staging retaliatory attacks on Palestinians. Conflict intensified, emotions flew, skirmishes and outrages took place, and the British further suppressed Arabic opposition to their rule. There was an increasing separation of Palestinians and Jews. To pacify Palestinians, the British promised them independence by 1949 – though here the idea of partitioning the land was already forming.

The Zionist thinker Ze'ev Jabotinsky had mapped out an 'iron wall' policy in which Jews should use superior force to contain and oust Palestinians, bring advantage to Jewish interests and lay the ground for a state of Israel. The idea grew that, for the Jews to achieve a majority and self-determination, the Palestinians would have to be cleared or 'transferred' from what were to become Jewish lands. However, Jabotinsky also stated that a day would come when force would have to stop, and Israel would need to befriend its neighbours if the state were to survive longterm. This advice was later ignored and Zionism increasingly became a Jewish supremacist belief, not just a liberation movement, a programme for further colonising Palestinian lands and asserting muscle in the Middle East, whatever the cost.

In WW2 the Palestine Jews sided with the British. They opposed Nazi persecution, the Holocaust in Europe and the threat of a German invasion of the Middle East – the Germans sought oil and to seize Iraq and the Suez Canal. Palestinians were divided, some opposing British rule in Palestine and some implicitly supporting it by fighting against the Germans in Bosnia and Albania to protect fellow Muslims there. The British restricted further Jewish immigration, seeing trouble coming, and seeking to encourage Palestinian acquiescence to their rule.

Then Rommel's panzer divisions scorched through North Africa, scaring Jews in Palestine. By 1942 it looked as if the British were losing the war. They trained and recruited Jewish fighters, but Jews were losing faith in the British. The 1930s Jewish approach of retaliating against Palestinians morphed in the1940s into a plan to eliminate them – though, in the context of the Holocaust in Europe, Jews saw themselves as protecting their own survival, which was partially true, but it jeopardised Arabs. In later years this self-defence rationale was used to justify aggression, gradually becoming something between a myth and a self-fulfilling prophecy. It continues today.

By 1944, as the war turned against the Germans, Jewish factions plotted to get rid of the British, whose control of Palestine was loosening. The British sought to reduce Jewish immigration to keep things under control, offering destinations such as Uganda or Mauritius for Jewish refugees. But it was too late, the Jews were determined: they just needed to go home and home was Palestine.

Beit Jala, a Christian town that remained in Palestine

133

Pictures of Palestine

In 1947, planning to withdraw, Britain handed Palestine's future to the new United Nations. Naively, the UN voted to divide Palestine into two states, with Jerusalem and Bethlehem to be internationally-controlled. It failed to realise that substantial ethnic cleansing of Palestinians would result and war would break out. The Arab state was to have 43% of Palestine, mainly in the highlands, and a Jewish state was to have 56%, mainly in the coastal lowlands and the Negev Desert in the south. At the time, Palestine's population was 67% Palestinian and 33% Jewish. Something wasn't right in the calculations.

The international community, while officially standing in the role of mediator, was siding against the Palestinians – mainly out of sympathy for the Jews, who had suffered so much in Europe, but also because newly-decolonialised Arab countries weren't good diplomatic persuaders. Palestinians turned down the UN deal, since partition was unthinkable for them, the calculations were all wrong and they stood to lose too much. Internationally this was seen as obdurate uncooperativeness – the world wanted a quick fix. Things were moving fast and the world's attention lay with a plethora of other global crises, so the UN plan prevailed and the Palestinians failed to gain support for their case. They had little leadership or support.

In 1947, the Jews started effecting their plans to 'transfer' Palestinians out of the promised Jewish areas called 'Plan Dalet'. Most Palestinians simply could not believe such a thing could happen, and at first failed to defend themselves. The Zionist plan was secret, unknown even to many Jews and, of those who knew, some opposed it, some overlooked it, some disbelieved it and others simply went along with it.

By 1948 open war developed, in response to Jewish massacres and clearance of Palestinian villages and urban quarters. Palestinians were uprooted and sent packing to the West Bank, Gaza, Jordan, Syria and Lebanon. Things became desperate: to the Palestinians, this was the *Nakba* or disaster. Newly-independent neighbouring Arab countries were quite unprepared for conflict. It was Iraqi troops who were the most effective in protecting Palestinians, but the Jews had military superiority and total resolve.

Pictures of Palestine

By the end of the war the state of Israel was declared by David ben Gurion – far larger than the Jewish portion allocated by the UN. The UN-proposed international enclave around Jerusalem and Bethlehem never came to pass, 530 villages were systematically destroyed, thousands of people, mostly Palestinians, were killed and wounded, and 70% of Palestine's Arab population was uprooted.

The British, who shamefully withdrew without intervening, nevertheless secretly supported the annexation of the West Bank by the new state of Transjordan and of Gaza by Egypt, to protect the Palestinians. The British, together with the new Arab states, had voted against the UN partition plan, but they applied insufficient diplomatic pressure to prevent it. At least 700,000 Palestinian refugees fled or were driven from what became Israel, following shocking atrocities. Most expected to return but, when some tried, they found their homes and villages occupied or destroyed.

There followed an enormous population transfer. In the three years after 1948, 700,000 Jews immigrated from Europe and others (*Misrahi* or Sephardic Jews) came mainly from around the Middle East, where they were by now unpopular or threatened. 10,000 Jews lost their homes in Palestinian areas, moving to Israeli areas. By the end of the 1948 war Israel controlled 78% of Palestine, not the 56% they had been allocated. The UN drew a ceasefire line, the Green Line, to formalise a new boundary reflecting this. The Jews now had a nation and the Palestinians didn't.

Some old Palestinians still regard the British Mandate, though a foreign military occupation, as a lesser evil than what followed. But patterns had been set during British rule which determined later actions. Nevertheless, British visitors are largely welcomed today. I had a long discussion with an old gentleman historian who showed me some inter-war British Palestinian passports issued by His Britannic Majesty, with a stamp inside stating 'Not eligible for residence in Britain'. As a Brit I am not proud of this period of history. The British played a double game, and Palestinians paid the price. The price the Jews paid was that Israel was born under a shadow of blood, theft and injustice.

17 Fun in Beit Lahem
bagpipes and saxes in the Old Town

Arriving back in Bethlehem from Ramallah, I went to Adnan's shop to sit down, with the intention of soon afterwards getting a sim card for my new phone. But something else happened: music started playing down in Manger Square. It turned out to be a Palestinian Christian marching band playing, to my surprise, Scots bagpipes and drums. The shutter on my camera was busy for a while.

This was a throwback to the days of the British Mandate. The band, clothed in smart uniforms with red berets, marched around Manger Square, then up Al-Najmah Street into the Old Town. It was rousing music, yet coloured with a wry sense of historic tragedy, a hint of wishful thinking of former days. It faded into the distance, there was a pause and then they came back down again, with gaggles of people in tow and others hanging out of the windows watching. The band marched around the square again and then stopped. People hung around, chatting and the atmosphere on the square was sociable and upbeat.

Then something else started up: the unmistakeable sound of ragtime jazz, coming closer down Al-Najmah Street. As I went down to see, seven Austrian musicians appeared, dressed in comical clothing and followed by a happy crowd of kids and adults, all now entering the square. Everything and everyone perked up and people flooded into the square from all directions. Eventually hundreds were gathered, young and old. The jazz band stood in a semi-circle, striking funny poses, eyeballing people as they played, taking turns

136

to do solos, and people gathered around, taken with the witty ragtime music. It was good music, skilfully played.

Bravo to them. The group had come to Palestine to entertain, and they were succeeding spectacularly. Their crazy humour connected well with Bethlehemites, everyone smiling and chuckling. Christian monks in their habits hung around, chatting with the remnants of the marching band; boys on bikes weaved around them, and families, old ladies, kids and sundry foreigners all were drawn in by the happy din.

My eyes were becoming moist – the scene was so poignant. Here was an imprisoned people chattering, laughing, hanging out. This musical intervention is *real* aid and development, providing an ignition-spark to raise people's spirits, give youngsters ideas, remind

oldsters of happier times and simply to exorcise all current gloom. Bethlehem broke out into a smile and tapped its feet while the trombone, clarinet, cornet, trumpet and drums blasted out jazztime ditties and the Austrians sweated in their funny costumes.

A number of private initiatives like this do happen in Palestine – people come here bringing spirited cultural and human input. They bravely contribute what they're good at to a remarkably grateful and responsive audience. Carrying a trombone through security checks can't be the easiest thing to explain to a sceptical Israeli officer.

I heard of a project by a Dutch rock band, half of them working in Israel, half in Palestine. They held drumming workshops on both sides to train people up for the main event. They got loads of people drumming on anything they could find, all ages joining the training. Then one day everyone trooped upstairs through the buildings on each side of the separation wall on to the flat rooftops, where they played together for hours, across the concrete curtain of the security wall. Apparently it was quite a gig.

Some years ago a German installation artist came to Palestine, mobilising people to assemble junk, wrecks and bits of old metal, of which there is plenty. Then he set to welding them into massive statues outside various Palestinian towns. After completing one junk-sculpture, he would move to another town, leaving a series of sculptures which are mostly still there.

There was also a woman from Switzerland, whom I helped to get fixed up, carrying out her own aid initiative. She taught the European Computer Driving Licence, a certificate course in computer and software use. Her aim was to teach five Palestinians whom she would then set loose to teach others, and she would return later to supervise developments. She had discovered the Hope Flowers Centre in Deheisheh as a place to help facilitate this process – they had a newly kitted-out computer room funded by a European charitable trust.

I talked her through a few facts of the game, and she was receptive. This was a good sign: many Westerners have difficulty encompassing the differences between Palestine and the West. I told her that the basic efficiency standards we take for granted in the West were unlikely to work here – people turning up on time and things happening as planned. She wouldn't achieve her teaching task in just a few days, as she first had anticipated. I advised her to give it a few weeks, and she'd probably need to do more supervision and follow-up than intended, but her students would be intelligent and motivated. She would also make many friends and might even

fall in love with the place – these are the truly human spin-offs that can arise. She got the message and I think it rather excited her.

This kind of thing can be problematic though. As Hope Flowers' webmaster, people e-mail me with offers of help, but they don't necessarily understand the realities involved. There's an expectation that Palestinians will jump to attention and accommodate their generosity, and it's not quite like that.

One lady from New York City wished to teach cartoon-drawing to the children, to help them deal with their trauma by externalising their life-stories in cartoon format. A very good idea! Except that she wanted to have everything lined up so that she could do it in just one day. This was just not doable: it's not possible to move everything around to accommodate the urgent timetables of a visiting Westerner. People wouldn't be convinced of the value of cartooning until they tried it. To succeed in her mission, she would have to adapt to the situation, give it time and take things as they come. I had to decline her offer and regretted that.

A charity in California wanted to send vitamin pills for the school kids, another wonderful idea. Usually they sent them to Africa or to disaster areas, so they didn't quite understand the unique political circumstances here: the Israelis would not allow such a consignment through. The charity could not believe this – after all, Israel is an ally of USA, isn't it? Well, that makes no difference.

There's an extra twist to this. It's not just a question of straight, oppressive restrictions. If the charity gave the school money to buy the vitamins from abroad, then the business would go through an Israeli importer who would profit from the transaction and, eventually, *inshallah*, the vitamins would probably get through. The fact that this was an *aid donation* made it different, since Israeli policy firmly has it that there is no humanitarian problem in the West Bank, so no aid is needed. The charity got upset with us because they thought we were being ungrateful and obstructive.

Such ungratefulness also happened with a charity seeking to send Christmas gifts. Theoretically a good idea, except that Muslims don't do Christmas. A consignment of gifts was sent but Israeli customs got hold of them, so Ibrahim worked hard to release the gifts. Eventually they arrived long after Christmas, with most gifts removed and distributed to poor Orthodox Jewish families, whose parents don't work for a living. Disappointingly, only the boxes and a few leftover gifts were allowed through. Ibrahim told the charity not to send more gifts the following year but they couldn't believe that the Israelis would block such a donation. Surely corrupt Palestinians had embezzled the gifts instead?

There's another issue here: *cultural sensitivity.* Palestinian children don't need Santa socks. As for cake with brandy in, books with Bible stories or plastic toys that break on day two, forget it. So, the thought is nice, but it's necessary to find out what's *actually needed* or to send some money, or to come over to visit and find out what will work and why. We might ask for art materials or photocopier spare parts, or even money to cover the accountants' and auditors' services that Western organisations often require, to prove that we're not embezzling funds. Westerners' generosity is sincere but it doesn't always have the intended effect and the hassles incurred can be immense. Or the aid that is sent mainly benefits educated, well-connected Palestinians who need it less than the underprivileged. Complications that are encountered can cause charities and well-wishers to withhold support, which in turn increases Palestinians' feelings of abandonment.

The street-level aid and support ventures that individual people think up and carry out are heart-warming, imaginative and, at times, genuinely helpful – often in different ways than first conceived. Healers, artists and all sorts of people come here, and the locals appreciate it. Fancy taking an initiative yourself? Someone might fix you a piano, a room or a crowd of people. If not, something else will happen. But it's probably best to make a reconnaissance trip first, to find out what reality looks like in Palestine.

18 **Old Mrs Mobarak**
healing the side-effects of conflict

I went to see Albert, an old friend in the Christian Quarter. Finding his house, I rang the bell and the gate lock buzzed, so I let myself in. Albert wasn't there – he was visiting his wife, who was at a Catholic care home because she had multiple sclerosis. He spent a lot of time with her. When I visited in 2005 she had been living at home, still reasonably able to function, but now her condition had deteriorated (eventually she died in 2011).

Albert earns 2,000 shekels per month working for UNRWA as a security guard. This sounds like a good wage, but it was only £300, €360 or $500 per month at 2009 rates. Albert also cleans out wells and fixes things for property-owners. He's a real character and a true altruist. Once he was a wheelchair-smuggler, bringing them in from Jordan, fixing them up and giving them to disabled Palestinians, even smuggling them into Israel for MS sufferers there.

Around the time of my 2005 visit he had managed to persuade the Italian consulate in Jerusalem to provide a supply of an expensive drug to allay his wife's MS symptoms, on the basis that he was descended from Sicilian Crusaders from 800 years earlier. He's a bounder and a pirate, our Albert, in the nicest of ways and always for everyone's benefit. The world needs more people like him.

Since he was not there, I sat talking with the old lady, his mother. She was perhaps 80 years old. Once the formalities were done, she started a sad lament, showing me her knee, badly damaged from a fall. *The doctors ask too much money,* she said in halting English. Then she showed me her arthritic hands with bent, knobbly fingers and told me about her aches and pains. Oh dear, this lady was down in the dumps and feeling hard done by.

I offered her spiritual healing – a discreet element in my humanitarian toolkit. It's easier to offer to Christians than to Muslims. Palestinian Christians, belonging to Melkite, Syriac, Catholic and Orthodox churches, accept that angelic presences or the grace of God can work through some people – it's not something one would raise quite so easily with a Muslim. Well, 'angelic presences' is how I put it to them for explanation, though I see it as 'cosmic energy'.

I had her sit down with eyes closed and, adopting a calmly authoritative voice, asked her to pray to God to bestow His blessing. As I centred and connected myself downward to the Earth and upward to infinity, a palpable stillness came about the courtyard – I could feel her noticing it and becoming immersed in it.

I brushed down her aura to smooth it out, then placed my hands lightly and steadily on her shoulders, opening up the top of my head, letting a bi-directional energy-stream crank up. Down and through my left arm came a stream of light, bathing and illuminating her with an effervescent blessing. Up through the right arm and out through the top of my head came a stream drawing away her pain and impurities. (I'm a left-hander, and for right-handers it might be opposite.)

After a while I put my forefingers on her temples, circulating light and connectivity through her worried, tight mind, stiffened as it was by decades of tension and concern. Then my left hand went behind her heart, to imbue her with love and grace. Then in front of her I knelt down and did similar movements through her feet. Each move took a few minutes.

Then I focused on both knees since, although only one was damaged, I could detect strain in the other arising from added weight-bearing. I held my hands with my palms an inch away from the knees on each side and my fingers started twitching involuntarily, which they do when they're charged up and radiating. I noticed her looking at my hands, eyes agog.

I said soothing words to her: the angels will walk with her; her
errors and weaknesses are forgiven; she is supported and blessed;
through being generous she will receive God's blessing; the past is

over; her sorrows are melting away. She wept tears of self-forgiveness gently, peacefully, and I dried her eyes.

I brushed down her aura again and drew uplifting energy down into the top of her head, then I held my radiating hands a little way away from her shoulders, standing behind her. She thought I was finished. "I get up now?" "No, sit still." I stopped her locking back into that duty-driven, burden-bearing habit that was, in my estimation, a root cause of her weak knees – she was carrying too much psychological weight.

Finally I brushed down her aura and said a prayer out loud. *May God bless you and keep you, cause his light to shine within you, and guide your way home.* Then a long, silent pause. "Okay, now I am finished..." She leapt up, slightly shocking herself with her lightness, and turned around to face me, eyes glowing. It was wonderful to see. When she was young she must have been quite beautiful.

I sat down and she brought me some cherry juice. She told me that her husband was dead and her daughter, Albert's sister, lived in Miami. The shop that she and her husband ran had been burned down by Israeli troops, who had looted all their money, during the occupation of Bethlehem around 2001. Her daughter had invited them to Miami and they had gone there, but she didn't like it so she returned to Bethlehem to live with Albert and his wife. Her husband stayed for hospital treatment, paid for by the Church, but he died before she ever saw him again.

It's really sad, this kind of thing. You hear many such sagas. Bearing witness to people's grief, sadness and frustration is a major service any visitor renders by coming here, by *just listening* and by observing people's lives. It works wonders for these folk who feel abandoned and mistreated, shut behind someone else's concrete walls, and it helps them objectivise their situation from an outsider's viewpoint.

Perhaps it was God-given that Albert wasn't there. The angels had a gift for his mother, using me for the purpose. The best healings come when these gifts are drawn out in timely situations and through sheer need. I would visit Albert another time.

19 **Aida**
women's empowerment

Ibrahim rang on my mobile. He would be arriving in fifteen minutes to take me to Aida refugee camp. *Ah, okay, alright.* Down went my breakfast, on went my clothes, my bag was packed, then I was out of the door, struggling with the funny school locks that seemed to work only when they wanted to, and I stood outside in the hot sun, waiting. Ibrahim was running on Palestine Time. I shambled along toward the Hebron Road half a mile away.

Waad Rahal Road, leading from the Hebron road to the school, is dusty and bumpy. It hasn't been fixed since the Israelis wrecked it with tanks and dozers in 2003, declaring it closed and leaving it for someone else to deal with. The school's international friends were mobilised and made a fuss, so the Israelis eventually permitted the road to be opened. Well, not quite: they permitted it to be *not closed*, if you get the difference. It was wrecked, hardly passable, but technically open. In 2009 it was still a wreck, suitable only for deft second-gear pothole-avoidance. Ibrahim nagged the Bethlehem governorate to fix it but since the school was at the far end of Al Khader, it was out of sight, out of mind, so they made promises to fix it and promptly forgot about it again.

But there's more: a jurisdictional issue. The school is in Area C, Palestinian-majority but Israeli controlled. The Israelis do not extend the idea of control to mean looking after the needs of a place, so both Israeli and Palestinian authorities left this area to its own devices, claiming it was not their patch – except, of course, when they wanted it to be. Thus, the road remained a mess, and the school could not afford to fund road-fixing itself.

146

Pictures of Palestine

Ibrahim arrived by the time I reached the main road. Off we went into town, to pick up an UNRWA worker who had been helping to select disadvantaged women for a new women's empowerment course that Hope Flowers was to run for women from the Aida refugee camp. (Aida is pronounced *Ay-ee-da*). She was nice. I listened to intense yattering between her and Ibrahim, trying to identify sounds and syllables as part of my ongoing attempt to infuse my creaky brains with Arabic. We wove through the streets of Bethlehem and soon reached Aida.

The refugee camp nestles uncomfortably beneath the high concrete Israeli security wall. It was overlooked by a watchtower manned, no doubt, by bored young Israeli troops half-heartedly watching for security risks down below and, quite likely, drumming their fingers waiting for their next period of leave. The wall intrudes right into town here, overshadowing the refugee camp and separating off Rachel's Tomb, a biblical site, once part of Bethlehem but now appropriated by the Israelis. It's a travesty of town planning, to say the least. Imagine part of your town being walled off and occupied by strangers.

This isn't a camp with tents as it was 50-60 years ago. Refugee camps are nowadays the equivalent of social-housing estates, dense-packed, largely self-built and higgledy-piggledy, constructed with materials supplied by UNRWA or scavenged from rubble tips or the remains of houses demolished by the Israelis. They're social traps, like 'sink estates' in Britain but notably without the drugs, alcoholism and crime. The inhabitants take quite good care of the neighbourhood too, to maintain what pride in their area they can.

Older people are true refugees, while most are the descendants of refugees. But younger people share with their elders the dubious honour of having few rights and no secure property or financial resources. There is no social security system here except what is provided by extended families and clans, or by UNRWA and NGOs such as UNICEF or Christian Aid, which provide social services and education.

Pictures of Palestine

The Hope Flowers Centre in Deheisheh was organising the women's empowerment course. Ibrahim liked this, not least because he came from a former refugee family. He favours a hands-on approach to running courses, avoiding working through normal bureaucratic channels, where confident, assertive and educated Palestinians tend to do best and then choose their own kind to follow them up the ladder. He and his family had picked themselves up, pulled themselves out of destitution and got somewhere. The Issas had what it took to get out of the rut, but many people don't and Ibrahim wanted to work close to the ground with people left behind who genuinely need support.

We went down some stairs, entering a big, echoing room with a circle of seats already filling with thirtyish women in traditional dress – decorative long dresses with headscarves – ranging in age from twenty to sixty. Ibrahim asked them whether I could take photos: answer, *definitely no*. They were polite about this, but they didn't instantly trust someone from Britaniyya – after all, we Brits had bombed Iraqis and also supported the Israelis in some of their recent pranks. I had to respect this even though, privately, it was hurtful to be identified with British policies and actions with which I disagreed, but the ladies weren't to know.

The UNRWA worker introduced Ibrahim and he started explaining what the course was about. Intelligent eyes watched, some looking interested, some a bit sceptical, but he carried on. He has a good style, and he's an approachable and likeable person who knows how to handle a situation like this. Many knew the Issa family, holding them in high regard.

He spoke Arabic of course. Apart from picking up words like *hamdillah* (thanks to God) and *inshallah* (if it is the will of God), I didn't understand much. Then came the word 'computrr', and eyes visibly lit up around the circle. The computer means access to modernity and the wider world, especially for the younger women. The course also included counselling and psychological groupwork, skills development, business management, food hygiene training (for home food production), techniques for handling meetings and officials, and child development and family psychology. He'd hit a mother-lode, a magic key, with this formula, and discussions became animated. Ibrahim had achieved lift-off; his humility makes him persuasive.

The computer bit had the strongest response but they also got the message about the complete package. They weren't dumb, this lot – it's just that they had no experience of some subjects such as family therapy and personal counselling. I noticed that, when the clipboard went round for names, they were all fully literate – Palestinians aren't backward, they're just disadvantaged, and the general standard of education is high. The empowerment package was aimed to help these women train up, to form a women's cooperative, sell products they made, improve their lives and make their way in the world. After twenty minutes, the whole circle was alight. The women were by now convinced, jabbering excitedly, and they were coming next Monday to start the course. The UNRWA worker was visibly relieved.

She was one of the lucky ones in UNRWA who hadn't lost her job. UNRWA in Bethlehem had just fired 360 workers, owing to a shortage of promised funds from international donors. Payment arrears to the UN from donor countries amounted in 2008 to $1.28 billion, 67% of this owed by USA. The economic meltdown, or lack of political will, caused donor governments to cut UN contributions even more in 2009. Governments habitually make grand promises but don't necessarily pay up. This underpayment hit the UN system drastically, just at a time when there were increasing calls on its resources – hence the redundancies in Bethlehem.

Paradoxically, managers, administrators and security guards were largely retained. Buildings need guarding and maintenance and management tasks continue during cutbacks. It's the social workers, teachers and hands-on people who are deemed expendable and lose their jobs. The delivery end is thus reduced. This is one of the soft institutional crimes of our time – the favouring of managements over people-level services at the coalface. It means that much of the money doesn't get down to ground level.

I found out a few weeks later that the UNRWA worker herself, overloaded with extra duties, had taken shortcuts, thus failing to select course applicants well. So there was a high drop-off rate from the course, despite the enthusiasm shown at the meeting. This arose partially because of hurried selection procedures and partially because the ladies themselves were unused to having self-improvement courses offered to them. Often they were overwhelmed with family and community duties, and many forgot the explained benefits of the course, overwhelmed by other demands and simply failing to turn up.

There's an additional factor too – a psychological one. When you're poor, you get so used to things going against you that you distrust that things ever *will* go your way. You focus on *getting by*, not getting on. You get used to self-sacrifice, to mishaps and absorbing the tasks and burdens that successful people drop on you as they scurry past, chasing busy timetables and important priorities. These ladies were psychologically geared to failure and complication – it's also a gender-related issue. The idea of prioritising something to benefit them personally was unusual for them. If little Hamid turns up crying with a bloody knee, mother drops everything; if her husband has pressures at work, or no work, she deals with the issues he cannot or won't handle, and thus there was a big drop-off rate. Self-improvement is something other people do, yet those who believe this are often those most in need of help.

So the course was delayed for a month until Hope Flowers ferreted through the eligible women and made its own selection, using recommendations and introductions. This is a classic complication in Palestine and it also made things more complex for me: I needed to write a report for a British trust that was funding it. It would be tricky explaining to them how such delays happened, and how it was not the fault of Hope Flowers but a simple occupational hazard. Empowerment meets disempowerment, head on.

The meeting ended and we were out, back in the car and driving into Bethlehem. Ibrahim had some office work and was then to visit Ramallah again. He left me sitting in the foyer of the Hope Flowers Centre, blogging on my laptop. And waiting. Waiting until my real work here could start. Ibrahim was busy, his administrator sister Ghada was overstressed and pregnant, and Ibrahim's wife Maram, running the centre, was flat on her back with a slipped disk. I was busy waiting for each of them to supply me with materials for the school website.

This doesn't happen only in Palestine – at least half of my website clients in the West are like this too. But among Palestinians such a situation gets accentuated. They've had so many decades of disruption, calamity and disarray that the whole nation has learned to function in a perpetual crisis-management mode. Orderly planning and execution just doesn't happen. One must take each day as it comes and do whatever yells loudest each day. So I got on with those things I *could* do, awaiting a time when the space might appear in others' lives to supply me with the material I needed. Running a school and education centre is not easy anywhere, but in Palestine it's an uphill struggle.

20 Revelatory Revelries
arak and the oudh

I drink alcohol only occasionally, and one night I downed two sizable glasses of *arak*, an aniseed spirit rather like Greek *ouzo*. That was a lot for me.

Muslims don't generally drink but *arak* drinking by Palestinian Christians is another matter. On occasions they can get transcendentally intoxicated. It points to the ancient Greek origins of the Christian community here, with its Dionysian, Classical Greek and Byzantine roots – nine centuries of Greek influence, from Alexander the Great's invasion in 334BCE up to the Muslim invasion of CE633. The Muslims brought in new moral influences and, with them, a disapproval of alcohol – itself a response to alcoholic and violent excesses that had prevailed in Arabia until the Muslim period started.

The gentlemen with whom I shared the evening definitely got plastered. My fun-loving friend Albert had invited me to an evening of classical Arabic music and my expectation of what would happen was woefully out of step: I thought 'classical' would mean staid and serious. Not so.

After a long day's work, I had ridden into Bethlehem with Ibrahim, who had been at the school with his architect brother Abdul Nasser from Amman. They had been discussing building a new Japanese-financed rainwater cistern to cater for increasing water shortages. Together, these two brothers were in their element – an architect and a former engineer. The cistern was to be built in a month's time.

Pictures of Palestine

As we drove into town, Ibrahim was apologetic for paying insufficient attention to me and the work I had come to do – busy and preoccupied, he felt guilty about it. I had come here knowing that plans and Palestine don't mix easily, but it *was* rather problematic, since I needed to discuss details and issues and get on with it. The Issa family was overstretched. A few days before, shedding tears, Ghada said she hadn't had a holiday for eleven years. I wished I could magic her over to Cornwall so she could walk the Atlantic cliffs, watching seals, gulls and kittiwakes and letting the wind blow through her hair.

Albert was also under strain – it's not uncommon for Palestinians. A security guard for UNRWA, he sometimes did 16-hour overnight shifts and recently he had worked 72 hours without sleep. He takes life in his stride but this, plus caring for his disabled wife and living his rather riotous life, was taking its toll. He's one of those tough-it-out types who carries on regardless, disregarding his own needs, and I worry about him.

On my way to meet Albert I sat awhile with shopkeeper John's son, an intelligent man with good English and a ginger-haired European look – Crusader genes. He voiced opinions many Palestinians would agree with. He had offered me a cup of tea and I observed that the English solution to many things was to have a cuppa – even after terrorist attacks, of which, with the help of the IRA, we Brits had some experience. That set something going.

We launched into terrorism, which he said no longer served a purpose in Palestine – especially when it mainly killed innocent Israelis in buses and cafés. He was glad it had died down. He reckoned the rockets fired from Gaza, though causing few fatalities, also served little purpose – especially since, every time an Israeli dies, scores of Palestinians have to die in the backlash. He lamented the toll this took on Palestinian society. As a Christian he didn't concur with the Muslim idea of martyrdom, which he believed underpinned the Palestinian style of military resistance – though I ventured that, for my parents' generation in WW2, dying for their country was tantamount to the same thing.

Pictures of Palestine

He noted one thing concerning armed strategy: both Hezbollah in Lebanon in 2006 and Hamas in Gaza in early 2009 had successfully broken the invincibility-magic of Israeli forces. Israel had failed to achieve its objective – to destroy them. Israel's problem is that, in any conflict, it has to win decisively to prove its point. But its opponents just have to stand firm and survive, knocking off or capturing a few Israelis in the process for its shock-value. In doing so, they undermine Israel's sense of security, causing Israeli society to eat away at itself and activating worldwide public disgust over the scale and violence of Israeli assaults. This is 'asymmetric warfare' – how a small guy can fight a big guy. In biblical imagery, it's the story of David and Goliath. Except this time David symbolises Palestinians and Goliath the Israelis.

He, like so many Palestinians, was fed up with fighting and just wanted this nightmare to end. He longed for a decent and secure deal for Palestinians and a liveable life for his family. He respected Israelis as long as they stuck to their own territory, stopped messing with the Palestinians and acted as equals. His own family had lost land to settlers just north of Bethlehem, with neither compensation nor legal recourse.

Despite all this, it's impressive, the extent to which Palestinians accept their lot, and this is not just victimised resignation. It's a profound acceptance and forgiveness. Palestinians aren't willing to concede *everything*, but most of them seem willing to concede the land Israel gained in 1948, though not what it took in 1967 – the occupied territories.

I had to go and walked along to the Christian Quarter. There was Albert, waiting in the street to take me to his friend's house. Suleiman is a professor at Al Quds University, East Jerusalem, an educated man with near-perfect English – and a musician. We piled into his VW Golf, drove down to Beit Sahour to pick up another musician and then headed back through Bethlehem, up the long hill to Beit Jala, down some side-roads and through a narrow gap between the security walls, past the Israeli settler road by-passing Bethlehem, into a country area and along a winding, hilly back-road.

Pictures of Palestine

Eventually, as dusk fell, we reached a restaurant stowed away on a hill near Al Walaja for a night of classical Arabic music, a monthly event. The group, in which Suleiman was violinist, also consisted of the gentleman from Beit Sahour playing *oudh* (a lute) and another playing hand-drums and singing. After tuning up, off they went, starting in a measured way and then progressing into a pretty riotous and exciting performance.

People sat around at tables, chattering or listening, joining in singing at times, downing *arak* and looking radiant. It was difficult to believe we were in an occupied country where, a few years before, an Israeli tank manned by troops fresh out of school could easily have blasted this restaurant away at the slightest whim.

Part way through, people sprang up to dance. One young woman did a very impressive traditional belly-dance with an incredibly fast hip-wiggle, hands spooning through the air and a beatific smile lighting her face. Her husband circled around her, hands raised, index fingers pointing to the sky. Her dance was loose, fluid and controlled. While her hips vibrated rapidly, her shoulders and head were steady, her eyes gyrating and feet stamping the ground. This was something ancient, traditional and very much alive, yet she was dressed in a way which would have worked equally well at a hip-hop all-nighter.

Pictures of Palestine

The evening rolled on and dips, hummus, salads and other edibles were set in front of us, scooped up inside pittas and washed down with *arak*. Albert's son, eighteen, a brainy and serious young man, sat disapprovingly tolerating it all with an aloof air. He made sure I knew he didn't like this kind of music: he was a music genius who played Chopin and Liszt. I wouldn't mind betting that he'll later join the tragic stream of gifted Palestinians leaving the country for pastures green.

But these emigrants never lose their allegiance and they raise Palestinians' profile globally, sending back money and returning home periodically, some of them eventually moving back, qualified, confident and experienced. Emigration has mixed blessings, losses and gains. Most families have one or a few sons and daughters in Denmark, Wisconsin, Kuwait or Chile, and clans have international networks which prove useful in many ways. The Palestinians are one of the world's most highly-qualified ethnic groups.

The musicians were having a fine time. Looking at them, you wouldn't tag them with a label of 'oppressed Palestinians' – they were respectable gentlemen, adept in their art and deserving of a stream of recording contracts and concert performances. I had a fine time too. Earlier in the day I had been bugged by personal issues about work and my future, and this evening lifted my spirits. By the time it was finished I was worn out, sozzled, floating around in another world and grateful for a lift back to the school.

But I still had to get up those stairs and that was a heave. When I looked out of the window before staggering to bed, there was the Israeli watchtower with a spotlight beaming from it on to the hill below. I used my telephoto to take a closer look, wondering if something interesting was going on. No, they were probably just bored, tracking one of the wild dogs that live around the wall, with its cleared area on the Palestinian side which, in many places, acts as an unintended nature reserve. There's nothing much for these poor young conscripted soldiers to observe here, except dogs, lizards and the sailing antics of the moon.

21 Surrounded
Israel's future

Some might think I'm anti-Israeli, but that would be incorrect: I believe that, whatever has happened thus far, Israel has good reason to exist and have a future. So does Palestine. It's not Jews or Judaic culture I have a problem with – Jews have played a significant role in my life – but the current behaviour of the Israeli state and of certain assertive elements in Israeli society. They might believe God and rightness are on their side, but God is bigger than that, and rightness is a relativistic judgement. Imperialistic Brits, with our God-given 'mission to civilise', discovered this during the 20th century as our empire subsided and fell.

I'm involved with Palestinians yet my aim is to help catalyse resolution for everyone – not just an end to hostilities but a change so profound that hostility becomes history. Israelis' aim in building their nation has been to provide a secure place for Jews to live, to avoid being others' guests or beholden to their manoeuvrings and cruelty, but I feel Israelis go about it in a way which won't ultimately succeed or fulfil their great-grandparents' dream. Something will change to correct this, bringing a new future for both Israelis and Palestinians, but when and how?

Peace will come when Israelis respect the needs and perspectives of their neighbours. This will be reflected back with respect, which already exists as much as it can. By *peace*, I mean mutually-assured security, shared appreciation and multicultural interchange – nothing less than a rebirth of the whole area and its constituent societies.

Pictures of Palestine

It's fine for people to be different, and this adds to the remarkable social-cultural variegation in our world. But it's no longer workable for our differences to remain unreconciled, unresolved. Israelis are an integral part of the variegated patterning of humanity and they have a right to exist and coexist without harming others' right to the same thing. But living in a nation surrounded by barbed wire, concrete walls and gun emplacements does no abiding good to a nation and its people.

Since the building of the security wall, the schizoid difference of opinion, experience and worldview between the two sides has widened. The wall acts like a two-sided mirror so that each side sees only its own *projected image* of the other side. Real-life contact has largely been lost. Most Palestinians meet only armed Israeli soldiers, and most Israelis have little personal contact with Palestinians. Israelis do meet Israeli Arabs, but they have an underlying feeling that Arabs are a threat. Only a few people form real intercultural friendships or act in a truly neighbourly way.

The watchtower over the valley from the school,
with some Israeli soldiers checking out the area

Each side thus has a constellation of inaccurate impressions, fears and fantasies concerning the other. This is a psychological *apartheid* where close neighbours live in thoroughly different worlds. They dehumanise each other and this permits ideas to flourish that otherwise wouldn't exist, allowing actions to be carried out that wouldn't otherwise happen. It allows injustice and justice is a key ingredient of peace.

Israel is a brave settler project. Israelis, six million of them, have achieved great things in a short time. They have made their country green, an agricultural powerhouse, and have built new towns; they're brainy and energetic, big in trade, computers, finance, technology, specialist professions and a range of other industries, including weapons. Theirs is a Western-style country plopped amidst adjacent Arabic countries. Israel makes a big mark on the world, and it certainly has personality.

The climate is good, though they could do with more rain. Israel is full of ancient sites and history, going back millennia. Within its current borders are the sources of the Jewish and Christian faiths, and one of the three holiest sites of Islam. The Jewish population is made up of a mixed bag of nationalities and groupings, and there's a host of languages present amongst this relatively small population.

It is part-secular (centred on Tel Aviv), and part-religious (centred on Jerusalem). An impressive place that leaves a mark on memory, it's well worth a visit. It has survived threat and the IDF is one of the world's more effective armed forces. There are a lot of illusions and prejudices about Israel, both positive and negative – it's a treasure-chest of exaggerated, contradictory imaginal certainties over which people far and wide love to argue.

Jews have a long heritage, and at times they have had a very hard time, which has had a defining effect on Israel's character. They are a unique ethnic group who, when chucked out of the area between 2,600 and 1,900 years ago, stuck together by choice, though spread widely. They dispersed as far as India and China, around the Middle East, into Europe and eventually to America – there's even a Jewish enclave or *oblast* in Siberia. Many Jews, such as those of Khazar and

East European origin, are only faintly descended from this original stock, so the idea that, as a chosen people derived from one genetic source, they are entitled to this land, is weaker than their cultural narrative would like it to be.

Many stayed within the Jewish fold while in exile, maintaining distinctive identities and customs, while others dispersed by migration, intermarriage, conversion, pragmatism or simple lapse of allegiance, melting into surrounding populations – there's a significant hidden Jewish gene-stock in such places as Kashmir, Afghanistan, Spain, Italy, Iran and the Caucasus, for example. Many became educated specialists – doctors, money-handlers, artisans, scholars and scribes – ensuring their security by making themselves invaluable. They became influential, forming noted communities in great cities such as Baghdad, Damascus, Alexandria, Cordoba, Rome, Istanbul, Venice and Samarkand. Even in remote Cornwall, where I live, old Jewish communities go back many centuries.

At times in Europe they attracted resentments which eventually became fatal, although this did not generally happen in the Muslim world or Asia. In Europe it arose partially from jealousy, prejudice and scapegoating by host populations, exploited by rulers and clerics, and partially from mistakes Jews themselves made – and both stoked each other. People love bankers, doctors and advisers only when gaining from them – and this became a problem for many Jews when attitudes turned against them. By 1900 the belief in Europe, from Russia to Spain, was that Jews had excessive power and influence, and this escalated from a prejudice to Hitler's 'final solution', a planned extermination of the entire Jewish population of Europe.

It gave Jews a deep-seated feeling that everyone was against them. But it also arose because of Jewish feelings of differentness and social exceptionalism, the distinctness that was a survival mechanism for an isolated minority under pressure. The Holocaust, killing one-third of the world's Jews, shames humanity to this day. It also affected the Roma, the mentally ill, gays, dissenters, leftists and others.

Pictures of Palestine

Of the Holocaust, a Jewish saying goes, 'There will be no peace and freedom without remembrance'. But also, referring to Vietnam but applicable here, Michael Herr, scriptwriter of the film *Apocalypse Now*, said in 1989: "All the wrong people remember Vietnam. I think all the people who remember it should forget it, and all the people who forgot it should remember it". Remembrance is a double-edged sword.

Ze'ev Jabotinsky, the Russian Zionist thinker, reckoned Jews and Arabs should live alongside one another. As the Holocaust escalated, Jews grew desperate and militant, realising that, without a homeland, they would never feel safe. During and after WW2 their cause became so urgent that they migrated to Palestine, sometimes with little or nothing, settling without due consideration for its existing residents or seeing the consequences of doing so. There was a wide range of viewpoints amongst early settlers – socialist, capitalist, secular, religious, and some just wanting a better life – and this led to strong differences over the aims of their new nation.

This led to a dilemma that continues today: should Israel be a democratic state serving all its inhabitants – Jews, Arabs, Christians and others – or a Jewish state in which Arabs and others become secondary citizens, or are exiled or annihilated? Both annihilation and 'transfer' are impossible in real life, so there is a deadlock and dilemma for Israelis which remains perpetually unresolved. The conflict of aims between Jews is arguably bigger than that with Palestinians, if truth be known, and this is dangerous for Israel.

Is Israel to be an ethnic Jewish state or an open, democratic society? Some resolve this dilemma by asserting that Israel can be a Jewish state *and* democratic. But 20% of the population isn't Jewish, and many Israelis don't agree with the 'Jewish state' concept either. Actually, the argument isn't between these questions: it's really between Judaic culture and Zionism. The Laws of Moses specify 'thou shalt not kill, thou shalt not steal...' and many Israelis subscribe to such values, but Zionism places Israeli expansionism over other options, and plenty of killing and theft results from this.

Pictures of Palestine

It costs Palestinians highly, yet it costs Jews too, in social and moral terms, and this could be to the longterm detriment of Israel.

This is a major weakness and there is a tendency to ignore the problem and hope it will go away, which it doesn't. Or there's a tendency to externalise the problem on to Palestinians and hit hard at them, to teach them that Israelis are right and Palestinians wrong, but the Palestinians draw different conclusions to those intended.

Israelis and Palestinians live in very different worlds. It is thus difficult to establish dialogue, particularly on crucial issues. It's tragic, a clash of incompatible certainties. This is exacerbated by an international tendency to stand back in confusion, or alternatively to side quietly with the Israelis while guiltily making supportive noises and dishing out cheques to the Palestinians. Hypocritical lectures from elsewhere about the need for peace don't help, when peace can come only when each side genuinely feels safe and that it has a fair deal, and when foreign, particularly American, influences stop reinforcing and perpetuating the conflict. To quote the philosopher Dr Karl Popper, "We must plan for freedom and not only for security, if for no other reason than that only freedom can make security secure".

The worst of all human conflicts are family arguments. Both sides claim historic descent from Abraham and they have many similarities and complementarities. They're a riven family and a family argument is worse than a clash between strangers, who at least can walk away or agree to differ. A family, even if its members disown one another, remains a family, tied by shared ancestry and characteristics.

The conflict is affected by the fact that the Holy Land is a focus for world polarisation and conflict. To some extent this conflict will be resolved as the world resolves its own addiction to strife and injustice, its glorification of military means as a solution to disputes or as a stimulant to artificial economic growth and social control. Conflict is a failure of relationship by other means, it's neurotic and suicidal for humanity.

Pictures of Palestine

Warfare is nowadays becoming obsolete because we are globally challenged by bigger factors, demanding that we cooperate, both internationally and domestically. This is a pragmatic issue, no longer an idealistic principle: humanity's survival depends on cooperation. The resolution of the Israeli-Palestinian conflict through peace processes is unlikely – we had our chance in the 1990s with the Oslo process. The conflict is likely to be rendered irrelevant by larger, wider issues which make both sides realise they sit in the same boat and must stop rocking it. A time of *force majeure* approaches, and this fact started rearing its head during the Arab revolutions of 2011, with their wider repercussions.

Israel's interests are not furthered by alienating people, making enemies and giving Palestinians a hard time. It's necessary to re-examine the mindset which affirms that everyone is against the Jews. The ghost of anti-Semitism needs deconstructing, both as a fear and as an actuality. It would help the whole world if all nations deconstructed grand illusions of their own too. We are all humans, and together we all have kids, eat food, use resources, face dilemmas and experience joy and sorrow. We're in this together.

A strongly-held belief creates its own reality and if that reality brings problems, then another belief needs creating. This isn't fast and easy, but a decade or two can bring a turn-around in the Middle East. It involves an Israeli choice to ratchet down its hellfire approach to Palestinians, Lebanese, Syrians, even Iranians, and it needs a positive response from these people. It involves taking brave risks and gradually building up mutual confidence. The Palestinian resistance movement needs to de-focus from the Israelis and concentrate on an internal cultural florescence, and the Israelis need to resolve their own dilemmas within Israel itself.

Without such internal resolution, Israel could indeed crumble, not because Arabs drive Israelis into the sea, but because Israelis become disheartened and begin to leave, squabble, fight or go into a funk. Even today, Jews argue over who is a true Jew and who is not, and some 400,000 Israelis are regarded by some Orthodox rabbis not to be Jewish. This is serious if Israel's identity is to be based on Jewishness. Some ideological settlers don't want West Bank settlements to be integrated into the state of Israel because they visualise the West Bank (Judea and Samaria) as the true Israel, unrestrained by the conflict of secular and religious aims within Israel proper. If divisive forces such as these reach a critical point, then the nation could be lost.

A glimmer of this surfaced during the 2006 Lebanon War. The Israelis pounded south Lebanon, collectively punishing Shi'a Lebanese to try to dissuade them from supporting Hezbollah, but the bombardment had the opposite effect: Shi'a support for Hezbollah grew. Hezbollah was founded in the 1980s as a result of Israeli assaults on Lebanon and, again, in 2006, Israel failed to see how its thunderous retributions create enemies and unite people against it. A new generation of potential Lebanese enemies was created – hurt children whose grudges could come back to haunt Israelis in future decades.

Pictures of Palestine

The war impacted on bombarded northern Israelis too, causing dismay and loss of heart to some. They had been through this so many times before. Some started trickling abroad, taking their kids to a more secure life. Not officially emigrating, they sought jobs elsewhere until things improved – but they still left. Another surge of demobilised, traumatised IDF troops went off to India to take drugs and forget. Each time, a proportion returns and others stay away. This is not talked about, but they're gone. One million Jews have left.

But the alternative isn't easy – making a change. A truth process and a squaring up with reality is inevitable, some time. The truth is that people of different backgrounds, beliefs and ways can and must live together. The question is how long it takes and what has to happen before we get there. We live in times of profound choice, worldwide. Israel, as a nexus-point for certain kinds of global issues, has key choices to make. Israel's future has little to do with its enemies: it's all to do with itself.

22 Teaching and Learning
each day, new lesson

"Don't *ever* do that again, right?" I had my hand skilfully gripping his throat, fingers on his jugular to convey serious intent. It's decades since I did martial arts, but it comes in useful occasionally. He was shocked. I had walked up, staring right at him, and grabbed him.

"Eh, Ingaleesh, he don't understand."

"Well, tell him what I said, then." The lads didn't quite know what to do – they didn't know what I would do next, but they heard that I meant business from the firm tone of my voice.

The lad muttered something. It was translated: "He say sorry".

I released my fingers and eyed him straight. "Tell him he may not throw stones at people, unless they have *really, really* done him wrong, and only if he has *no choice*. Tell him." I had to repeat it bit by bit, to help translation.

The lad looked down with shame. He had hit me with a stone after I had passed by. It was one of a barrage of stones and empty cans thrown at me, but this one had hurt. It had happened before. I'd had enough and I was letting them know.

"If you don't like me, there's another way to say it. Tell him." Pause. "Does he understand?"

Looks were exchanged. "Yes, he understand. We like you. We don't mean it."

"Good. Do you all get it? I am your friend, okay?"

"Yes, we get it. *Shukran*."

"I understand why you throw stones. But I am not an Israeli soldier. I come here to help you. But be careful with Israeli soldiers – you could land up in jail for fifteen years, or you could even be shot. I know it's difficult for you, though – I know you'd love to be able to fight back."

I changed my body language and lightened up. I then put out my hand for a shake with the boy, in the Palestinian hand-slapping way. We clapped hands.

Then I leant on the wall, tired after doing town, and rummaged in my bag. I got out a small bag of abalone shells that a friend had given me before I left, for giving to kids. I picked one out and gave it to him. He fingered and examined it.

"Eh, Martin, can I have one too?" They think that's my name. Perhaps a previous volunteer at the school had that name.

"No. I make peace with *him* – it's for *him*. My name is Palden."

"Balden..."

"No, Palden. *Puh* – Palden. What's your name?", looking at the youth who had thrown the stone.

"Imad."

"Imad, do you throw stones at your grandfather?"

"No."

"I'm as old as your grandfather." Silence.

I stayed there with them, quietly holding them there. They didn't speak, except to ask what football club I supported. But they were watching, rather fascinated by now.

Last week I had said no when they wanted me to let them into the school playground to play football one evening. Ibrahim wouldn't want that. The boys hadn't liked it, they had been rowdy, pushy – local kids get like that sometimes, on days when the atmosphere is edgy, when frustrations are surfacing. On the gate, when I emerged next morning, was scrawled 'Martin – you dog'. A dodgy situation had been brewing.

After a while I got up, smiled and bowed to them slightly, "*Shukran, ma'asalama!*" and headed up the road. Then came the Pied Piper of Hamlyn scene: they all followed, chattering. A bunch

167

of parents was just up the road, watching all this. I wondered how they would react. One came out from the group.

"Eh, Mr Balden, you do good thing. These kids, they go too far. They need to learn. It's difficult. We try."

"Shadi, I know you try. It's hard. But peace is sometimes like war: to make peace, you sometimes have to be fierce, to help people *really understand*. Then you get respect, then you smile, and then comes peace. But I know it's difficult for you, dealing with your kids. Sometimes it's better if an outsider like me gets involved." He took my shopping bags and walked back with me to the school, talking, the kids still with us.

It is difficult for these parents: sometimes they see their youngsters throbbing with frustration at their life-situation. There's not much parents can do because, secretly, they feel the same feelings – and they feel shame and helplessness over it. Some young Palestinians see their parents to be failures: behind these houses is the security wall and on the hill is a watchtower, both symbols of Israeli

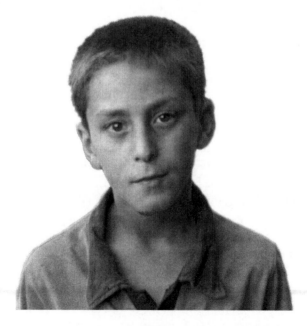

dominance – their parents had failed to hold off the Israelis. These kids have seen bad scenes.

"Thanks, Shadi. Goodnight, and bless you. Tell the other parents it's okay. I hope it's okay with all of them." I gave him a hug and, slightly surprised, he hugged back tentatively. I waved to the kids and disappeared into the school.

But today was not just a day for teaching a lesson. I learned something too.

Most of the time the school is empty, a little ghostly because of the school vacation, but that day noise had started up downstairs. I looked out to see teachers and children going into classrooms. What's this? Later I found out they had remedial classes, doing catch-up for pupils who weren't doing so well. I could hear the letters of the English alphabet and numbers being incanted, teachers talking and the shuffling of classroom furniture. I went down and walked around, taking photos for the website.

I was anxious to assemble materials for the website, such as photos, but it seemed that I had come at the wrong time of year for taking action shots of schoolchildren and I had almost given up. Suddenly I had a chance and grabbed it.

Finished, and pleased, I went and popped my nose into the school office, where Hala, coordinator of the teachers, was talking to another woman.

"Balden, you come to Centre tomorrow? I be there at eleven."

"Yes. Why?"

"I got many, many photo for you of school – childs, teachers, classes – I like take photos! I give you disk!" She looked at me, glowing with pride.

Brilliant! I beamed ear to ear. Bless her. With luck, my problem was solved. From then, my photo collection did start taking shape and by the end of my stay I had hundreds of images.

The lessons of this day were: *all things come to those who wait* and *sometimes you have to stand up for what you believe is right*. The challenge is that there are no clear or simple rules for what you should do when.

23 Greener on the Other Side
émigré issues

It was a hot day, the temperature in the thirties. I walked down to the main road to catch a service taxi (*'serrveese'*) to town. You stand anywhere by the side of the road, stick your hand out when one comes along and, if it has room, the yellow eight-seater taxi-van will stop and pick you up. You rarely have to wait long and it's a good form of cheap transport we ought to have in the West.

On the way I passed some men labouring on the road, making much-needed improvements.

"Where you from – Amrika?".

"Britaniyya." The workers gathered round, clearly not highly motivated to work. One complained that they were unemployed and it wasn't fair, saying they were paid only 50 shekels ($10) a day while people in the PA creamed off all the money.

"We live under double occupation", said one. "Israeli occupation and PA occupation – double occupation." The PA was arresting people, expanding its security forces, and was seen by some to be in league with the Americans and Israelis, failing to rate well for impartiality and justice. Double trouble with no let-up for ordinary people.

"You got a job here?" I was asked. I could tell where this was going. It was a reasonable question, because many Westerners here are well paid by governments and NGOs at Western rates, dramatically higher than Palestinian rates of pay.

"Yes, I'm working. No, I'm not paid." It was difficult to explain more than this to people with a small English vocabulary. My basic expenses were nearly covered by kind donations from people in UK and USA, but my bills back home and my extra costs were not. It worked as long as I lived cheaply and didn't sustain big, unexpected expenses.

Sometimes it's difficult explaining to Palestinians that I'm not a rich Westerner and I don't have my snout in the trough. You can't walk along the road without being honked at by taxi drivers, assuming you're there to provide business. Sometimes I'm overcharged, but I might not be in the mood to haggle or protest, and sometimes I'm unsure of myself. Some of my costs include occasional deliberate overpaying for things, just to help someone get through the day or buy something for their kids.

The West is rich. Therefore Westerners, as Palestinians see it, can afford to have money siphoned off them – after all, it's only fair. Relatively speaking it is true. But many Palestinians don't know how far from rich many Westerners are. We don't have extended families to rescue us either – we're on our own. They don't know how expensive life can be in the West, how much Westerners are slaves to banks, corporations, governments and shareholders. Palestinians who haven't been abroad tend to believe Westerners are all blessed with wealth and this makes us happy and free, always with cash to spare.

Pictures of Palestine

Around two-thirds of Palestinians live under the official poverty line, with 45% in poverty in the West Bank and 80% in Gaza, according to 2008 figures from the PA Bureau of Statistics. With the suspension of aid to Palestine in 2006 because of the Hamas election victory, the numbers in deep poverty (less than 50 US cents a day) nearly doubled to over one million, a fifth of the population. GDP in 2008 comprised 70% of that in 1999, before the *intifada*. Per capita GDP was expected to fall in 2009 by 7.4% and things were likely to get worse.

This is tough stuff, eating away at the hearts and self-esteem of many Palestinians, especially the young. The guys fixing the road understandably resented their situation. Conditions in Palestine have nothing to do with laziness or lack of enterprise – Palestinians are hard workers. It concerns *politics*, as defined by Israelis, Westerners and the Palestinian oligarchy in Ramallah. When ordinary Palestinians had their say in the 2006 elections, it was overridden – so much for democracy.

These economic figures must be qualified though. Most Palestinians live in families and clans which provide something of a support system and collective enterprise, so the effects of unemployment are not quite the same as they are in the West. The 'grey', unofficial economy is large, with many transactions taking the form of mutual exchanges, problems solved within the family, clan or neighbourhood, and with only some financial exchange going on – this doesn't show up in the figures. Not having a registered job doesn't mean Palestinians have nothing to do: they contribute to the flow of tasks within a family, clan and neighbourhood, and they have very busy lives whether or not they are classified as employed.

Here were these guys, building a wall as part of a rudimentary PA employment programme – paid for, no doubt, by a foreign agency. After our short conversation, one guy buttonholed me and kept on talking.

"You help me get to Breetin? You find me Breeteesh girl to marry? I work, I do anything, I try hard – you help me, yes? It

good in Breetin. You have human right. We have no human right
– PA, Fateh give no human right. I have no job. I find job in your
country. I need go to Breetin – you help me?"

Now how do you say no to that? How do you explain that Britain
is not heaven, that the UK immigration authorities would say
no, and that most British people do not consider it their duty to
help 'economic migrants'? How do you explain that many British
women are pretty selective and would not find the idea of rescuing a
Palestinian through marriage an attractive proposition?

"But Breeteesh people are *good* people – you are a good person.
You have a job in your country – we have no jobs. You help me, yes?
I have studied law with the Palestinian Bar Society – I am lawyer.
But now I build walls for $10 a day. It's all wrong, all wrong."

My heart was wrenching. It *is* all wrong. I tried to explain that
he would not find it easy in Britain. People don't care for others in
quite the way that Palestinians do and he would be disappointed. I
was getting emotional – this guy was pressing my buttons. The fact
was, when I returned to Britain I too was anticipating a hard time,
and it preyed on me. One reason I had come here was to draw a
line under the recent past and this guy was exposing my own raw,
unprocessed feelings. How could I explain?

"Look, when I go back to Britain, I will have no job. Many
people have no job! *Some* people in Britain are rich, but most
aren't. When I try for a job, sixty other people apply too – get it?
My job ended last year." I had been a book-editor in a sinking
book trade and a webmaster to small businesses in a recession,
so my income had fallen disastrously to one-third of its already
unimpressive level.

I'm a soft-hearted guy but I couldn't help him enter Britain; I was
here to help Palestinians improve their own country. I was willing to
talk and listen: he needed to talk, and he also needed freeing of the
expectation that the West would solve his problems. His issue was
probably political: he might be a Hamas supporter discriminated
against by Fateh people, but this was insufficiently life-threatening
to qualify him as a political refugee in Britain.

173

He wanted my phone number so that we could meet again. It was then that I discovered my phone had been stolen. That *really* pissed me off – it would cost 250 shekels to replace. I had had enough. We parted company and he shrugged his shoulders as if to say, *what's wrong with this guy?* Later I sorted myself out, came to peace on the matter and talked it over with him. He had made me aware of my own feelings about the way things had worked out for me. It's good, in the end, when people bring up awkward feelings – feelings you might not be aware of until that moment – but it's disturbing at the time.

As I wrote this in my blog back at the school that evening, I paused to watch the gecko doing an amazing gravity-defying act, chasing errant mosquitoes. I was missing my loved ones. I had been on the edge of tears for much of the day too: Hamid's was not the only sorry story this day had brought. I felt an incapacity to help and benefit people, to concentrate on work. Obstructed by my own feelings, I just want to curl up and rock myself to sleep. Poor me.

I had known I would be tested in Palestine, and the testing was now happening. The feral dogs were howling outside and the cacophony of the calling to prayers was sounding out – a right old din. It all added to my dismay. But still, I had to remind myself I was lucky.

For many people in this land, every day is just about *surviving*. Their prospects for much more than mere survival aren't great. Later, when I spoke to Hamid, I encouraged him to work steadily, taking a long term view: things always change, there's always something to learn, something to develop, in every situation we're in. Perhaps I was teaching him what I myself needed to learn.

This world is a vale of tears and I hope Hamid one day learns that being 'rich' is not the solution to all life's ills. Many of the 'rich' are deeply lonely, stuck in a narrow world of false freedoms and, when they fall, like the convicted Jewish-American banking fraudster Bernard Madoff who, that very day, had received a ridiculous 150-year jail sentence in USA, they receive little sympathy.

At least many ordinary Palestinians, hovering around that much-vaunted poverty line, have each other. I sincerely hope Hamid finds some personal success, fulfilment and security, because the poor chap genuinely needs it – his spirits were struggling, and depression can be more difficult than poverty.

We in the West need to rejoin the human race, to relearn how much we *need* each other. Prosperity permits independence and evasion of life's bigger issues, but this is grinding to a halt for many Westerners now. Perhaps the Palestinians will one day counsel us on handling this, for this is where *they* are rich.

24 Ostensibly Nature Reserves
land appropriation and how it's done

I had chomped an incredibly hot chilli and my mouth was burning. Not the worst news of today. On the way up to Ramallah, Ibrahim had told me that the Israelis had just announced their intention to appropriate a lot of land east of Jerusalem and down to the Dead Sea. The Israelis didn't phrase it that way – to them it was a legal formalisation of property ownership – but that's what was going to happen. They were laying the ground for a strategic settlement bloc, of which Ma'ale Adumim was the start.

They do this by declaring the land disused or unregistered, requiring Palestinians to prove ownership and current use. Proof of ownership is tricky because much of this land has been owned by common law and by implicit public acceptance since long before the Israelis, the British or any of their property laws came along. Or they have old title deeds, or they started out as refugee squatters, or they had been required to register their land but the charges had been ruinously high, so they had left it.

Proof of use is tricky too, since much of this is desert or non-commercial farmland – quite a lot of it the ranging lands of Bedouin, used mostly by goats. The burden of proof of use lies on the ordinary person, and if he or she doesn't have the right paperwork or money to buy permissions, then all is lost.

Land deemed to have unregistered ownership is declared government land, using an old Ottoman law, meaning that the

Israeli government can allocate future use as it wishes – and it goes to Israelis and new settlements. This was not what the Ottomans were thinking of a century ago. Anyone living on government land is deemed an illegal squatter, to be thrown off without compensation or rehousing, and any obstruction causes the army to be called in.

This bulk confiscation will split the West Bank into north and south, also taking away valuable Palestinian open space – the desert hills. The Israelis gave two weeks for complaints to be lodged. Two weeks? The Ma'ale Adumim settlement, located amidst this land, was to be expanded, even though 30% of its houses were empty. As it is, much of the settlement sits on appropriated private Palestinian land and, even when proof is shown – often dating back a century or more – it isn't accepted as valid, and re-registration fees are unaffordable.

The Israelis thus wave a finger at the international community, knowing that the latter will utter lofty declarations while doing nothing much or insisting on talks. Such talks, or talks about talks, drag on for years, and meanwhile the Israelis create ever more 'facts on the ground'.

Then, if talks reach a conclusion, probably involving concessions from both sides, the Israelis will say that nothing can be done for their part because this will involve moving too many (Israeli) people and destroying too many (Israeli) livelihoods. Soldiers will refuse to enforce the law on their own people, and whole towns cannot after all be demolished, can they? Little will be said about the Palestinian and Bedouin livelihoods destroyed, or the open space – a key resource in a crowded country – that has been commandeered and lost, or about water drained from the water table to feed Israeli settlers' modern lifestyles.

Statements will be made internationally about the need for peace and a two-state solution. The US president will make a pious oration, the British PM might utter some verbiage, if pushed, and an EU special negotiator will talk to concerned parties, trying to restrain them and get them back to yet more talks. Israelis will bark loudly about anti-Semitic bias, and few will say much that's audible in return – themselves afraid of anti-Semitism accusations.

Hamas, crisis-managing Gaza and excluded from the West Bank, will be unable to lift a finger. Hezbollah in Lebanon will broadcast weighty speeches from their great leader, unwilling to invest much more in this issue. Ordinary Israelis might mumble reservations and shrug shoulders, while right-wingers will huff and thump, and some settlers will beat up a Palestinian farmer somewhere. Arab nations will rumble, fluster and hold a conference, or the 'Arab street' will buzz resentfully for a while. Europeans will mutter about peace; Russia will say some interesting things but go no further; India will sell Israel weapons made from British components; China doesn't let politics obstruct business.

The security wall might be extended to surround Palestinian towns and villages which once experienced the privilege of having space around them. Bedouins, not even registered as existing, will be squeezed on to marginal desert land further south. The north-south Palestinian trunk road might be re-routed 'for security reasons'.

Pictures of Palestine

Doesn't make sense? Well nothing much will happen to stop it. Little has happened to stop anything in recent decades. This is the drift of events here and it's all sickeningly predictable. The Palestinians lose land, from wilderness and farmland to village and city properties, and this incremental loss slowly eats away at the possibility of a Palestinian state, or a Palestinian *anything*. They just have to move over, making way for Israelis.

The Palestinian Authority will complain fruitlessly. It doesn't want war and it won't push Israel hard because it seeks to stay in power and earn the international community's approval. A few leading lights in Palestine will be invited to speak at conferences in Geneva, Milwaukee and Stockholm. Serious words will be uttered and nothing will happen.

It gets to you, sometimes – the ridiculousness and tragedy of this situation. The wider world consistently undermines Palestinians' chances and international institutions fail them. The confused world public, who lose track of events and their whys and wherefores, have other worries.

The Israelis driving this land-grab know this and that is how they get away with it. Not all Israelis support it, but the government and settlers carry on all the same. The measure will probably succeed – after all, it isn't settlement building, it's the establishment of nature reserves and military security areas. It's simply a matter of gaining land for future use, chipping away at Palestine. Today, another chunk started to be prised away.

Part Three:
Peace of the Patriarchs

25 Sixty Years of Triumph and Disaster
wars and peace processes

Here's some recent history, from 1948 onwards. This was the year of the *Nakba* or Disaster. By 1949, Jordan controlled the West Bank and East Jerusalem, Egypt controlled Gaza and Israel had the remaining 78% of former Mandate Palestine. This division continued through the 1950s as Israel established itself, growing in population and vigour from small, vulnerable beginnings to become a regional power backed by international Jews and propped up with sympathy from Europe and America.

Palestinians and Arabs from neighbouring countries maintained an ongoing resistance against which Israelis fought doggedly, developing a strategy of hitting hard to assert military superiority. This hammer approach characterised Israeli strategy, wreaking enormous damage, and in the last twenty years it has damaged Israel's moral position too. Despite the efforts of both sides to deliver knockout blows and deter further aggression, the ongoing conflict escalated in scale and violence through the 1950s, with neither side backing down.

Meanwhile, refugees in Gaza, the West Bank and neighbouring countries lived a life of poverty, hardship and destitution, first in tent cities and then in the dense breeze-block housing replacing them. UNRWA, one of UN's biggest operations, was founded to provide basic services and humanitarian aid. It's still operating sixty years later.

Pictures of Palestine

The situation suddenly shifted in the 1967 Six Day War when Israel, anticipating an Arab attack, pre-emptively struck its neighbours. Israelis always claimed that Arab countries wanted to eliminate Israel but the truth was that they never dared – it was a rallying-cry, not a serious threat. However, they did want to protect Palestinians from further incursion.

The world raised its eyebrows as Israel spectacularly wiped out neighbouring countries' air forces and occupied the West Bank, Gaza and the Sinai Peninsula. This defensive lightning attack was a ruse concealing deliberate territorial expansion – even Shimon Peres, now president of Israel, later admitted this.

The West saw Israel as a bulwark of its interests in the oil-rich Middle East during the Cold War, at a time when many Arab countries were forging connections with USSR, and it went along with the outcomes of the Six Day War, buying the idea that Israel's expansion constituted but a temporary security measure. Yet hawkish elements in Israel had other designs.

The official causes of the Six Day War were various: rivalries over water rights in the upper Jordan valley; the porous and troublesome frontier of Israel with the Jordanian-ruled West Bank, extending into Israel and rendering vulnerable to attack the populous narrow coastal strip linking northern and southern Israel; Syrian shelling of Galilee from the Golan Heights; Israeli fears over the Egyptian insistence that UN peacekeepers leave the Sinai (they had been there since the 1956 Suez Crisis); and the blocking of Israeli sea traffic by Egypt in the Red Sea Straits of Tiran (the right-hand fork at the top of the Red Sea), affecting Israel's Asia trade from the port of Eilat.

This war initiated the long Israeli occupation of what became known as the Occupied Palestinian Territories (OPT). Israelis, in a triumphalist mood, proceeded to colonise the West Bank and build settlements there. Palestine now had no political status except as a destination for international humanitarian aid. Incredibly, Golda Meir, an Israeli prime minister, even denied that a Palestinian people existed. Some Jews asserted that Palestinians had immigrated into the area after them. Palestinians were on their knees, in utter shock.

Israel's move was claimed to be temporary and strategic, but Zionist elements sought to perpetuate the occupation, pushing their case in the Israeli political arena and winning. A battle for the soul of Israel, between Jews who simply wanted a secure homeland and Zionists who wanted all of former Mandate Palestine, was won by the Zionists. Returning the West Bank evaporated as a possibility.

Arab nations, shocked and militant, agreed 'The Three Nos': no recognition of Israel, no peace and no negotiation. Israel meanwhile accrued new self-confidence, though soon it was in for a surprise: in 1973 Syria and Egypt, Soviet-armed, staged a surprise attack, the Yom Kippur or Ramadan War. Complicated by Cold War geopolitics, it risked conflict proliferation, drawing in the great powers. After initial losses, Israel staved off the attack, but a tide had turned. From this time on US military and economic support for Israel escalated.

Israel now stood at a junction-point and chose to dig in its heels – as is its habit. The country fell victim to its sense of uniqueness and exceptionalism, exempt from international norms or laws. When in doubt, Israeli voters tend to head for the simpler certainties of right-wing politicians, and this they did in the later 1970s, ending the former left-leaning period since Israel's founding. In effect it committed itself to permanent militarisation, to live permanently at odds with its neighbours and to be domestically steered by military, nationalist and right-wing interests. This alliance of interests was from then on to dominate Israel, though the moderate, secular and internationalist part of Israeli society nevertheless did its best to present a more reasonable, compliant face to the world.

International involvement in peace negotiations frequently erred on Israel's side, and US foreign policy made sure Israel remained shielded. Things went little further than declarations, conferences and peace processes, under the cover of which Israel incrementally strengthened its occupation, building more facts on the ground. Peace negotiations dragged on year after year: Israel customarily refused to budge and the Arabs didn't always play their diplomatic cards well. Israel avoided a comprehensive peace treaty, negotiating separately with those countries it chose to negotiate with, and not at all with the Palestinians, a squarely defeated, annulled people.

By 1979 Israel had signed a treaty with Egypt, returning the Sinai peninsula, taken in 1967, in exchange for passage rights through the Suez Canal and an end to Egyptian attacks. Gaza stayed in Israeli hands: here began Gaza's long isolation and sidelining by the international community, to become 'the world's largest prison'. Arab countries were no longer a united bloc, and the Palestinian resistance, the PLO, was also by now splintering. The Marxist PFLP staged dramatic hijackings and killings in the 1970s, of its own initiative. Much later, in 1994, peace was made with Jordan as part of the Oslo Accords.

In 1970 Jordan had expelled the PLO after the latter's attempted violent takeover of the country, where 60% of the population was of Palestinian extraction. The PLO fled to Lebanon where it then staged raids into Israel and bombarded it. It upset an already escalating civil conflict in Lebanon and played a bloody role in it between 1975 and 1982. To deal with the PLO, Israel invaded and occupied south Lebanon in 1982, advancing to Beirut and adding to the destruction wrought on Lebanon by the civil war.

Multiple atrocities occurred, including the notorious Israeli-sponsored massacres at Shatila and Sabra, and also outrages committed by Yasser Arafat's frantic PLO. Eventually defeated, the PLO escaped to exile in Tunisia in 1982. Palestine was now at a low ebb, since the PLO had been its sole source of political leverage and representation. By 1985 Israel withdrew from Beirut, finally leaving Lebanon much later in 2000 after a long occupation. Israel's Lebanese invasion cost it highly: it lasted 18 years and led to serious repercussions, caused largely by overdone aggression. Israel caused far more damage than it incurred, thereby creating trouble for itself with Lebanon in the long term, pursuing a narrow and violent definition of its own national interest.

One of its main perverse achievements was to provoke the Lebanese public into an adverse reaction to Israel's invasion, giving birth to Hezbollah in the early 1980s. By sheer determination, discipline and ferocious guerrilla tactics, Hezbollah gradually pushed Israel back, expanding as a combined militia and social reform party – the only body offering protection to Lebanese Shi'as. Much later, by 2006, Hezbollah engaged in war with Israel and, by not losing this war, in effect it won. Shi'a Muslims paid dearly in death and destruction – 1,200 died, mostly civilians, while 160 Israelis died, mostly soldiers – yet Hezbollah checkmated Israel, shattering its armed invincibility and ending Israel's threat of reinvading Lebanon. Hezbollah remains a latent threat today.

Other things had been unfolding too. In late 1987 the first Palestinian *intifada* erupted. Civil disobedience and street violence broke out, egged on particularly by young people. *Intifada* means 'shaking off'; it started as a spontaneous outbreak of frustration, though in its midst new ideas and a new Islamist element was emerging, Hamas. Foolishly, the Israelis had secretly funded Hamas, seeking to divide the Palestinians and weaken the PLO.

Meanwhile, the PLO, exiled in Tunisia and thus upstaged by events and by Hamas, quickly gave its support to the *intifada*, while being heavily pressured internationally to talk peace. It was blocked from entering peace talks until it recognised Israel and renounced warfare, which eventually it did by 1993. The PLO had been on its way to negotiating for peace, but the *intifada* demonstrated that a shift had occurred for Palestinians. A home-grown resistance had emerged, fired up by a younger generation born in the 1960s and 1970s, now disappointed in the old leftists and liberation warriors of the PLO.

But the PLO gained recognition by Israel as the legitimate representative of the Palestinian people – perhaps because Israel preferred the devil it knew. Yet the strongest grouping inside Palestine was now Hamas, a popular, lively, moral and social resistance movement.

Pictures of Palestine

Yasser Arafat led the PLO, an umbrella group of Palestinian factions in which his own party, Fateh, a nationalist party founded long before in 1959, was dominant. By 1988, after two decades of warfare, Arafat turned from fighter to statesman, making an historic speech at the UN in New York, engaging in negotiation and espousing a two-state solution. This was a big shift, accepting that Israel was a permanent fixture which could not be dislodged. Islamists in Palestine believed Arafat was corrupt, handling the Israelis too softly. Yet regardless of their belief, most Palestinians looked on Arafat as their leader and father. As the Oslo Accords took shape, they gave negotiation a try, and Arafat and his men began moving back home, returning to Gaza in 1994.

The 1990s brought a series of acts of faith by Palestinians, hoping that negotiations would work and the international community would guarantee a fair deal. In the Oslo Accords of 1993-95, Israel and the PLO ended open conflict. Palestinian nationhood was to come to pass in 5-10 years if various agreed conditions were fulfilled. The PLO, returning home, morphed into the Palestinian Authority or PA, in which Fateh was the biggest political party.

Palestine was to control Areas A and B of the Occupied Territories, with the prospect of expanding its control to Area C and further later on. Area A, a series of Palestinian urban islands, was to be fully Palestinian controlled, while Area B, generally surrounding Area A, was Palestinian-controlled but under ultimate Israeli control – Israel could intervene militarily in Area B but not in Area A. Meanwhile, Area C, Palestinian populated, was completely controlled by Israel – and here grew many of Israel's settlements.

Much rebuilding took place in Palestine, funded particularly by EU countries. But there were two major snags: the PA couldn't fully control violent Palestinian factions and suicide bombers, and the Israelis wouldn't ease their repression of Palestinians. They accelerated settlement and infrastructure building, land-appropriations, checkpoints and repression in Palestinian territory. In doing so, they undermined the PA's capacity to fulfil its own side of the deal, some would say intentionally. Here we see Israel's dual approach at work, with a peace wing and a nationalist-Zionist wing acting as good cop and bad cop.

Israel's political direction swerved as a result of the decisive 1995 assassination of its peacemaking prime minister Yitzhak Rabin by a young right-wing Israeli. The right didn't want accommodation with the Palestinians, and the assassination, passed off as the action of one deranged individual, changed everything and killed the peace. No one could step into Rabin's political shoes and a hardening of public attitude followed.

Then came the 1996 ascendancy of the nationalist PM Binjamin Netanyahu, who had little interest in concessions. Tunnel vision and bunker mentality waxed strong and disappointment with peace processes set in. In 1999 Netanyahu was replaced by the leftist ex-general Ehud Barak, who sought to revive peace negotiations, but the damage was already done.

Around 2000, in the Camp David negotiations chaired by US president Bill Clinton, to everyone's dismay Yasser Arafat turned down Barak's 'generous offer' to return to the Palestinians 73% of the West Bank, all of the Gaza Strip and some Bedouin-populated bits of the Negev Desert. But this offer did not include East Jerusalem, the Palestinians' capital and the site of the Muslim holy places. Jerusalem was to be Jewish and non-negotiable. Arafat would not negotiate without East Jerusalem being included, and without the removal of many Israeli settlements in the West Bank, so he walked out. From then on, most Palestinians no longer believed in negotiating. Arafat later died in 2004 following a long, punishing Israeli siege of the *Mukata'a* (his Ramallah HQ) during the second *intifada*.

Significant improvements thus failed to develop after Oslo. Yet Palestine had also changed, becoming more stable, more of a functioning entity. The conflict-weary Palestinians sought peace and regularisation but frustration simmered at the lack of progress. Palestinian suicide bombings by renegade factions, including Hamas, hit at the Israeli public to try to make them pressure their leaders to sue for peace, applying the 'collective punishment' tactic

Israel itself practised. Israel meanwhile refused to relax checkpoints, its military and economic stranglehold and its building of facts on the ground. Palestinians lost heart.

Israel's position reflected a vain hope held by Zionist factions that Palestinians would get up and 'transfer' out of the country if life were made difficult enough. Hardly likely for five million people with historic roots in the area and nowhere to go. This tension culminated in Ariel Sharon's provocative personal incursion in 2000 into Haram al-Sharif, the site of Al Aqsa and the Dome of the Rock in Jerusalem's Old City (Jews and Christians call it the Temple Mount). Mastermind of the earlier Lebanon invasion, Sharon sought to be Israel's strongman, garnering the insistent energy of the growing settler and nationalist movements.

This incursion, together with nervy Palestinian frustration, triggered the second *intifada*. Starting with street protests, the Israelis retaliated and it progressed to violent confrontation. There followed four years of Israeli troop incursions and sniper attacks, tanks on the streets, house searches and demolitions, curfews, arrests, assassinations and imprisonment of Palestinian leaders and activists. Palestine was in turmoil, undergoing hardship, trauma and insecurity.

The *intifada* petered out by 2004 after many horrific scenes. Ariel Sharon engaged in a strategy of unilateral action, building the separation wall around Palestinian areas, expanding settlement-building and consolidating Israel's strategic hold on the Jordan valley, thus surrounding the West Bank. Sharon imposed a forced calming on Israeli terms, tactically withdrawing from Gaza in 2005 and reducing military incursions in the West Bank as the wall was built, although this was actually a consolidation of the occupation rather than peace-building.

Much remained unresolved for Palestinians but they were exhausted. Their attacks and suicide bombings died down – after all, the Israelis kept winning, gaining added American support and international acquiescence. Palestinians had no way to progress, either through resistance or negotiation.

Pictures of Palestine

The occupation meant intense control and complication of Palestinians' lives, giving young Palestinians no sense of future and preventing economic development. Palestinians who could do so left, often to study or get jobs abroad. The wider world diligently applied double standards, sending aid while acquiescing in most of Israel's actions and generally subscribing to its narrative.

The next peace plan was the Roadmap outlined by US President Bush in 2002, to be jointly overseen by a body called the Quartet, made up of USA, EU, the UN and Russia. Peace plans were now

a joke both to Palestinians and Israelis, each for their own reasons. The Roadmap was a diplomatic checklist and timetable of actions which sounded good, but it had no teeth.

This checklist included an end to Palestinian violence (achieved by 2005); Palestinian political reform (mostly done); Israeli withdrawal and a settlement freeze (not done); Palestinian elections (done in 2006 but nullified by Israel and the West); internationally-sponsored peace conferences (hardly done); establishment of an independent Palestine with provisional borders (not done); multilateral engagement on water resources, environment, economics, refugees and arms control (partially done); an international conference to establish a final agreement, borders and clarification of the future of Jerusalem, refugees and settlements (not done); and Arab states' agreement of peace deals with Israel (partially done but not accepted by Israel).

Nothing much has happened since then, except for the Dayton Accords of 2008 and Obama-sponsored negotiations in 2010, neither of which made any difference. Peace processes are seen by Palestinians as a charade, while Israelis regard them as a foreign imposition useful only if they keep the US and EU quiet. Israel's best option is to leave things unresolved, permitting it leeway for taking unilateral actions. Palestine effected many of its Roadmap agreements but Israel refused to stop settlement expansion, and the international community failed to proceed with the necessary conferences, or with *anything* really, except for signing cheques to keep Palestinians quiet.

This situation was implicitly supported by the international community's tendency to avoid interfering in the domestic issues of sovereign nations – at least, when it so chose. This shielded Israel, for which, technically, Palestine was a domestic issue. Except it wasn't – and this is where law and justice clash.

That's where things stood by 2010, a long seventeen years after Oslo. Israelis by then suffered a form of victorious hubris, continuing to consolidate their hold on the Palestinian territories. The boldness of Netanyahu's 2009 government upset even Israel's chief supporter, USA, while causing other countries to groan. Israel edged toward pariah status in the world's eyes, confirmed in its confrontation with the Freedom Flotilla off Gaza in early 2010. Some Israelis saw this antipathy to be unjustified anti-Semitism, while others worried that Israel's soiled reputation would one day catch up with it.

With all avenues to resolution blocked or exhausted, something happened in early 2011 that started a process of contextual change for Palestine: first in Tunisia, then Egypt, then elsewhere in Bahrain, Yemen, Libya, Syria and Jordan, the Arab protests and revolutions broke out. These represented an irreversible historic shift, prompted by declining Western influence and an overdue swing of Arabic public attitudes against bad government, top-heavy elites, corruption and injustice. It was driven particularly by younger people – half of the population – reacting against the now old-fashioned fundamentalists and Arab nationalists who had defined the course of previous decades. These events represent a permanent change, shifting the balance of power in the Middle East.

Palestinians went quiet after 2004, getting on with life and hoping something would eventually emerge. World governments did nothing significant, even though global public opinion was shifting against Israel, except in America. The media and diplomatic worlds muttered airily about peace processes and disproportionate aggression by Israel. Matters remained unresolved for Palestinians and frustration lurked ominously under the surface, concealed beneath an aversion to further conflict and a yearning for a normal life.

The Arab revolutions removed a burdensome onus for initiating change from Palestinians' shoulders, yet they implicitly brought change by transforming the wider Middle Eastern context in which Palestine and Israel both sit. Frustrated with the semi-benign stranglehold exerted by Fateh in the West Bank and Hamas in Gaza, Palestinian youngsters, seeking justice and a better life, demonstrated for an end to the Fateh-Hamas divide and a revival of Palestinian unity – without which dealing with Israel was pretty futile.

193

But it also changed Israel's position in several ways. No longer able to claim that it was the sole democracy in the Middle East, and with weakened support from the West, Israel couldn't form a clear response to the changes developing around it. As usual, it didn't budge an inch. To Israel's advantage, the moral leadership of Iran evaporated and Syrian support for Hezbollah and Hamas weakened but new possible threats emerged – of an unravelling of treaties with Egypt and Jordan, of friction with Turkey and an upstaging of Israel by change in the Arab world. All this led to ramped-up settler moves to complete the job of colonisation in the West Bank. World sympathies for Palestinians, jaded disbelief of Israel and international tiredness with the Israel-Palestine issue also constrained Israeli freedom to act, except perhaps furtively.

This tectonic shift represents a parting of the ways and a change of pattern which will unfold in years to come. Palestine's conflict cannot be resolved without wider international change, but wider change is now happening, sucking the conflict along with it. In Palestine there has been talk of a third *intifada*, against both the PA and the Israelis, who are to an extent seen to be acting together. Yet international PA political initiatives are also approaching a critical point, in which the PA seeks international recognition as an independent state within the pre-1967 borders, whatever Israel thinks.

Change is gaining momentum, and the Great Unknown yawns wide. Meanwhile Palestinians, wary of bloodshed and disarray yet needing change, carry on with daily life. This is their strength. In one crucial way they have been perpetually successful: they haven't gone away and, whatever anyone thinks, they aren't going to.

26 Al Quds and Other Stories
complex social ecosystems

Just a day after returning to Bethlehem from Ramallah, I was on the move again – this time to Sheikh Jarrah, part of Arabic East Jerusalem immediately north of the Old City. As I sat blogging in a café, there was no mistaking that I was in the developed world – Israel. This was a Western-type café, though Arab-run, in the style of a burger joint, while cafés in the West Bank are distinctly Arabic in style, with a family-run feel and usually with tiled, somewhat unattractive decor.

Arab Israelis live quite different lives from West Bank Palestinians just ten kilometres away behind the walls. They're theoretically better off than West Bank people, yet the cost of living, taxes and other constraints in Israel are high. Israeli Arabs are distinctly disadvantaged and they feel like guests in someone else's country, though they lived here long before most Israelis. Their rights and security are subject to the inconsistent whims and political tides of Jewish Israelis. Someone once observed: "Israel is democratic for Jews and Jewish for Arabs".

There's a greater alienation here in Jerusalem, less of a sense of communal solidarity, and people's faces wear more frowns. The city council, theoretically running the whole of Jerusalem, operates patchy and inferior civic services in Arab areas. Israel has annexed the whole city, asserting Jews' right to live anywhere in it, and Arab areas are eaten away and crowded out by Jewish settlers. Yet Arabs may not move to Jewish areas in West Jerusalem or return to pre-1948 properties they lost when the Jews pushed them out.

195

Orthodox Jews in 19th century garb walk around with a proprietary air. They aren't aggressive – they just disregard you – and my rural British habit of nodding hello to people felt out of place here. Many Israeli Arabs seem less easygoing than West Bank people, more bound up in their own worlds, busier, less open, though they're decent enough when you engage with them. Arab traders in Jerusalem can be quite money-grabbing and surly – one, from whom I was buying some perfumes for folks back home, complained that I was taking too long and using up his time, so he lost my business forthwith.

The last 24 hours had been eventful. I had visited Ramallah, gone back to Bethlehem and now I was in Jerusalem. Not a long distance, but big jumps nonetheless. Ibrahim and I had been to Ramallah for another meeting with the deputy minister about the proposed radio station, but we didn't get past a departmental director, who spent much of the time berating Ibrahim for seeking to talk to the deputy minister rather than to him. Ibrahim was not happy when we emerged. He stood there outside the ministry, quietly fuming, frustrated as much with the territorial illogicality of the PA system as with the director's spiky performance.

Mercifully, before the director arrived, a female administrator had taken a liking to Ibrahim and supported the proposal, taking notes and saying that, if Ibrahim sorted out the necessary paperwork, she would shunt the matter through the system. She was interested in the proposal and judged Ibrahim to be worth dealing with.

Only some public servants, like her, are really in it for public service. This is one way Palestine scuppers itself. Some within the power-structure betray public interest in favour of self-interest, though at times both also intersect. This is a mindset, not just individuals on the make, or it's a situation that people get sucked into even when they started out with good intentions. There are exceptions, good-hearted public servants and ways of getting things done, and the secret is to know the right people or have the right approach – and trust in Allah for good measure.

On the way back to Bethlehem we hit a roadblock with long tailbacks, up in the hills near Abu Dis. There didn't seem to be a major security issue going on but the Israeli soldiers were clearly taking no risks and the queues piled up. The soldiers suffered more than everyone else, dressed up in boots, fatigues and bulletproof vests, carrying heavy guns and roasting in mid-thirties temperatures. The Palestinians in the queues were just bored, sitting in their cars and service taxis waiting, watching, but the soldiers were having a hard time. They pay a price for serving their country – national service is after all a form of slave labour.

People watched as I trolled along the stationary queue toward the checkpoint to get some telephoto shots. They possibly assumed I was a Western journalist. In situations like this, journalists with cameras and microphones are welcome since they give a 'world is watching' feeling to Palestinians and sometimes restrain Israeli soldiers' excesses. My Nikon, given by a well-wisher, being far beyond my means to buy, proved useful sometimes – it said 'international observer'. I got my photos, chatted to people and wandered back. Eventually the roadblock opened and we were on our way. An officer had made an operational decision, and a thousand people could get on with their lives.

We reached Bethlehem and Ibrahim dropped me off. I sat in a café drinking fresh juice, then a bottle of water – it had been a hot day. Then to Adnan's for a chat, then a few more tasks.

I met up with Albert at the Catholic Centre, an enormous Vatican-financed complex with cultural, swimming and sports facilities, placed high on the edge of the Christian Quarter, with a view stretching as far toward Jordan as the Middle Eastern smog (thick today) would allow. The breeze up there was cooling after a hot, clammy day. Older gentlemen sat in groups playing backgammon and young people footled around enacting coy

teenage embarrassments. It could have been anywhere, yet here we were in a walled-in, occupied land. Albert nattered on about wells he was currently clearing out – one of his several jobs – and about the spiders, gunk, junk and historic artefacts he found inside them. Some wells go back millennia.

Albert's extended family had been in Bethlehem for eight centuries since the Crusades. They once occupied a whole street in Bethlehem, named after them. His clan numbered thousands, though most now lived abroad and, were it not for his old mother and disabled wife, he would have left too, trying Scandinavia, where he believed his handyman's and construction skills would be well rewarded. But here he remained, with a left-behind feeling not uncommon for Palestinian Christians.

I asked him whether there ever was conflict between Christians and Muslims, since they're visibly different ethnic groups. He said no, there was remarkable solidarity, except when ruling regimes set them against each other, such as during the British administration. The British drove communities against one another to strengthen their overall control. They were wary of public figures capable of uniting disparate communities against foreign rule, and in the 1930s they murdered two popular singers and various clerics and activists who attracted significant followings. This turned Palestinians against them, and a revolt broke out in 1936. The British exiled or killed much of the leadership of Palestine and this gave the Jews an opening to gain the upper hand. Later in the 1940s, when the Palestinians needed leadership, none was available.

Had they been wiser, the British in the interwar years would have built up social harmony, trust, fairness and mutuality. Back in Europe, they could have acted diplomatically to restrain pressures on Jews, thus reducing Jewish despair and their subsequent resolute immigration into Palestine. They could have acted to limit the growth of Zionism in Palestine, encouraging a more integrated society, or at least a multiculturalism based on coexistence.

It was within the power of the Brits to do this, and some British diplomats pushed for it. Arabs would have accommodated moderate Jewish immigration and Jews would have had to be more realistic about the land they were entering. These were difficult options for both parties, but still easier and better than what actually unfolded. Christians and Muslims became united against the Jews by the *Nakba* of 1948. Yet over the centuries, Jews, Christians and Muslims across the Middle East had lived in largely peaceful symbiotic coexistence. Things could have developed very differently. Something went very wrong, and the British, as arbitrating rulers, let it happen.

Albert, in his mid-fifties, is a commanding drama-king, rich in character, who can be both entertaining and demanding as company, yet he's a good-hearted man. He lives, plays and works hard, and he's a pillar of the community. That night he saved me. After an evening with him and his friends, watching them playing billiards, Suleiman gave me a lift back to Al Khader. That was a relief – I was weary. He drove off and I walked the last half mile to the school.

When I slipped the key into the gate padlock, it would not turn. Trying again, it still would not turn. I had to get a grip. No, it definitely wasn't turning. Strange. It was approaching midnight. After more trying, I gave up. Next day, it turned out that the lock had been changed because children had stuffed sand in it – and someone had forgotten to tell me to collect a new key. I rang Albert to ask if I could return to his place. Later he told me that, normally, he switched off his phone at bedtime, but this evening he hadn't. That was a godsend – I wasn't fit to handle a bigger crisis at that moment.

Next morning, it was an early rise at Albert's. More stories from him over breakfast – this time about monks at the Catholic school he attended when he was young, who had had a penchant for fierce punishments and sexual delight in little boys. He had strong feelings about this, saying that some people he knew had paid a high emotional price. I think he was speaking for himself too: it had made him a defiant prankster with a disrespect for authority. When the Pope visited Bethlehem in early 2009, he had planned a theatrical protest, having read of child abuse scandals amongst priesthoods in Ireland and America, but his friends put a stop to that and bundled him away so that he wouldn't endanger himself during the high-security crackdown accompanying the Pope's visit.

Off he went to work and I took a service taxi to Bab al-Zqaq, where the Jerusalem bus leaves. I hopped on the 21, a comfortable, air-conditioned bus, making use of the opportunity to sit still and gather myself together. As we neared the Gilo checkpoint, a young woman in front of me took out a British passport, and I started talking to her. We had to get out, queue and have our passports examined. She was a Christian working with micro-finance schemes for women's cooperatives and arranging joint church activities on both sides of the wall. She had been here three years, formerly working in Hong Kong. By the way she described her life, she, like me, was on a semi-conscious mission to redeem some of the shadows of the British empire.

She was fascinated by my stories about Hope Flowers and we exchanged numbers. Her people could do with our experience in women's empowerment, and we could do with their experience in micro-finance. We discussed the dangers and complexities of working with both Israelis and Palestinians. One person she worked with in Haifa was being chased by Hamas, another in Bethlehem was suspected of collaboration with the Israelis when, like Ibrahim, he was simply trying to bridge the sectarian divide. She was straddled between different kinds of people and risks, and we discussed our rather schizoid situation of working with such people.

Either of us could easily blow it for someone, or we could be suspected by a variety of different parties of crimes we were not knowingly committing. There are many human hazards to contend with – Israelis, Fateh and Hamas, and religious, political, official and tribal interests, each with their own agendas. Within the Christian community alone there were disparate groupings to handle deftly. You have to discern what kind of person you're talking to at any moment and we agreed on a need to be wary. We parted company and I never saw her again.

Pictures of Palestine

Jerusalem is intense, crowded, multi-ethnic, loud, confusing and exciting, modern and historic, commercial and spiritual. How it functions I do not know, but it does, and it's quite prosperous. It's not unfriendly, but it's shifty and you need your wits about you. Jews, Muslims, Christians and others mix more freely than the foreign media would have us think, but there is still an implicit *apartheid*, and some people betray this in their behaviour. Arabs and Israelis travel on separate buses and live in segregated areas. People are exceptionally varied in opinion – a spectrum wide and intricate. But they seem to rub along, for most of the time at least.

It was time to leave the café in Sheikh Jarrah to attend a meeting at a radio station – in the end a non-event. Next I had a meeting with some American researchers investigating citizens' peace initiatives, then I made calls at two shops. Finally I reached Ibrahim Abu el-Hawa's house up on the Mount of Olives, east of the Old City. His was an open house for peace-oriented internationals, where I was to stay the night. Some hours and ten people later I was glad to get to bed. What a day.

27 The Twenty-One Bus
holy intercity bus service

I confess that my heart lifted a notch when next day, on my return to Bethlehem, we passed the sign just outside Beit Jala which says 'Entry forbidden to Israelis'. This is the border, though the checkpoint there is now dormant, replaced by the big Gilo checkpoint a few miles back. The Israeli authorities and army cannot guarantee the safety of Israeli civilians in Palestinian-controlled Areas A and B, so entry is discouraged and this *apartheid* system is a loss for Israelis as much as it is for Palestinians.

Strangely, it's also a protection for Palestinians since Israelis impact on them far more than Palestinians impact on Israelis. So the relative absence of Israelis in the West Bank makes Palestinians feel more secure. *Apartheid* manifests differently for West Bank Palestinians than for Israeli Arabs: the former experience a certain personal freedom within their collective imprisonment while the latter experience a personal unfreedom, even though officially they have greater rights within the Israeli democratic system.

While we're on it, this apartness is multi-level. Vying for bottom position are desert Bedouin and Gazans. Many Bedouin villages and their inhabitants are not officially recognised and they have few rights, since they aren't registered as citizens. Gaza is under siege and Gazans have for some time been deprived of basic rights, travel, supplies and access from outside. Neither Bedouin nor Gazans officially exist, except when they attract military or humanitarian attention.

203

The Gilo Checkpoint with Beit Jala behind it

Next up come Palestinians with permits to live in Jerusalem, who either have Jordanian or no passports, with no right to vote and diminished legal rights in Israel. This is a leftover of the 1967 invasion when Jerusalem Palestinians were offered a choice of Israeli citizenship or to retain their Jordanian nationality – and many chose to stay Jordanian, believing the occupation would one day end. These people exist officially, but they're treated as foreigners, sometimes 'infiltrators', even when their families have lived there for generations.

Then come West Bank Palestinians, with rights within the West Bank, though only some have rights to enter Israel and, if their papers are incorrect, they nowadays risk deportation as 'infiltrators' – excluding them from their own land.

Then come Arab Israelis (and Druze and others) who have the vote in Israel and theoretically full rights, though they are discriminated against in multifarious ways. They are politically disunited and their rights are subject to the whims of Israeli courts, governors and officials. Druze, living in northern Israel, have somewhat greater rights than Palestinians – they are more trusted by Jews.

Then come non-Jewish people, *goyim*, in the form of residents (many of them Western Christians), guest-workers (cheap labour from Africa, the Philippines and elsewhere, with diminished rights) and visitors, with visitors' rights and recourse to their own governments' protection. As a tourist you find yourself slotting into the *apartheid* system whether you like it or not, and in this group you stand. In 2010 the Netanyahu government started deporting or refusing entry to certain NGO employees and activists, and a new discretionary entry visa allows entry to Israeli or Palestinian areas only, but not to both – and it's applied selectively, just to confuse things.

Top of the pile are Jews, though even here there are stratifications, with Euro-American Ashkenazi Jews at the top and Sephardic (*Misrahi*) Jews next down. Russian and American Jews immigrating in recent decades are very influential. Secular and religious Jews vie for influence. *Sabras*, born in Israel, can be elbowed around by immigrant Jews or *olim*, many of whom are settlers. It's complex, and there's an arbitrariness and variability to it, depending mainly on one's ability to stand up for oneself and who one is talking to. Also, as everywhere, money affects one's rights and freedoms.

So all is very complex in this kaleidoscopic land of just ten million people, and yet it could be a wonderful place if everyone got on – a proper holy land.

After people-working hard, I had been glad to board the 21 bus from the Damascus Gate in East Jerusalem to Bethlehem. We drove through Jerusalem's suburbs down the Hebron road, which used to lead straight through to Bethlehem. But now the security wall and the Rachel's Tomb checkpoint intervene so Israeli traffic and the 21 bus turn right to follow a settler by-pass road leading toward the Gush Etzion settlement bloc and Hebron. It passes the controversial settlement of Har Gilo, for which, in the mid-1990s, a large expanse of virgin forest was destroyed, much to environmentalists' dismay. Once a woodland hilltop giving Bethlehem a sense of space and greenery, it is now a stacked-up concrete settlement, giving Bethlehem an overcrowded, hemmed-in feeling.

On the settler by-pass lies the Gilo checkpoint – a modern multi-lane checkpoint staffed with soldiers. If you have Israeli plates you drive straight through, but with Palestinian plates you stop if you're entering Jerusalem, and sometimes when leaving it too. Today we went straight through – they weren't bothering. The by-pass road skirts Bethlehem, with the security wall between it and the town. It ploughs through dramatic scenery of high tree-covered hills and deep valleys, through tunnels and over lofty bridges, with concrete walls alongside it in places to prevent anticipated attacks. They don't happen, unless the odd football accidentally flies over the wall, but the Israelis take no chances. After the checkpoint the bus pulls sharp left onto a side-road winding uphill to the 'No Israelis' boundary sign, and down through the narrow winding streets of Beit Jala into Bethlehem.

Pictures of Palestine

Beit Jala, a pleasant, antiquated Christian hilltop town, clings to its hill with quaint bravado. It is the highest part of the Bethlehem conurbation, which itself sits on a plateau. The conurbation accommodates between 70,000 and 100,000 people – I've never seen a reliable population figure. Palestinians count the old towns of Beit Jala, Beit Sahour and Bethlehem as separate towns, which once they were, but now they're joined together. Each has a long Christian heritage.

The reason my heart lifted on returning to Bethlehem is that the atmosphere in Jerusalem is rather intense and heavy. Its population is 700,000 and it's crammed with traffic, people, separated communities and tightly-packed buildings although, naturally, it has some beautiful and impressive aspects, pleasant suburbs and of course a rich history.

Bethlehem is far more congenial, on a good day a good-natured and nurturing city. That's not just because it is smaller: it has an us-together atmosphere, nowadays reinforced by the security wall separating it and Jerusalem, insulating it from Jerusalem's jangle, bustle and simmering discordance. People say hello in the streets, expressing interest in their fellow humans, while Jerusalem has the alienation and insecurity of a big, divided city. Jerusalem also has a latent aggro, a sub-explosive intensity not present in Bethlehem.

I saw this aggro when sitting at a bus stop in Jerusalem. Drivers parp their horns at the slightest obstruction, even when a bus ahead slows for a bus stop. Excuse me, but is a bus not *supposed* to stop at bus stops? People project their frustrations and feelings in no uncertain terms. Like when I had a ride with Itzhak, down a steep, winding hill from the Mount of Olives to the Old City. We hit a narrow bit where some cars were coming up. No one yielded to anyone else: they just pushed forward expecting the other to get out of the way and then scowled through the open window if they didn't.

Itzhak was genuinely stuck, sandwiched between upward, downward and closely-parked cars. Then a yelling match started, resolved only by some skilled manoeuvring on Itzhak's part, battling with hand-brake, accelerator and the steep hill. British eyes might have anticipated a fight brewing, but no, it's just the way people here relate to one another, pushing at each other to see who will yield first. Most adults are ex-soldiers, after all. Mercifully, Itzhak is nevertheless a philosophical negotiator by nature. Through this experience I realised that my mild-mannered, polite Britishness looked, from a bullish Israeli's viewpoint, cowardly and worthy of disdain. Perhaps so, but I'm glad the whole world isn't like this.

Before coming to the Holy Land, some friends had been nervous for my safety, but I can happily assure them that the biggest risk here is not from soldiers or terrorists but from Israeli car-drivers. Watch out, and get across that road as quickly as you can, because they're coming at you and it's *your* problem!

This pushiness was visible in an Israeli settler building that Itzhak showed me on the Mount of Olives. Boldly decked with resplendent Israeli flags, the settlers were barking 'screw you' at everyone around them. The house had been Palestinian, and the owner had sold it to a Jordanian. It had a lovely view over the Dome of the Rock and the Old City. But the Jordanian was an agent acting for American-financed Israeli settlers. The owner, who would never knowingly have sold the house to settlers, was deeply aggrieved, accused of betrayal by fellow Palestinians, and he escaped abroad for his safety. This is how many properties in East Jerusalem are acquired by Jewish settlers and their triumphalist Israeli flags rub salt in local Palestinians' wounds.

Itzhak himself was unhappy about such things. He felt shame over it: this is not obedience to Moses' Ten Commandments, as Orthodox settlers might have it, but Zionist assertiveness and colonisation, arguably a major source of potential danger to Jewish people. He is enthusiastic for the Israeli national project and the Jewish vision, but he doesn't believe it has to bring others hardship or oppression.

Itzhak is warm-hearted and interesting, a mutual friend of the late British prehistorian John Michell and, like him, a student of ancient

geometry, mathematics and cosmology. We first crossed paths years ago in England. I rang him while in Jerusalem to see whether he might like a visit from me. He asked where I was and, hearing I was on the Mount of Olives, said, "Ah, Ibrahim Abu el-Hawa's – I'll be over in an hour". Which was a relief, saving me another taxi fare. Itzhak is one of those Jews with no qualms about entering Palestinian areas, since he counts many Palestinians as friends and is respected by them. Palestinians generally judge people not by ethnicity or belief but by manifest behaviour.

I had shared a room the night before with a delightful English expat called David, who had been here for eleven years. A retired surgeon and a magnanimous, eccentric, gentlemanly Christian, he wandered around promoting peace and reconciliation, with a "How marvellous, just fascinating, God bless you!" approach to life. Having no residence rights, he left and re-entered the country every three months and, the antithesis of a terrorist or troublemaker, he clearly charmed the uniformed ladies at the Israeli border into letting him in again.

David also knew Itzhak. David and I sat for an hour drinking English tea that I made with milk and no sugar, which delighted him – Palestinians drink tea with no milk, mint leaves and half a ton of sugar. After joining us and chatting awhile, Itzhak took David and me to a sanctuary garden on the side of the Mount of Olives with a dramatic view of the Old City.

Geomancer that he is, he told us, waving across the amazing panorama, that the Kremlin is due north of Jerusalem and the Golden Temple at Amritsar is due east, forming a triangle, and that there were also geomantic triangles linking Jerusalem with the Pyramids, Mecca and the High Altai mountains. He then talked of an alignment in the Old City between the Muslim Dome of the Rock and the Christian Church of the Holy Sepulchre.

All of which goes to show that different faiths and cultures are not quite as different as we believe. This point is what Itzhak chips away at in his rather scholarly theological work. While Jewish and a Kabbalah student, he promotes the idea that Jews, Muslims and

Christians can live together, using meticulously-argued scriptural justification to do so. After this memorable interlude in the sanctuary garden, via the aforementioned high-tension traffic-jam, he had taken me to Damascus Gate, dropping me outside the bus station – with a car behind parping appropriately as I got out – so that I could catch the 21 bus.

One more thing. Ibrahim Abu el-Hawa, whom I had been visiting, is one of the Jerusalem Peacemakers. He was sad that I was leaving his house. I was, to him, sensible and a good contributor, and he looked bereft when I packed up. Poor old Ibrahim, he's a saviour and a saint, welcoming all and everyone to his open house, then regularly getting into money trouble because his guests make insufficient financial contributions to help him run the place. He takes Muslim hospitality a long way, bless him, and then the Israeli authorities take him to court for unpaid bills.

He's a generous, hospitable Muslim living in a country operating on tighter Western rules, with a dose of occupation controls thrown in. I was unhappy to leave Ibrahim but I needed to get away. I gave him a $100 contribution, knowing he hoped for $10,000, and left with Itzhak and David. Ibrahim is another of those Palestinians I wish I could wave a magic wand over. His soul no doubt stands well in the eyes of God, and he's an underrated asset to the world. A community father with an enormous family, his folks have lived on the Mount of Olives for 400 years, and his open house has been a haven of reconciliation for many people.

On the 21 bus, my welcome refuge after Jerusalem, I had the opportunity to gaze aimlessly out of the window and let my thoughts drift. Once back in Bethlehem, I went to Adnan's shop, rested on his Bedouin rugs and found myself chatting with a Pole and some Germans, then some Americans, then two Brits. Where had all these internationals suddenly come from? Adnan is a magnet for such visitors, serving tea and hospitality. Like Ibrahim Abu el-Hawa he's perpetually broke too, but for different reasons – he tries hard to sell his stuff, but somehow it just doesn't work.

Pictures of Palestine

One well-known guest of his had been the British mural-painter Banksy, who painted cheeky political artworks on the security wall while here. One was of a big window with a lovely pastoral scene visible through it – a comment on the unsightly architectural atrocity of the wall. Another was of a little girl body-searching a soldier, he with his hands up. Another was of a girl using balloons to lift her over the wall. Brilliant. On another occasion, a large group of Italian art students came and covered a considerable expanse of wall. However, some Palestinians disapprove, regarding this as decorating an atrocity to make it more acceptable. Whatever you do in this complex land attracts opposition from someone!

The security wall had been built close to Adnan's village, and they'd lost land to settlers. Not far from his house, over the wall, lived the dreaded Avigdor Lieberman, the controversial Israeli foreign minister at the time. Lieberman, a Lithuanian Jew, advocated 'transferring' all Palestinians abroad – yes, five million of them! Where to, Greenland? 'Transfer' is ethnic cleansing by another name. Palestinians, foreign diplomats and commentators know not whether to laugh or cry over Lieberman. Even so, in the days when Adnan's villagers and the local Jews met each other on a daily basis before the wall came between them, Lieberman and his mates played friendly football matches with the villagers, just another strange paradoxical inconsistency.

Life here is a stretching, fluid, volatile thing, with glimmers of light, darkness, joy and sorrow. In the West we know a more organised, regularised social environment, while here your boundaries are pummelled, tested, rubbed and stimulated in, shall we say, richly character-developing ways.

This indeed *is* a holy land, scintillating, energising and enlightening, yet tragic, contradictory, densely-populated and rubble-strewn too. Despite its bizarre and challenging aspects, it's a remarkable place. The hand of God moves in *very* strange ways.

28 Those Notorious Settlers
West Bank settlements and outposts

ethlehem sits on a high plateau with quite steep sides. If you go along Manger Street, the historic main road from the Nativity Church toward Jerusalem, the route sweeps in a series of curves along the high edge of the plateau, affording fine panoramas, until it joins the old Hebron Road. There sits the Rachel's Tomb checkpoint and the security wall, nowadays marking the northeast edge of town, separating Bethlehem from Jerusalem and blocking interaction between people lacking the right permits.

That view from Manger Street looks over a sweeping valley. On the far side rises another prominent hill – again, once covered with forest, felled in 1996-97. On the hilltop arose the Israeli settlement of Har Homa, a commuter settlement incorporated into the Israeli-created Greater Jerusalem area. An ugly, snaking fence with a cleared security zone on the Palestinian side separates Har Homa from Bethlehem.

This modern concrete monstrosity, with a population of 4,000, glowers over Bethlehem like a hilltop citadel. It always astounds me that Jewish people want to live there, with a commanding view over Arabic Bethlehem, which Har Homa residents cannot visit, and from which the Muslim calling to prayers resounds throughout the day. Surely that must give Jewish housewives headaches? But then, many of the inhabitants are neither the privileged of Israel nor the troublemaking ideology-soaked settlers who hit the headlines – they're working couples with families, drawn there by the facilities, cheap property, tax breaks and financial incentives. These people are the more innocent and numerous of the many different kinds of West Bank settlers.

Israel is a settler country. The vast majority have immigrated over the last century, and settlements have been a major mechanism in the staking out of territory. In the West Bank they have taken on many different forms – urban, dormitory and industrial municipalities, city neighbourhoods (in Jerusalem and Hebron), religious and secular townships, farming communities and colonial outposts in the wilderness. Nowadays, in the political controversies over settlements, their variety is not widely understood.

The 1948 war left Palestinians with 22% of former Mandate Palestine. This they lost in the 1967 war. This occupied land was not incorporated into Israel proper, except for Jerusalem. The West Bank is run either by a military 'civil administration' or by the municipality of Jerusalem, and Palestinians occupy 54% of it, or 12% of 'historic Palestine' – the rest is Israeli settlements, military zones, nature reserves or government land. There are settlements northwards in the Golan Heights too (taken from Syria in 1967) and they existed in the Gaza Strip until Israel withdrew from it in 2005.

Hara Homa Settlement (behind) overlooking Bethlehem (foreground)

Pictures of Palestine

Settlement blocs have eaten into large chunks of the West Bank, either on its edge (such as the Etzion bloc west of Bethlehem, containing Efrat, Kvar Etzion and Betar Illit), or penetrating deep into wedges of the West Bank (such as the Ariel and Ma'ale Adumim blocs, orbital to Tel Aviv and Jerusalem respectively). There are farming and military settlements and zones in the Jordan valley and corridors of land, settlements and outposts breaking up many parts of the West Bank, leaving Palestinian enclaves with limited or circuitous connections.

Settlements are largely officially sanctioned, though naturally it's complex. Some are not, and most of those are officially overlooked. They're another masterpiece of exceptionalism, all stridently variable, yet they're all part of the same overall colonising strategy. Smaller outposts are largely the initiative of independent settler groups and they're often illegal in Israeli law, which is only sometimes enforced. Or they are officially illegal at first, then they are legalised as time goes on. Under the military administration, Israeli laws are applied selectively in the West Bank. 'Security measures', meaning 'what the military administration wants', are the mechanism by which things usually happen – and there's no questioning a security measure. It's a military dictatorship, really, for Palestinians.

Some ideological settlers want the occupied settler areas to become a 'new' or 'other' Israel, subject to Orthodox Jewish rules and autonomous from Israel proper. This is a potentially dangerous state of affairs which could blow up into a conflict between the state of Israel and renegade settler groups. There's already a low-level war going on between these settlers and adjacent Palestinian communities.

Outposts – often trailers, cabins and tents – are the way that settlements are established and extended. Settler pioneers head out, take some land, defend it, hold out for a while, then develop and expand from there. The authorities conveniently build roads and services for them, and the army guards them when called on.

Some settlements are full-scale towns, such as Pisgat Ze'ev (40,000), Ramot Alon (40,000), Ma'ale Adumim (30,000), Modi'in Illit (27,000), Ariel (16,000) and Betar Illit (25,000). Others are more like suburban dormitories with a few thousand people. Some are populated by special interest groups, whether ultra-orthodox Haredim in Betar Illit and Modi'in Illit, or Russians in Ariel, or supporters of parties such as Labour or Likud, or ex-army people.

Some are city neighbourhoods carved out of Palestinian urban areas – 35% of East Jerusalem is now made up of Israeli settlements and neighbourhoods. Some settlements (such as Gush Etzion) are former Jewish settlements founded in the 1930s, abandoned in the 1948 war when Jews had to retreat into Israel and later reoccupied after 1967. Some are outposts of followers of certain rabbis or sects, or they're alternative communes or run by independent-minded pioneers ('Jewish rednecks', an Italian activist called them) with a penchant for building and farming.

The purpose behind settlements is strategic, to obstruct an Arab re-invasion, a Palestinian revival or the expansion of Palestinian towns. Or it is religious, to fulfil the biblical notion that the land was given to Jews by God. Or it is economic, to allow Jerusalem and Tel Aviv to expand. Or Zionist, based on an expansionist and colonialist impulse.

Settlers you hear of in the news, encroaching on Palestinian farmland, uprooting trees, attacking Palestinians, setting fire to fields, houses and mosques and causing other trouble are a minority. They are ideological, religious or cowboyish settlers with overblown *chutzpah*, ranged particularly around the biblical towns of Hebron and Nablus, or out in wilder rural areas. Most settlers are more harmless, there because of economic incentives or a need for a home, and many are immigrants of the last few decades.

In 2007 there were 485,000 settlers, of whom 280,000 were in the West Bank, 190,000 in East Jerusalem and 19,000 in the Golan Heights. Eighty percent of settlers live within commuting distance of Jerusalem. Added to settlements are infrastructure such as security walls, which break up the West Bank and isolate Palestinians from each other, together with settler roads and bypasses, military zones with restricted access, nature reserves, appropriated farmland, industrial sites and land reserved for settlement expansion.

Settlers can thus range from secular commuters, disadvantaged families and new immigrants to orthodox religious nationalists, farmers and idealistic Zionists. The overall effect is that Palestinian lands have been sectioned up, rendered into patches which can no longer form a proper contiguous Palestinian state. The Arabic word for settlements means 'colonies'. Colonisation is the reason for their development.

Irrespective of their legality in international law – which states that all settlements on the Palestinian side of the Green Line are illegal – facts on the ground have been established to make any abandonment of settlements difficult. Large numbers of Israelis would have to be moved and much infrastructure would be destroyed – something no Israeli administration would willingly do, especially if it relies on settler or right-wing nationalist parties to keep it in power. There have already been cases where soldiers refuse to move settlers or, if they do, the action is symbolic and settlers simply move back afterwards.

Ironically, much settlement and infrastructure construction work has been done by Palestinians, simply because of their need for employment and income. They are hired as cheap labour without being subject to Israeli employment laws, which don't apply in the West Bank. Up to 2009, 12,000 Palestinian building workers gained permits each year to work in settlements. Controversially, some Palestinian construction and materials firms have been involved as well – the West Bank has plenty of good quarrying stone. The PA decided in 2010 to end this divisive system, though whether there will be jobs to replace those lost is a moot point. Settlement-building will become more expensive as a result. There are also international moves to obstruct the settler movement through selective boycotts and disinvestment, and product-labelling and trade restrictions on goods exported from the settlements.

Aside from considerable losses and hardships incurred by Palestinians, I have two worrying concerns. The first is space, both geographical and psychological. The West Bank is densely populated and settlements have been dropped into small spaces, not only impinging on Palestinian farmland, villages and towns but also dominating them since they are often high up, overlooking Palestinian areas. A wall or fence is built around settlements, usually more visible and humiliating to Palestinians than to Israelis. So life has become more claustrophobic for Palestinians.

The second concerns the settlements themselves, modern concrete estates with little spare space – though their elevation compensates for this. Innocent kids' bike-rides into the country are just not done unless overseen by soldiers. These places are incubators of social problems and mental illness, sharing the ills of faceless dormitory towns worldwide, dependent on car transport and, in times of economic downturn and oil-price hikes, potential prisons.

Though Israelis are the apparent winners of this population-and-location game, their settlements are not naturally-evolved, full-spectrum communities, and thus they are susceptible to serious social issues. Settlements have narrow demographics, housing people of certain age-groups, belief-groups or social types, leading to problems arising from a deficient social spread. Other issues such as environmental and resource stress, effluent disposal, water aquifers, social polarisation and humanitarian, economic and social impacts on Palestinians all add up to a future headache of enormous proportions.

About 40% of settlements sit on private Palestinian land. Ottoman law had it that, if land was registered, farmed for ten years and taxed, ownership was recognised. If not, or if farming lapsed for three years, it reverted to government land. However, the later British-run registration process was incomplete in 1948 when Israel was established and the West Bank was occupied by Jordan. The Jordanians let people stay where they lived, intervening only when there was a dispute, so there is still much unregistered land.

Much was communally owned, therefore not technically 'private', and much land had only common or customary legal standing, without contractual ownership. Many ownership rights have been overlooked by the Israelis anyway, and land has been forcibly occupied by the army, settlers, court judgements or construction

firms, walled in or otherwise appropriated for security zones or
other purposes – especially in the case of large tracts of land in the
Jordan valley. Eighteen percent of the West Bank is made up of
Israeli military zones.

So it's all suitably complicated – a nightmare to sort out and,
in the Israeli way of things, intentionally so. This complexity
obstructs any unravelling of the settlement project. If the
evacuation of settled land were called for, then Israel would be
responsible for doing it. It is therefore unlikely to be done, however
many UN resolutions are agreed. The prospect of foreign troops
battling with settlers to enforce laws, resolutions or treaties is a
nightmare no one wishes to take on.

Some have suggested that settlers could become Palestinian
citizens, but this is improbable and wouldn't be accepted by many
of them, given their nationalist zeal. Some would fight and some
reckon that, since they are enacting the Law of God, they are
fighting God's war and that human rights or political decency play
no part. It is God who decides these things, not humans, so this
interpretation of God's Law is a moot point. Some settlers oppose
the idea of the state of Israel, though they're happy to call in the
Israeli army to protect them if necessary.

This is a success for the 'facts on the ground' strategy, adopted
before Israel was founded. But this strategy isn't unique in history:
in the occupation of America, Australia, Siberia and the past
colonial enterprises of European powers, laying facts on the ground
was standard practice. The main difference is that Israel's colonial
enterprise has taken place in modern times. Key principles are
thus involved here which, because of the passage of time, morally
override earlier colonial precedents.

The first principle is that, whatever Israelis believe, Palestinians
have needs and rights which are equal in *all* respects to those
of Israelis. Second, whatever the historic and biblical claims
of Jews, most Palestinians were living in Palestine before most
Jews immigrated. Religious Jews reckon this land is theirs by
God's gift, but some assert that other Jews have not fulfilled the

Pictures of Palestine

Covenant by which God granted them this land, and that the killing and stealing accompanying the occupation breaks the Ten Commandments. All this doesn't mean Jews should leave, but it does mean, as in post-*apartheid* South Africa and other post-colonial countries, that the needs and rights of the original *de facto* inhabitants must be respected, accommodated and even prevail, especially if they are a majority.

Third, the right of invasion and occupation was legally abolished in 1920 by the League of Nations – this distinguishes the Israeli settler movement from earlier colonial enterprises. Fourth, it's commonsense that all people must have a fair deal, with equal access to and responsibility for the space and resources of the Earth. That's the bottom line and, in time, that's what must prevail. Worldwide, if we cannot cooperate, all of humanity will suffer in the 21st century, Israelis included.

When I looked out from my workplace at the school, over the valley I saw a collection of portable cabins, a settler outpost at the northeast end of the rather long, thin settlement of Efrat. Efrat has a population of 7,000, and it is part of the Etzion bloc. The outpost has been there a few years, making a statement and

Over the valley behind the incomplete wall lie the cabins of an outpost of the expanding Efrat settlement

creating a fact on the ground. Efrat will one day extend right up to the wall. That's why the watchtower on the hill, overlooking Al Khader, is retained. Efrat is financed by a property developer who made his millions by running bingo gambling joints in USA. He offered a large sum of money to the Issa family to get them to move the school so that the settlement could extend to the edge of Al Khader – the money was refused.

It makes me wonder whether, eventually, the school and the Palestinian houses on the hill around it, located on the Palestinian side of the wall, might nevertheless be forced to move. After all, the Palestinians over here are second-class citizens, whose needs and priorities are considered less important than the march of Israeli progress.

Encroachment on Al Khader could be prevented in the unlikely event that a peace agreement established clear borders and rights, permitting Palestine to become a proper country. This is one reason why, over the decades, Israel has prevaricated, delayed and dragged its feet over peace agreements. Such delay allows Israel to carry on its quiet invasion, its incremental conversion of a military occupation into a full appropriation of what remains of Palestine.

Settlement-building might, in international law, be illegal, but Palestine is not thus far a legally recognised nation, so its claim on the land is technically tenuous. Yes, Palestine doesn't exist. In this political void, anything may happen. That's why the international community quietly allows this situation to persist – it's a convenient abrogation of responsibility. The right of invasion has been abolished, yes, but this applies only to recognised nations with legally-sound borders, which Palestine is not. Neat, huh?

29 Korea meets Palestine
the Hope Flowers story

Iawoke at 5.30, bolt upright. Staggering into the kitchen, I gazed blearily out of the window. A lovely dawning light blessed the monastery village of Irtas down the valley with a misty goldenness and, looking over at the watchtower, I wondered how those soldiers were doing. They might themselves be staring at this liminal dawn, wondering exactly why they need to keep watch over such a sublimely tranquil scene.

I started my day, blogging over breakfast. Around nine a taxi drove up. Visitors for Ibrahim, by the looks of it. I trotted downstairs. It was a Korean TV man with a multilingual visiting card and a Palestinian taxi-driving fixer. The Korean was concerned that Ibrahim was not on time – and where were the children?

"Welcome to Palestine! Well, Ibrahim's running on Palestine *Inshallah* Time – and it's the school holidays!" The taxi driver grinned, giving me a look as if to say "Sorry about this".

I brought them upstairs. By the time the kettle was on, Ibrahim arrived, and they found themselves going back downstairs again, minus tea. Welcome to Palestine indeed – just take each moment as it comes!

After a while I went downstairs to say hello. Ibrahim asked me to take over an interview with the Korean, for TV. He had a security problem – the Issas were being watched and he said he was unsure about what to avoid saying, whereas I was a foreigner who'd be out of the country when the programme was broadcast. If something was problematic, they could blame it on me.

Well, yes, I *could* do it, but I needed twenty minutes to smarten up, and I was unprepared – I was still getting over yesterday in Jerusalem. Soon, two cameras were rolling, and I was answering questions about Hope Flowers.

I explained how the school had been started by Hussein Issa, a refugee raised in the Deheisheh refugee camp down the road. Working hard, he later studied social sciences and education at Bethlehem University. He knew that the effort he had made to change his life was not possible for all refugee children. In 1984, at age 36, he started a Montessori-based kindergarten up towards Beit Jala called *Al Amal*, Hope, for refugee kids.

Before long he discovered the extent to which children's learning capacity was marred by psychological damage, undernourishment and disadvantage – he'd been like that himself. He developed ingenious methods to shift things, and thus began Hope Flowers' innovative war-zone educational programme, from which nowadays other schools seek to learn.

As the children at Al Amal grew too old

for kindergarten, it wasn't right to consign them to ordinary schools where they could pick up destructive ways and neither was it right for them to have no education. So Al Amal started extending its brief. After seven years, following the first *intifada* of the late 1980s, it grew into a full-scale school, Hope Flowers, moving to its current building in Al Khader.

In the first *intifada* teenagers had thrown rocks and stones to battle with Israeli soldiers, and reprisals were heavy, long and disproportionate. Fathers were carted away, people died, there were lengthy curfews, houses were demolished, tanks rolled and shoot-outs echoed in the streets. This was witnessed first-hand by children. In the second *intifada* these children were teenagers, and their childhood experiences fanned the flames.

At Hope Flowers in the 1990s, a new emphasis on trauma recovery was needed to create a ground-level 'deep peace' to complement the Oslo Accords. This was not only for the children but also for teachers since, no matter how dedicated to peace teachers were, they still tended unconsciously to convey their stress and disturbances to the kids – teachers' tolerance levels were themselves sometimes frayed. A counselling system was developed and new peace-building techniques were built into the curriculum. These included dealing with difficult situations, handling frustrations, articulating one's thoughts and feelings, participating and voting in meetings, managing edgy situations and generally tackling life's rigours.

These were not theoretical lessons in peace studies: peace-building and democratic practices were incorporated into school activities to train children personally for real life – it concerned their current situation. Language lessons taught real communication skills. Art involved drawing and painting traumatic situations, to help kids work out their feelings and transform their memories. Mathematics involved calculating quantities for reconstruction of buildings. Nature studies concerned actually growing food crops, and science involved learning how to fix the electrics or work out the volume of a water-cistern.

Pictures of Palestine

Families were found to unintentionally reinforce destructive patterns as a result of their own tensions, undoing the good work of the school, so family counselling and parenting groups were introduced. This became the basis of the school's *Listen to My Voice* programme, which has over time attracted much attention and support from abroad. Its methods were evolved spontaneously, on a shoestring. Some methods such as 'compassionate listening' were imported, adapted and taught by foreign volunteers versed in psychotherapy and personal growth.

Up to 1999 there were Muslim, Christian, Jewish and secular children at the school. Religious teachers and community leaders from all faiths visited to teach the beliefs, customs and views of their communities. Children learned to understand people different from themselves. Arabs were taught Hebrew and Jews were taught Arabic, both also learning English. This interfaith aspect ended thanks to pressures from people and authorities on both sides, and the school became Palestinian only. But the kids are still taught intercultural understanding and a global perspective, to connect them with the wider world.

In the 1990s the school expanded on a wing and a prayer, driven mainly by faith and determination. It was partially supported by trusts, foundations and grant-givers in the West – these were the times of the Oslo Accords, when a sense of future was dawning in Palestine, and the West was investing in it. Money and practical support also came from the wider, extended Issa family itself. But there were still difficulties with the occupying Israelis, who performed house-searches and troop incursions, making everyone feel insecure.

In 2000 the second *intifada* broke out in response to the failure of the peace process. Hussein Issa also unexpectedly died from heart failure – overstrain – at the age of 52. The school went into survival mode, but Palestinians know that it's important to keep things going even under duress. After a time of soul-searching, Ibrahim returned from the Netherlands to run the school with his mother Hind and sister Ghada, later joined by another sister, Hala, and assisted by a board of trustees, with a dedicated staff who all kept on with the work irrespective of events or finances.

They were under intense pressure and times were difficult. In 2002, despite active liaison with the Israeli authorities to protect the school, it was shelled, scaring the kids and their parents and damaging the school. Giving kids a feeling of safety, containment and security was essential and difficult, since *everyone* felt unsafe. At times they didn't know whether there would be a tomorrow.

The age-old tourist trade in Bethlehem had collapsed and the local economy was crippled, forcing some parents to withdraw their children from school. Sometimes it was difficult or dangerous for children to get to school.

There were long, arbitrary

curfews, food shortages, sleepless nights and sundry privations, water and power were intermittent, and prices rocketed.

Pupil numbers at Hope Flowers sank from 600 to 150, though by 2009 they were back to 350. Classes for older students were shut down because science and computer facilities, plus advanced teaching, were prohibitively expensive. Palestinians were becoming increasingly isolated behind the separation walls that were enclosing Bethlehem. School fees, $250 per year plus $250 for transport, meals and uniforms, became prohibitive for many, and the school's scholarship fund, already over-subscribed, dwindled rapidly. It was an endless struggle to keep going.

Jewish children were withdrawn and joint projects with Jewish schools were cut by the Israeli authorities. This led to a bizarre situation where school groups would sometimes fly to Germany or France to meet groups from Israeli peace schools. The separation wall stopped children from outlying villages from coming to school and volunteers from abroad diminished in number, particularly because the school could not guarantee their safety.

At times the staff continued working unpaid. Sometimes they came to school upset, after sleepless nights and military actions, and sometimes they needed more attention than the children. Things were insecure, tetchy and funding from abroad nosedived. The road to the school was shut by the Israelis; there were local troop incursions; a few neighbouring houses were blown up and left as piles of rubble, since the Israelis believed they harboured terrorists. Ibrahim visited the West, doing presentations and interviews to raise support, and Ghada made grant applications back in Bethlehem but it was an uphill grind.

Things started improving from 2004 onwards as the *intifada* subsided and the Israelis pulled back, but life was tough. So much damage had been done, including psychological damage to children, families and whole communities.

Then there came a new threat: the separation wall was to be built across the edge of the school's property, demolishing the school cafeteria and cutting off the school from the countryside. The wall and an armed watchtower would be built right next to the school. This threatened to neuter its peace-building work.

Christians were leaving Palestine, Palestinian public opinion was polarised and resentment and extremism escalated, affecting the school. The depressed economy brought serious poverty to families, so the school started feeding kids. Children were edgy and traumatised.

I remember a touching story of one girl woken up by Israeli soldiers in her bedroom, pointing guns at her and shouting. Her hair turned white at the age of six. Many of these soldiers are themselves young, their social skills unformed, and their training prepares them only to shoot first and think later. Kids were peeing their pants in class, becoming disruptive or unmotivated. School property was wrecked; teachers were going nuts; Ibrahim was arrested by the Israelis, suspected of harbouring a terrorist. Later he was accused by Palestinians of collaboration with the Israelis, and he was penalised badly by both in turn.

It was a long, long nightmare and only the remarkable commitment and dedication of teachers, staff, counsellors and trustees held the school together. Support from abroad gradually increased again as the troop incursions subsided – this was when I got involved – but it was always insufficient, and generating support was hard work. The school nevertheless struggled along.

Things slowly got better and a semblance of regularity returned. The Israelis generally stayed away after the building of the wall. It is now further away from the school over the valley, thanks to pressure from international supporters. A new military watchtower glowers down, but from over on the far hill rather than on top of the school. Teachers and students learned to accept this, but visiting internationals still feel intimidated by it.

Hope Flowers then started a Community Development Centre, first at the school, later in Deheisheh, to run extramural programmes for adults and youth. It runs women's empowerment courses, micro-business and teacher training, it trains helping professionals and civic workers in handling conflict-related situations and it carries out parenting classes and family therapy, engaging in a wide approach to community reconstruction. All this arose from the observation that children are not separate from their families' and wider community issues, and the whole spectrum of relationships needs addressing if a society is to revive after experiencing horror.

International support provides only part of the funding needed and little steady, consistent funding supports the basic, regular overheads. Paying teachers' already modest salaries is always a worry. Funding trusts are rigorous in their requirements, few of them knowing how things actually work in Palestine – things don't happen as efficiently or according to plan as in the West, so trusts sometimes believe the school is ineffective. They seek accountability, research figures and independent verification to a level that diverts resources from the school's core work.

It's a lot of run-around for a small organisation with insufficient staff and resources. Each grant application is a lottery, with a long wait and a high chance of refusal. Frequently a grant application is turned down not because of the merits or demerits of the application but simply because there were too many applicants chasing too few funds.

It's tricky assessing how much foreign funding actually benefits the school, since the work-input doesn't necessarily match the benefit. But the school perseveres since it cannot do without these funds. Some locals think the school is rich, receiving millions, and suspect that it taps a motherlode of foreign funding – they are incorrect. Foreigners think the school is such a good cause that *surely* it *must* receive generous funding – they too are incorrect.

In 2007 Pam Perry and I wrote a £180,000 application to the UK government to teach the school's methods to 180 teachers from around the West Bank. After six months' work, a visit by Ibrahim to Britain and 37 pages of submissions, it came to nothing. The government changed its policies after our application had been submitted, switching aid from education to law enforcement and media. We had been encouraged by an official to apply on peace-educational grounds, then on anti-terror grounds, then back to peace-educational grounds – each demanding a re-write – but the effort was in vain. One official said ours was the best submission he had seen for years, but he was posted to Singapore and we lost our champion.

Working with international volunteers also had its difficulties. They frequently applied to come for only a week or a month, often at the wrong time of year, during summer. Trouble is, it can take a month to get used to being here. Most spoke no Arabic, and many failed to understand beforehand how rigorous life can be in Palestine, or they get upset when things get challenging or chaotic. Checkpoints, soldiers and life in a different culture can be demanding for young people. They came and went, disrupting the normal flow of the school and themselves requiring support and supervision. So the volunteer programme has been scaled down, made more selective. Not a happy decision, but necessary.

The school's great asset is its knowledge and experience. As an independent school operating in a situation where real results have been desperately needed, it has innovated and experimented its way through life, developing advanced expertise. One helpful factor was the relative weakness of government intervention, in the earlier years of the 1980s when the PA didn't exist or in the 1990s while it was in the process of organising itself. This allowed the school to develop its own standards and methods, making it a standard-setter. This is why I was here, not just to support Palestinians, but because it's a 'beacon school' in the field of conflict-transformation, worldwide.

So, welcome to Hope Flowers. It is of considerable consequence in our day, contributing to dealing with the effects of conflict by addressing its social-psychological causes. This is the gist of what I told the Korean TV man on camera. Korea and Palestine share some history, both being countries that were partitioned in the late 1940s, with chronic and acute conflict alternating ever since. Perhaps that's why this man came.

The Hope Flowers website: **www.hopeflowersschool.org**

30 Reconciliation under the Full Moon

peacemaking around a campfire

I
t was one of those terribly tangled days. Something went wrong and, when that was sorted out, something else went wrong, and so the story continued. I got through it all but, by late afternoon, I felt pretty ragged. Then the taxi was 45 minutes late. Eventually I reached the All Nations Café and things changed as I stepped into the tranquil setting of a nature reserve.

All Nations is not a physical café but a regular peace-building meeting in the Rephaim Valley at a deserted Palestinian village called Ein Haniya, northwest of Bethlehem. The valley is lined with derelict agricultural terraces going back millennia – a Jewish lady told me that when the Hebrews came in the time of Joshua, the valley-bottoms were occupied by Canaanites, and the Hebrews settled the hilltops, building farming terraces down the hillsides. Jewish hilltop-bagging has a long history.

Dhyan, a genial and freethinking Israeli ex-soldier and peacemaker, runs the group, with the help of his friends. They persuaded the Israeli army, government and local Palestinian landowners to permit the project to meet at Ein Haniya, in a nature reserve in a kind of no-man's-land which, thanks to a fluke in history, was neither clearly part of Israel nor the West Bank. The group helped stall the building of a separation wall across the valley, backing the original Palestinian residents in retaining their land rights even though they were no longer permitted to live there. Meetings are held monthly around an outdoor campfire, with 'talking circles' involving people from both sides and of all

231

persuasions. Dhyan busily rushes around making a fire, brewing coffee, providing snacks and getting the group going.

Poor chap, he came under fire that evening. The circle was full of Palestinians. Of the two Israelis, one disappeared before things properly started and the other said her bit and soon left, saying she had an appointment. This struck people as stereotypical Israeli arrogance. When various Palestinians expressed their frustration over this, they looked at Dhyan. They weren't exactly blaming him but, like it or not, he embodied the Israeli nation there and then, being the only Jew present. When his turn came to speak, he pointed out that the previous meeting had had eighteen Israelis and two Palestinians, and the Israelis had been annoyed. There were chuckles and the situation was accepted as an ironic mishap. That's what peace-building is all about – building up understanding and separating out the threads that create misunderstanding and friction.

Pictures of Palestine

Truths had been spoken, and that's what we were here for. Sometimes in discussion circles, arguments and sticking points arise over the utmost trivialities, but they ventilate deeper questions and boundary issues. If people have an attitude of resolution and they stick with the process, then sooner or later resolution happens.

One man had observed something I too had noticed. Enlightened Israelis tend to take a sociable, genial approach to meeting with Palestinians – they like discussing worthy peace-building issues and this is good. But Palestinians need to talk serious stuff about grievances, difficulties and real life challenges; they suffer greater factual hardships and their need for specific solutions is more existentially pressing. To Israelis, peacemaking is a noble spare-time option, rather like saving the planet is for many people worldwide – *important of course, but, well, I'm a bit busy right now...*

Many Israeli peace supporters reach out to Palestinians and carry out very brave deeds, but others seem to feel that it's sufficient to make friends and to overcome the conditioned Israeli belief that Palestinians are dangerous and not entirely human. Again, good, and such people are at least meeting 'the enemy'. But this is the graciousness of the privileged. Meanwhile Palestinians have real concerns affecting land, prospects, families and future – it's closer to the bone for them.

There were some powerful sharings. Two Palestinian peacemakers came from Hebron, a conflict hotspot. Hearty people, they made lucid statements about the need for peace. Back in 1994, a settler called Baruch Goldstein had walked into Hebron's Ibrahimi Mosque with an automatic rifle, killing 29 and wounding 150 innocent Palestinians, and another 25 died outside in clashes with soldiers, trying to assist those inside. This was a tipping-point announcing the slow death of the Oslo peace process.

Fareed eloquently yet measuredly described how, in most cases, outbursts of conflict were provoked by Israelis, not Palestinians, and he was genuinely vexed about what to do about it. This indeed is true, a pattern recognised by the UN. Such information rarely emerges in the media since Israelis portray themselves as victims who are justified in taking pre-emptive military actions. Palestinians, provoked, then make a pained or robust response which, when it meets up with Israeli troops, gets nasty. This of course further reinforces Israelis' justifications for their actions, proving yet again that Palestinians are savages.

Palestinians are not wholly innocent, and at times they can be politically inastute or emotionally over-reactive. But still, as Naima, the other Hebronite, said, it's time for Israelis not just to *say* they believe in peace but to *act* that way too. Palestinians had complied with the terms of the Oslo and Roadmap agreements far more than Israelis and Israelis oppressed Palestinians far more too. The Palestinians haven't been invading Israel.

Naima stated movingly that she was willing to spend the rest of her life working to end conflict and to understand Israelis' viewpoint, because there is no alternative. She mentioned the Holocaust and the anti-Jewish pogroms of 19th and 20th century Europe as valid sources of pain for Israelis. She wished they could be satisfied with what they had gained in recent decades, leaving Palestinians in peace, for Palestinians would respond with peace. She recognised that Jewish suffering was deep and historic, while Palestinian suffering went back just a few generations. Palestinians therefore could forgive more easily, but it wasn't Palestinians that Jews needed to forgive – it was Europeans.

A former PFLP fighter was more impassioned. The People's Front for the Liberation of Palestine was famous for dramatic plane hijackings in the 1970s. This man had come to peace by the 1990s. He wanted a return to the pre-1967 borders. Most reasonable Palestinians want some variant of this, largely accepting facts and conceding the lands they lost in 1948. They recognise Israelis are *here* and need a home. But Palestinians want East Jerusalem as their capital – and it's fine for West Jerusalem to be Jewish. "This is a unique land, and here it is possible for one city, Jerusalem, to be capital of two countries", said the former fighter.

"I cannot believe people when they talk about peace unless they *behave* peacefully. This would make me totally committed to peace. Peace should be practiced, not just talked about. Everyone talks about it as a theory. My wife has cancer and she needs to go to hospital in Jerusalem. I cannot get a permit for her because of things I myself did 25 years ago, so she will die. This is an act of war. We Palestinians live like sparrows in a cage, and Israelis treat us according to the propaganda they're fed. Peace will come only when we really understand each other and our real concerns. We cannot be superficial with each other."

When my turn came, I talked about being born shortly after WW2 and how, during my lifetime, Britain and Germany had joined in an economic-political union – the impossible was proven possible. I was not proud of my country's history and the role it played in seeding the Israel-Palestine conflict, neither did I agree with the way Britain and France divided the Middle East into small powerless states. I was here now to help heal some of my country's role in Palestine's history.

Pictures of Palestine

I talked of my grandfather fighting Germany at the Somme in WW1 and my father in the Libyan desert in WW2, of the Protestant-Catholic strife I grew up with in Liverpool, of the trouble I got into as a peace activist and my involvements with Ulster, Kosovo and exile Tibetans. Time eventually brings peace, but it's a long historic process – often too long. Tel Aviv and Gaza could in future suffer flooding more than bombing, and this is what we should focus on now. War stops us attending to bigger questions.

There was much nodding, with sincere handshakes afterwards. I hugged the PLFP man and wished him and his wife well. "We must all stand back and see our children's children's view", he said. "We must look at what we share, for all of us are *people*. Allah helps us and tests us all, teaches us all together." Here's a former Marxist talking about God, a former fighter talking peace.

I found myself reflecting on how some of the best people I have met are those who have been criminals, terrorists, drug addicts, alcoholics and sundry sinners – they've seen hell and returned changed, committed to doing good. Here's a former PFLP fighter, and there's a former IDF soldier, Dhyan. Thank you, Dhyan, for your work bringing people together: you're a hero, a patriot, a veteran your country should be proud of.

The lift home with the Hebron contingent was welcome. Late-evening Bethlehem was heaving with people under a bright full moon as another day came to an end. Well, not quite: this obsessive blogger stayed up late, chronicling the day. All was quiet by the time I went to bed – just crickets and a peacock stirring the tranquillity that had settled over Al Khader and the Irtas valley.

31 What's All the Fuss About?
Palestine's political situation

Worldwide, people get tired of hearing about Palestine and its woes. The whole thing has gone on for *such a long time.* The conflict started before most people's birth. It's so complex: we're fed snippets that don't seem to fit together, and there's no visible rationality to it.

Assessing fairly the competing claims and viewpoints is like fitting together jigsaw pieces that refuse to fit. The media feed us a steady diet of violent conflict situations, polarised extremism and the narratives of politicians, spiked with disinformation that even knowledgeable reporters fall for and the saga wearily drags on.

Why haven't the Israelis and Palestinians sorted things out by now? Worldwide, people wring their hands when they see yet another round of bad scenes in Palestine. Stereotypical shots of keening mothers, angry youths or piles of rubble float across our screens. We fret, then we shrug shoulders and forget – there's so much else to attend to.

Many people sincerely wish to support peace in the Holy Land. Trying to be fair, they often see Israel and Palestine as equal partners in conflict, equally able to create peace between themselves. This is seriously inaccurate and, sadly, such an approach helps prolong the conflict. The conflict has always been one-sided: one side is occupying the other's land, one side is armed to the teeth, and the other side sustains far greater loss of life and property. Peace negotiations have to be weighted to reflect that.

Pictures of Palestine

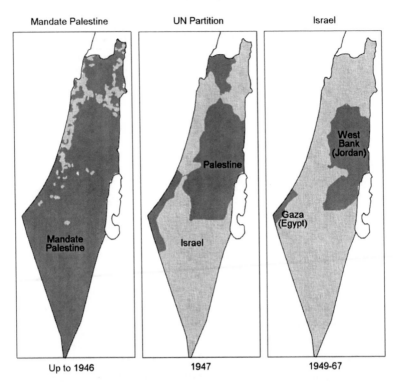

| Mandate Palestine | UN Partition | Israel |

Up to 1946   1947   1949-67

A quick look at the five maps sums it up. On the left we see the land where Palestinians lived during the British Mandate, up to about 1946. Next comes the proposed partition agreed by the UN in 1947, then the actual area the Israelis took in 1948. On the fourth map is the situation following the 1967 war. Finally we see the extent of Palestinian control today, following the 1993 Oslo Accords. Map 4 shows how, for 26 years from 1967 to 1993, the Israelis controlled the whole lot. The only thing that has changed since 1993 is the return to Palestinians of parts of Gaza in 2005 – and a lot of talk.

In 1989, during the first *intifada*, the international community realised they had to do something. The Oslo peace process gave Palestinians patches of land (Areas A and B) that the Israelis found too difficult to control, shown in the fifth map. This doesn't

Pictures of Palestine

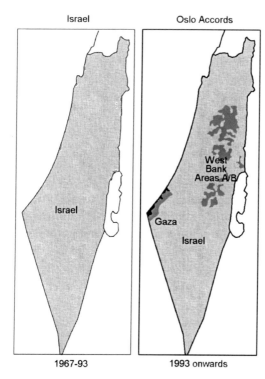

Israel — 1967-93

Oslo Accords — 1993 onwards

West Bank Areas A/B

Gaza

Israel

show areas where Palestinians *live*, only those areas they control. One million also live in Israel and others live in Israeli-run areas of the West Bank (Area C). Even so, the Palestinians will in coming years become the majority in Israel and Palestine added together.

Israel is technically a democracy, and Palestinians in Israel proper, 20% of its population, have representatives in the Knesset, the parliament. The PA in the West Bank and Gaza has a parliament too, but the Israelis jailed sufficient of its MPs in 2006-07 to make it lose its quorum and render it ineffective, unable even to amend the Palestinian constitution or elect a president. Those MPs were members of Hamas. The party in power in the West Bank (Fateh) is not the one that was elected in the last election in 2006 (Hamas). So democracy in Palestine is a moot point, wanted yet lost. The West Bank and Gaza are now under separate administrations, largely because of foreign interference. More about that later.

The PA's patch in the West Bank is made up of non-contiguous enclaves separated by Israeli settlements, appropriated land, security zones, government land and nature reserves. Palestinian areas are often surrounded by fences and security walls and, to get into and

239

out, one has to go through checkpoints which can be randomly closed at any time, delaying and complicating Palestinians' lives and making reliable arrangements difficult.

Checkpoints are humiliating and at times deadly. Between 2000 and 2006, at checkpoints there were 112 deaths of people on their way to hospital treatment. There were 35 stillbirths, five deaths of women in labour and 69 births in the back of vehicles or at the roadside. Things have improved since then, but the same problems still occur.

Israelis continually eat away at Palestinian land. They take it or nibble at it, and if there is resistance, settlers harass people until they leave, or the army comes in to defend Israelis if Palestinians resist. Houses are demolished by armoured demolition machinery supported by troops. Palestinian farmland is fenced off so that its owners cannot get to it – then it is classified as unused and reverts to the Israeli government. Settlers take initiatives and the army and authorities turn a blind eye. The idea is not just to gain land but also to make life so hard for Palestinians that they leave – except they don't.

Pictures of Palestine

Palestinians are consistently admonished by the international community to stop violence – such as the suicide bombings of a decade ago or the rockets fired from Gaza in recent years. However, there is little actual violence, and the world conveniently overlooks periods of calm – they're not newsworthy. Most violence happens to come from Israel – Palestinian deaths and injuries happen daily. And by what article of the law of war should the weaker side disarm itself when the stronger side uses arms against it?

The Israeli government requires Palestinians to fulfil quite ridiculous conditions before it will talk peace – that's a ploy making it look as if the Israelis *want* to talk peace. It's made to look as if the Palestinians are intransigent and argumentative but mostly it's the other way round. Meanwhile, Palestinians are willing to negotiate if settlement-building and land-appropriation stop, since these are acts of war without shooting, but the Israelis see this as unreasonable.

There is ongoing debate amongst Palestinians about how much to resist Israeli pressure and how much to negotiate. Resistance is usually supported by Hamas and negotiation by Fateh. The Israelis have until recent years had the propaganda edge, and the world has tended unthinkingly to believe that Palestinians should simply negotiate and yield – anything for peace. It's all been one-sided, and the Palestinians have had few consistent champions internationally. Neighbouring Arab states theoretically support them, but on balance they tend to perpetuate the problem and at times betray the Palestinians. These countries have until recently been pressured by USA to stay in line – their governments stay in power thanks to aid, oil and corporate business, so they must behave themselves. But the balance is shifting, especially since the Arab revolutions of 2011: Palestine's credibility is rising, and Israel's is subsiding.

This said, the Palestinians are not always good at diplomacy, propaganda or strategy – though the recent administration of Abu Mazen and Salam Fayyad has bucked the trend. This doesn't remove the fact that Palestinians are seriously under threat and their position, space and resources are continually eaten away. Some resent what Yasser Arafat agreed to in the 1990s when he signed the

241

Oslo Accords, awarding Palestinians control over the 'bantustans' they were allotted – they believe it was a sell-out. Arafat took this as a starting point for future gains, but he underestimated the extent to which Israelis simply would not budge and the international community would fail to follow up its talk with effective action.

There is an influential Israeli minority that wants Palestinians simply 'transferred' to Jordan, or anywhere, as long as they're gone. God's promise of the land from the sea to the Jordan river is non-negotiable and they regard Israeli Arabs as potential traitors, Gazans as sub-human and West Bankers to be obstructers of Jewish destiny. Israel is a democracy where the government is made up of multi-party coalitions where small religious, nationalist and Zionist parties often hold a casting vote, and its electoral system has a fractured randomness permitting powerful influences to tip the balance their way. Ehud Olmert, prime minister from 2005 to 2009, was the first for nearly 40 years who wasn't an ex-army officer.

The key point is that Palestinians are penned in, literally, by walls. So are Israelis, on the other side of the same walls, but the one who makes the choice holds the power, and the victims of that power feel more closed in. The Israelis obstruct Palestinians' lives, clamp economic growth and deprive them of much of the necessary capacity to improve their lives. Abroad, they make it look as if they are being perfectly reasonable. The Hebrew word for this is *hasbarah* – 'explanation' or 'spin'.

Here's a local example of *hasbarah*. On the hill over the valley from the school is a mosque at the centre of a small Arab village which is becoming surrounded by the new Efrat settlement. The local rabbi opened a one-room clinic for the Arab villagers. That was considerate and charitable. However, it was followed by the appropriation of much of the villagers' farmland by the rabbi's flock of settlers. The clinic was built so that the settlers could say, "But we gave them a clinic, and these Palestinians just keep complaining!". It was a cynical PR stunt. The Palestinians, meanwhile, were portrayed as hopeless bleaters and, with media attention trained on the clinic, the loss of their land was conveniently overlooked.

The main Palestinian aims are:

- an end to settlement building, wall-building, house demolitions and land incursions
- lifting of roadblocks, border controls and the throttling of Palestinian society
- East Jerusalem to be Palestine's capital
- joined-up Palestinian land, enabling viability and security as a nation
- the right of exiled Palestinians to return, visit, own property or invest in Palestine
- decent restitution arrangements for those who don't return
- proper Palestinian statehood and control of its destiny
- release of Palestinian political prisoners from Israeli jails
- withdrawal of Israel to the pre-1967 'Green Line' (with leeway for local land-swaps by negotiation)
- connection of Gaza with the West Bank and free passage between them (possibly by way of a sunken road)
- access to the sea and natural gas deposits off Gaza, and proper Palestinian borders with Jordan and Egypt, without Israeli interference or obstruction

Most ordinary Israelis are themselves victims of this propaganda. They are taught that Palestinians are dangerous, seeking to drive Israelis into the sea. They are given to believe that their government seeks peace and that the Palestinians don't. Hamas are a bunch of terrorists and Palestinians have no right to East Jerusalem. Settlement-building in the West Bank is justifiable and Palestinians' refusal to negotiate until settlement-building ceases is unreasonable. Israelis are given to believe that the absence of progress in peace negotiations is Palestinians' fault.

Of course some Palestinians get angry – and you might too, especially if you were young, with little future – but the vast majority of Palestinians indeed want peace and decent rights. They're also notably patient: a key Palestinian virtue is *sumud* – steadfastness.

Of course the Israelis need a decent life and security guarantees from Palestinians, together with peace – that's fair and proper. The Arab states have proposed a comprehensive peace deal that is well worthy of discussion, and the Palestinian majority consensus wants peace and some sort of regularisation of daily life.

Even Hamas has proposed a ten-year truce, a *hudna*, permitting minor agreements to be made over immediate pressing issues, followed by a pause and a final agreement after some time has elapsed – recognising that only a future generation can truly make peace. It is often said that Hamas wants to eliminate Israel, yet it is pragmatic and it really wants a return to the pre-1967 borders. It can convince its radical Islamist elements to agree to this only once there has been protracted peace to calm tempers. Arguably, Israel has maintained the Gaza siege to keep extremism alive in Gaza, thus justifying its own tough strategy.

The conflict will take one or two generations to fully resolve, but confidence-building and calming are possible within a few years if we start now. This would act as a foundation for further steps later on. But extremist elements in Israeli society will not desist from expansionism and hyper-control, and militant elements in Palestinian society resist negotiation and compromise too, so they both feed off each other. The winner from this impasse is Israel, permitting it to continue its colonisation project by furtive means. On both sides, and internationally, there are interests who prefer perpetuating the conflict because they profit from it, or too much would unravel if conflict ended.

So there is a stalemate in which peace processes, despite the rhetoric, have exhausted themselves. What is needed is *calming* – 'peace' is not a useful term. A key ingredient would be genuine even-handedness from the international community, and the linking of American economic and military support of Israel to the achievement of specific peace-building goals. American military support amounts to more than $2bn per year.

My hypothesis is that the only way to break this deadlock is the arrival of new factors which would render the current situation untenable, obsolete or upstaged. This has now started happening with the Arab revolutions, but it could also concern climate, public health, politics, economics and other pressures, or an unforeseen crisis. I don't advocate crisis, yet crises do change things, shifting the game-plan. Sometimes a crisis can be symbolic or catalytic more than damaging – an example being the almost-coincident death of Yasser Arafat in late 2004 and the disabling stroke of Ariel Sharon in late 2005, affecting only two people yet changing the context of the whole scenario.

Another longterm factor is the possible uniting of the Middle East in some form of economic and political union. Globally, big countries now dominate the international arena, so small countries need to coagulate into regional blocs to participate in the new multi-polar global configuration. Yet another factor is the decline of Western dominance, reconfiguring the Middle East and most likely obliging Israel to begin to make friends with its neighbours.

A further possible factor is a simple and momentous change of heart, as we witnessed in South Africa around 1990: it was simply decided that *apartheid* didn't work, and a new consensus suddenly pertained. If something changes in the wider context, placing Israelis and Palestinians in the same boat, we have lift-off.

Or, of course, another option is further conflict. If that starts, anything can happen. The odds are that Israel would be unlikely to win outright because its military strength no longer achieves the sought-after outcomes – as we saw in Gaza in 2009 and Lebanon in 2006. A third *intifada* could take place, fomented by a new, restless generation, but its outcomes would be unpredictable. There's also a risk of confrontation between Israel and Hezbollah, Syria or Iran, though the Arab revolutions have made this less likely.

Yet something else is happening underneath – a global tectonic shift of geopolitics. The international community might at last be forced to help Palestine because the cost of not doing so would be higher. That means you and me, and getting over our feelings of incapacity to do anything. The wider world plays a large, determining role in this conflict. We need to get out of the way.

32 Sad Stories, Happy Stories
weddings and house demolition

I went to a stag party – and it was just great. Ibrahim's nephew was getting married. Yet for the school the wedding meant loss, since the bride was a counsellor at the school and she was moving with her new husband to Ramallah. That's typical of the mixed stories I bore witness to that day.

In the afternoon I was down at Manger Square, interviewing Adnan for a podcast about life and business in Bethlehem. At the time he wanted to leave Palestine since he had lost so much trade and could not survive. He's a social psychologist with a degree from Bethlehem University, but he runs a shop since there was no work in his field. The shop had declined, thanks to the isolation of Bethlehem by the separation wall and the shrinkage of tourism. His wider family had also lost land, now on the Israeli side of the separation wall and being used by settlers.

Later, I talked with Ibrahim Issa, who told me some tragic news. The Israelis had just sent stop-work orders to the house-owners surrounding the school in Al Khader. The owners were forbidden from making improvements to their houses and land without Israeli authorisation – that's code for an impending possible takeover and demolition of the area. The school itself was safe, as far as Ibrahim knew – it would presumably be left standing in an open wasteland where the houses used to be. The locals might be able to retrieve the situation, but the chances were slim, he felt. One hundred people could lose their homes.

Pictures of Palestine

They wanted to designate the area a security zone. I could see the strategic reason: the houses and school sit on a hill overlooking Al Khader, and the Israelis probably wanted to observe and control the town. Al Khader is in Area B (Palestinian-run with partial Israeli control) but the hill is in Area C (Palestinian majority with full Israeli control). Also, they didn't like the idea of Palestinians living on high ground overlooking an Israeli settlement in the other direction – even though the settlement had encroached on Al Khader, not vice versa. Either this, or the Efrat settlement's American private developer was just plain acquisitive and the 'security zone' was a ruse for settlement expansion.

The doubly-cruel element here was that local people were conflict-weary and good-natured, so this security zone was militarily hardly necessary. Even during the Gaza devastation at the beginning of 2009, Bethlehemites did not rise up – they anguished over the damage and hardship in Gaza, and they could hear the bombing in the distance, but they didn't want to start fighting again. The risk of Al Khader being a conflict flashpoint is slim. This possible demolition was excessive, reflecting the Israeli tendency to see threat and enemies everywhere. It was sufficient to have the security wall

where it was, over the valley. But strangely, the wall had not been fully completed, and there was something fishy about that.

I had been talking with Ibrahim about water shortages and he replied that the next war, if any, could be over water resources. The Israelis were taking too much water, droughts were increasing and the Palestinians were running out. This is a survival issue. Apparently, when a leak is found, the water authority, one of Palestine's more efficient public services, comes very quickly to fix it, since water is costly and valuable.

Later I chatted with John, a Christian neighbour of Adnan's, asking him why, as it seemed to me, Palestinians seemed happier and more secure than Israelis, even though Palestinians are the oppressed ones and Israelis the winners. He said simply, "Well, most Israelis come from America, Europe and Russia, where they saw such tragedy before they came. You Westerners are *so alone*, so concerned with your private property, your own interests. You have so much pain and fear of each other. We have a different culture: we are *together*, we look after each other. Muslim and Christian, we are together. This is why we are happier. Yet our situation is worse than that of the Israelis". That was very perceptive and charitable of him.

It's also an observation on *social capital*. Israelis have prosperity and military might but Palestinians have more social resources – strength and vigour of family and community networks, feelings of togetherness. The more Israelis try to divide Palestinians and wall them off, the more Palestinians grow stronger, since their relationships, their families and clans, are all they have left. Every time Israel bombards or blockades Gaza, it increases the inherent social resistance of Gazans.

Perhaps it is affluence and militarism that ultimately break up societies, more than oppression and hardship. In former times hardship caused Jews to develop tremendous solidarity among themselves – a solidarity which disintegrated after 1967 as Israel grew powerful and successful. Palestine is strangely blessed because much of the development frenzy pervading the world has bypassed it: this might become a key asset in times to come. In the 1990s

Pictures of Palestine

Martin Bell, a veteran war correspondent, observed: "Peace and freedom can be defined as the peace that makes traffic jams possible and the freedom to sit in them". Palestinians have to an extent by-passed this situation – most traffic jams are at checkpoints.

The day had been hot and when the cooler evening arrived Bethlehem came out on to the streets. Manger Square filled up with people chatting, hanging out, demonstrating Bethlehem's remarkable social inclusivity. Bethlehemites are not *always* like this – at times they can be visibly weighed down by their situation, like caged animals. But sometimes they just drop it all, let go and break out in shared geniality. I loved the atmosphere on Manger Square that evening and felt very much part of it.

Later, at the stag party, the joy was climactic. I was welcomed into a gathering of some 300 men out on the street in Duha under bright lights, with loud music and revelry. Immediately I noticed the drinks: not a drop of alcohol was there – just coffee and juice. But Palestinians, when they get going, are unstoppable

fun-lovers. Men greeted each other with hugs, dancing together to wild modern Arabic music, whirling around the bridegroom with arms linked, jumping up and down, raising him – and later his father-in-law – up on their shoulders, giving the groom a rousing send-off into the world of marriage.

It was energetic, a show of male solidarity. There was no sign of the excessive, drunken and sad behaviour you often see in the West. These men were brothers letting loose, dancing their socks off. The older guys sat at the back chatting, watching and smoking *shisha*, water pipes. The children were safe, running around or sitting watching the proceedings, occasionally joining in. It was a rite of initiation.

The only drugs Palestinians imbibe are tobacco (which they smoke furiously) and coffee (they take it strong). The flavoured tobaccos smoked in water pipes are entirely innocuous, a social thing. Palestinians are remarkably well-behaved, with strong shared moral principles. This is arguably a positive consequence of the 60-year conflict they've been through, a social consensus hammered out in response to a tough situation.

Fun is something Palestinians just love and this highlights a big paradox: the Israelis have won the war, but the social price they pay is *enormous*. They have their times of joy and celebration like anyone, but there's a big hidden elephant in the room. They seem to have lost their way, boxed into a bundle of certainties that seem final and fixed, yet with a creeping hubris pervading their lives. Israelis are relatively prosperous, but income disparities are significant. Meanwhile in Palestine people hang together, even when they're divided. This suggests a deeper, hidden, longterm trend: the eventual true winners of this conflict might not be the Israelis after all. I don't mean this militarily – I mean *socially*. Or perhaps it's evidence that a conflict is *never really won*: there can be military or political victors, but look again.

You can't help wondering whether it has to be this way. Why do the people of Al Khader have to watch their houses being demolished? Why does the lovely city of Bethlehem have to be throttled? Is it something deeply perverse in the human psyche that permits such things? Is this what life on Earth came about for? Is this what the Holy Land is really about?

The day after, I attended the wedding reception. The wedding ceremony was a family affair but hundreds of people were at the celebration afterwards with their kids. It was dynamic, inclusive, delightful to witness and loads of fun. Palestinians give their marrying couples an amazing blessing and send-off.

The guests were offered only soft drinks. Instead of food, the Issa family gave the money they would have spent on it, 30,000 shekels, to poor people in Aida refugee camp. Most people at the wedding were well enough fed and much of the food would get wasted anyway. Wasn't this a good way to bless a marriage, through charity?

The music was crazily, thumpingly, swirlingly modern Arabic music. Everyone, young and old, was heartily involved. I did what I often do, standing on an unobtrusively positioned chair at the back, taking copious fly-on-the-wall photos to give to the family. I close in with my telephoto to catch people's facial expressions and in one photo I caught the bridegroom flying in mid-air, thrown up and caught by his male relatives.

These people live in a land where there is so much tragedy, but they know how to let rip when their spirits rise! If you're planning to get married, you might consider doing it in Bethlehem. You'd certainly remember that for the rest of your life.

33 Things Hotting Up
pressure building

It rained! For the first time I saw rain in Palestine! It lasted ten minutes and then the rather lonely cloud drifted away south-eastwards. The air was transformed, the land changed hue, nature's aromas wafted around gently and we were blessed with a sprinkle of grace after a dramatic, window-rattling windstorm the night before. How amazing.

It's funny how things go. That weekend I had been deeply stirred by the combination of the joyful family wedding and the sorrowful news of the stop-work order delivered to homeowners around the school. The paradox and poignancy of human life were exhibited in full contrast with this dual pincer action.

The demolition threat affected both the residential houses on the hill and the smallholdings down in the valley. The locals were doing all they could to make improvements to the area: the Israelis presumably wanted to claim it was unused land (ridiculous), allowing them to reclassify it as a security zone. The security of Palestinians, under threat right now, was of no import. Local landowners were improving the roads in the valley, trucking in new topsoil for the fields and doing up houses in an attempt to save this area, and the Israelis wished to prohibit it. Most residents had been here for decades, some for generations. I could hear a man downhill hammering on top of his house.

After the rain I sat down to trawl e-mails, and my antennae were suddenly tweaked. I looked out and there on the opposite hill just by the watchtower was a collection of armed soldiers. Out came my telephoto to get a closer look. They were having what seemed to be a site meeting, surveying the valley below and the hill on which the school stood. There were discussions going on, with much pointing at various buildings and features, then they all trooped off. Judging by this, demolition might happen anytime now.

Unless the troops got rid of me, I would be a witness. Hope Flowers was apparently safe, but who knew what would actually unfold when the soldiers and bulldozers came? As you might imagine, I was *not happy* about this. I alerted people abroad about the possible impending action and sent out photos by e-mail. This area was *no* threat to the Israelis. The night before there had been loud parties with dance music resounding around the town. That's as noisy as it gets around here, apart from the barking of the wild dogs, some peacock screeching and the chirruping of my pet gecko.

Two days earlier I had gone down into the valley for a walk, photographing the ancient farm terracing and plant life, hanging out in the golden late-afternoon sun. A boy on a bike from one of the farms rode circles around me and we communed across the language barrier. I then climbed up toward the wall until a soldier emerged from the watchtower, telling me in English to go back – no cameras allowed. I wandered back and sat on a rock, watching a rivulet of busy ants exercising their rights to freedom of movement across the rocky ground. Further along, I was hauled in for tea and *shisha* by a family on the veranda of one of the houses. Friendly and bright people they were, and we had a fine two hours together, constrained only by my poor Arabic and their scanty English.

Their main disappointment was that I was not a supporter of Barcelona football team. Palestinian men are football-crazy. Having grown up in footy-mad Liverpool, I had developed an allergy to the sport when young, becoming a marathon runner instead. So, sacrilegiously, football teams had not been my major concern.

One bright-eyed, smiling member of the family had crutches. His legs had been hit in the shoot-out with the Israelis at the Church of the Nativity in 2002 during the second *intifada*. He seemed unresentful about it, smilingly reconciled to his disabled

fate – at least, that afternoon. We talked haltingly about the security wall and the watchtower looming over their house. They were enthusiastic about their land-improvement – it was their act of resistance, the only thing they honourably could do. But it might all be in vain and the crunch might come soon.

I felt for these people – harmless, good types who just wanted to carry on looking after their land. They were reconciled to the security wall glowering above them – a blatant symbol of Israeli occupation and their own powerlessness. Their family used to own the hill on which the watchtower stands and now they might lose their remaining land, their crops, fig, olive and plum trees and vines, all to be bulldozed for the security zone. The ecological effect of this is disastrous in this former land of milk and honey.

The area to be demolished stretched about 400m from the security wall, including the valley and the school's hill. The Israelis might not be *intending* it, but the net effect of a demolition here would be to stir things up. Presumably they don't think about the frustrating effect it can have on Palestinians and thus ultimately on Israeli security too. The best way to guarantee security is to ratchet down conflict but the Israelis seem to love stoking it up.

If you sought security for your people, would you destroy the homes of people on the other side, getting them angry? Would you alienate their kids, knowing that one day they'd be 20 years old and smarting? This is not a good security strategy. I sometimes wonder whether, now that most Palestinians want peace and a normal life, the Israelis have an unconscious need to keep conflict alive. Get the Palestinians angry, then the Israelis have an enemy and reason to defend themselves. This is a serious, perhaps unfair allegation but, even if it's untrue, the game still needs to change. This is what your taxes go on, dear readers: financially supporting arms provision to the Israelis and development aid to the Palestinians, to keep both quiet and keep the conflict alive.

Well, aside from the matter of house-demolitions, things were hotting up in another direction. Hope Flowers had been invited to send a representative to a democratic education conference in

Korea. Many teachers lack permits to travel, and Ibrahim could not go. So Ibrahim asked if I might go. Er, well, I hadn't quite considered going to Korea, though perhaps it was relevant to do so. But I was slim on finances – it was expenses-paid by the Koreans, though this wouldn't cover everything.

Such a conference was important for the school's networking. Yet something felt intuitively 'not right' about it, and it took a while to find out why. My priority was to complete the new website, and there was the matter of those Israelis with their armoured bulldozers – shouldn't I stay here to keep watch on the school? Clearly, I needed to think things through.

Lots of issues were crowding in. I was to attend a school parents' meeting, amass material for some podcasts and visit Hebron. I needed to make decisions, raise more money to cover my expenses, work like stink, keep myself fed, do my shopping and cope with everything else that came along. There was too much to handle and I risked losing my cool.

The reason I felt funny about the conference in Korea emerged a couple of weeks later. It was one of those lessons in trusting intuition, as something had felt strange about it all. Well, on the cut-off day when I needed to decide, I checked the conference website and, lo and behold, the conference was cancelled because an outbreak of bird flu in Korea. Situation resolved.

Later that day Ibrahim Abu el-Hawa came along from Jerusalem, bringing an Asian-American bearing a wonderful story. She was the widow of one of the astronauts who died in a space shuttle re-entry burn-up in 2006. She had subsequently visited Hope Flowers and was deeply moved by what she saw here. She had taken pictures of the kids, returned to the States and persuaded an astronaut to carry three of these pictures up to the International Space Station. They orbited the Earth 190 times!

I knew that Hope Flowers is a project of global significance, but I hadn't quite thought it would be demonstrated this way! Of all the kids to be taken into space, it was kids from a school in Bethlehem. At the school that afternoon, we showed a picture of a smiling astronaut with a photo of the kids floating in space next to him: the pupils didn't quite understand what they were seeing, but the magic saga had been taken full circle, back to the classroom.

Meanwhile Jane, a friend and colleague from England, was visiting. She had decided to take on Friends of Hope Flowers UK, to organise fundraising, networking and support-raising events in Britain. I was relieved. Since the death of Pam Perry in 2007, a super-trooper campaigner who had run HFS-UK, there remained a space, a hard act to follow, and I hadn't wanted to take on leadership myself, preferring instead to work in Palestine. Jane deserved a medal for taking on Pam's mantle, and it felt right. It was good for the school and I was happy to work with her.

I was grateful too for the support of my ladyfriend and cousin back in Britain. They stood by me, offering hearing ears. It's tricky being in comfortable old England while talking to someone on the frontline – a bit like being a family member of a soldier serving in Afghanistan, a world away, on a different planet.

Working for peace has some parallels to acts of war. The enemy in peacework is fear and the polarising tendency of each side to dehumanise the other. Even if you don't understand the people on the other side, it's important nevertheless to try to do so. Working for peace involves love-bombs, truth-mines and missiles of clear understanding – applied even to oneself – and there are no protective blue helmets.

Paradoxically, suffering people stand on the frontline of human evolution. Through the pathos and intensity of their experience, such people push forward the evolution and redemption of humanity by making personal sacrifices on humankind's behalf. They do this by encountering the hard truths, deep feelings and profound lessons of human life, thus saving others from having to do so, while also conveying some of that experience to them via the media. It took me a long time to understand this.

We who live in secure countries have peace because others, less fortunate than us, siphon off violence or hardship on to themselves – and unconsciously we dump it on them. Then we send them aid and relief to soften the blow. Yet in return they give us a gift of compassion, awakening us from our own kind of suffering, from our busy, humdrum, de-sensitised lives, reminding us of our humanity. I'm talking here about the collective unconscious and about humanity as an enormous organism. It's as if we are all the 'eyes and ears of God', acting unwittingly as parts of one great wholeness we fail to see. If we did see it, we'd do something to balance and moderate the extremes of privilege and hardship, wealth and poverty that characterise today's world.

In the end, change is created through *events* and the way we deal with them. Where the stakes are high and life's pathos is amplified, such as in conflict and disaster zones, collective life-experience is at its sharpest and most poignant. A lot of human feeling and grief is aired and there's a strange mixture of intensely human and inhuman experiences to be had.

Palestinians reap a tragic benefit from their experience – a certain spirited togetherness which many other nations lack. For Palestinians, the idea that many people in Western countries take their freedoms and comforts for granted is unbelievable. But then, we all have lives to live and viewpoints to hold, from the position of our own culture and experience and the tables also can turn. This is why compassion is important.

34 City of the Patriarchs
Hebron and the Ibrahimi Mosque

I visited Hebron, invited by Naima, whom I had met at the All Nations Café. A warm-hearted Muslim matriarch in her late forties, she was a peacemaker who had organised sport and social events to bring together Muslims and Jews in Hebron. She had been relieved of her job because the Israeli peace centre where she was employed kept recycling its Palestinian employees so that none could become too influential. She believed politics was prioritised over her qualities as an employee.

Hers was a lovely family, aged 11 to 27 – three males and one female, with two further sons living in Germany. Their father had abandoned them, leaving them without support, and I was impressed with the way they worked together and supported each other – an operational family solidarity many Westerners would long for.

We talked about life and the situation in Israel, in Iraq and the wider world – with translations by Yaqub, the eldest son. He was promising emigration material, with brains, computer programming skills and good English. Then we had lunch. At first vexed over my vegetarian diet, they cooked up something suitable, enjoying the challenge, and after sitting out the afternoon heat we went down to the centre of Hebron.

Here I should raise an incidental issue: Saddam Hussein. Whatever his sins, he supported Palestinians generously during his time. Yaqub had studied computer science in Baghdad, expenses-paid by Saddam's regime – it was one of the few open-door opportunities available to a young Palestinian at the time. When the Americans invaded in 2003, Yaqub went into hiding, losing his university qualification papers in the process. He subsequently got out. But he was left with a good impression of Saddam Hussein, one of the few politicians who unequivocally and practically supported Palestinians through their darkest years. This is remembered favourably, despite the unpopularity of this dictator.

In Western eyes, Yasser Arafat scored an own-goal when, at the time of the Gulf War in 1991, he voiced support for Saddam. But he did so, rightly or wrongly, out of a Palestinian's sense of honour. This dilemma would have been resolved otherwise if others had supported Palestinians in the 1970s and 1980s. But they didn't. Yaqub knew Saddam was no angel, but he wasn't impressed with what had happened in Iraq since his fall in 2003 either.

Hebron is Palestine's equivalent to Londonderry, Naples or Chicago – a shady, edgy and spicy place. From the rooftop of their house Yaqub pointed out a neighbour's house where they stole Israeli cars and had them dismembered within minutes, so that when Israeli troops raided them soon after, there was no sign of the cars. The guys there were arrested and carted off regularly. Yaqub also mentioned family and clan feuding in Hebron, which apparently can go on for decades. It's a hot'n'heavy place in some respects, but it has character.

Hebron is an ancient city, Palestine's third largest after Jerusalem and Gaza City, with a population around 180,000. On arrival at the town centre, Naima explained that this had been its centre for the last twenty years only. The old centre, the souk, was now semi-abandoned as a result of Israeli settlers' actions.

Being situated at one of the conflict's frontlines, there's more ill feeling toward Israelis in Hebron than in other Palestinian cities and I sensed this in the streets. Hebron is not quite as congenial as Bethlehem, yet I never felt in danger and, as a foreign observer, I was made welcome. People here feel left out and forgotten, so they appreciate visits by internationals. They also protect something important to Muslims worldwide – the Ibrahimi Mosque.

Pictures of Palestine

It was to the Ibrahimi Mosque that we headed. Naima felt it was important to take me and I was honoured to be taken. First we walked down into the benighted souk. It's quaint, with narrow streets and small shops on either side. The shops at the top end near the city centre are still active but lower down it gets quiet, with a sadly abandoned look, and the tragedy of Hebron becomes blatantly visible. I was shown buildings from which Israelis had shot into the crowds in the 1990s and during the second *intifada*.

Many of the old shops in the souk are closed, some with metal door fronts welded shut by Israeli settlers so that shopkeepers could not re-open. Some shops were deliberately kept open by Palestinians to maintain a presence regardless of their viability. The settlers occupy properties as soon as they can assert that they are unused – which somehow entitles them to take them over or seal them up, even if the owner is away only for a few days.

But Hebronites are firm about keeping the Old City going, despite everything. The souk had become dangerous for Palestinians, who were fired at or had rocks, sewage and garbage thrown at them and the deserted souk was depressing for locals to see, so they often stayed out. Yet the shopkeepers maintained a

presence here not just for sentimental and political reasons, but also because access to the Ibrahimi Mosque would be lost if they lost the Old City. To get to the mosque one had to go through the narrow streets of the souk.

Why all the fuss about the mosque? Well, here were the tombs of Abraham and Isaac, two great patriarchs of both the Jewish and the Muslim faiths. Abraham, or Ibrahim, is by tradition the genetic ancestor of both Arabs and Jews and the one who first spoke of the One God. By rights this should unite them, but instead it's a matter of contention.

The tradition goes that the marriage of Abraham and his wife Sarah (or Sarai) was barren so he had a son, Ishmael, by a servant girl, Hagar – a standard practice around 1800BCE, since servants were part of the family, and monogamous fidelity was not then the rule. Later, miraculously, and at a strangely old age, Sarah bore a son by Abraham – this was Isaac, who then went on to father the Hebrew people. Hagar and Ishmael were cast out into the desert because Sarai had a fit of jealousy, since Ishmael was the eldest son and thus presumably Abraham's inheritor. This was the mythic beginning of a long saga of strife between Arabs and Israelites, coming to an intense symbolic focus today at the Ibrahimi Mosque. Sarai is there too, as well as Isaac and his wife Rebekah.

We shambled through the Old City, occasionally accosted by shopkeepers intent on earning shekels. I bought a few things but wasn't awash with money. As soon as I reached into my pocket a flood of other shopkeepers would zoom in, smelling a rich Westerner. Such fraught hassling is uncommon in Palestine and it is easily seen off if you know the right hand-signals and remonstrate expressively enough. They were clearly desperate for business.

The good news was that the European Union had invested in improving the souk, paying for electricity and rents, subsidising shops to keep them open. The EU regards the Israeli occupation of Hebron to be incendiary and illegal, a breach of the Oslo agreements. By all means, Jews should have access to the Tomb of Abraham and, if they wish to live in Hebron, that shouldn't be a problem if done in peace and good-neighbourliness and by buying properties legitimately and respectfully.

But this isn't Israeli settlers' strong point. Hebronites were nervous not just because their country had been forcibly occupied in 1967 but also because the settlers, who arrived soon after and were backed by troops, acted threateningly, seizing property and getting rid of Palestinians through harassment. Rabbi Levinger was their ideological leader – an uncompromising, provocative type. They didn't acquire property by negotiation – they took it because they felt entitled to it and sought control. Many were Americans, some of whom come to Israel spoiling for a fight.

Peaceful residence in Hebron is insufficient for some religious Jews. They seized one-fifth of Hebron, put up checkpoints and a hundred urban roadblocks, sectioning off part of the city. They built new, segregated access roads to the Jewish Quarter plus a big settlement outside the city at Kiryat Arba. To protect them the IDF moved in, taking control of the whole city in 2002, despite post-Oslo agreements in 1997 to divide control into Israeli (H2) and Palestinian (H1) sectors.

The whole thing had exploded in 1994 with settler Baruch Goldstein's massacre of 29 Palestinians at the Ibrahimi Mosque. It should be said that the Palestinians have responded at times with violence to provocations like this, but usually in response to incitement. The outcome is that 180,000 Palestinians live in area H1 (about 80% of the city) and 500 Israeli settlers live in H2 (about 20%) – though the 7,000 settlers in Kiryat Arba and other settlements outside the city somewhat swell the numbers using H2.

It's very sad in the Old City. The Israelis had seized the higher places, even the upper floors of Palestinian shops and houses. They threw rubbish and bricks on Palestinians below, and I was introduced to a shopkeeper whose head had been cracked open in such an incident. He showed me the dual medical certificates, one Palestinian, from the first hospital he went to, and one Israeli, after an international uproar had forced the Israelis to conduct an enquiry. The Israeli documentation cited the man's injuries to be from a cause other than the violence and they asserted that the man had been assaulted by a Palestinian. Well, of course. That's *hasbarah*, assertion of information contrary to what's really going on, in order to bring reality into question and confuse the issue, so that everyone gives up.

Naima introduced me to some characters in the street. She had grown up and gone to school here. She showed me the wire protections paid for by the EU, installed over the narrow streets to protect people below from settlers' garbage and projectiles. She pointed out more welded-up shopfronts.

At one point we met two Danes in blue uniforms, one a policeman on a year's sabbatical, and the other an Arabic-speaking aid worker. They were from TIPH, the Temporary International Presence in Hebron, which kept a presence in the streets to restrain Israeli settlers and soldiers and Palestinian responses to them. A noble job they did, keeping the Old City open and quiet. TIPH was funded and staffed by Norway, Italy, Switzerland, Turkey, Denmark and Sweden, though its continued presence relied on an agreement renewed every six months between the PA and the Israeli government.

Their booklet, measuredly neutral and diplomatic in its wording, at one point states, "Permanent watchtowers were constructed [by the IDF] in area H1 [the Palestinian sector] in 2005. Since then the Israeli army operates over the entire area in violation of the 1997 agreements". That's as far as they go in their comments. To be permitted to stay here and monitor developments, international organisations have to watch their step, and their staffs occasionally take some hits too.

As we moved on, Naima showed me some of the tragic mess of the area – almost empty Palestinian streets with wire protections overhead, covered with rubbish, with settlers' abodes above them and blatantly-placed Israeli flags hanging over the street. I stood there shedding tears. How can people do this kind of thing? How can they live with themselves? Is this really the best way to get what they want?

Pictures of Palestine

Gradually we neared the Ibrahimi Mosque, but first, checkpoints. Not one, but three, each with a turnstile and a narrow metal-fenced single-file passage, so that passers-through could be singled out and inspected by the soldiers at the far end. Then it's emptying pockets, inspection of bags, questions. *Are you a journalist? Where are you from? Why do you have so many keys* (from the school), *what's this* and *what's that?* Naima kept them sweet and I played my courteous Englishman act. The rather stern officer at checkpoint two was twenty years younger than me, and I made sure he knew it, letting him know through calm body-language and steady x-ray eyes that I wouldn't permit him entirely to control our interaction.

The first checkpoint took us into the Jewish Quarter, the second to the outer part of the mosque and the third was at the very entrance to the mosque. The soldiers were okay, even guardedly friendly – there's little point giving these guys a hard time since they're just frontline subordinates, and there's little point causing oneself trouble either. Most of them were just bored, doing quite pointless duties.

Then into the mosque. Naima told them I was a Muslim, bless her, so off came our shoes and we went into a large, arched, carpeted hall, then across it to the tombs of Isaac and his wife. Their remains are presumably 3,800 or so years old. Next we went to Abraham's tomb – our side for Muslims, the other side for Jews. Naima and her daughter made prayers and I sat quietly in meditation. No one else was there.

It was a powerful atmosphere here, intensely still. I felt drawn deeply within myself into a markedly altered, spiritually-electrified state, a kind of potentised quietness. While Naima and her daughter made their prayers at the shrine, in meditation I contemplated my friends, parents and family, sending them a prayerful meteor of light from this place. I gave thanks for the privilege of being here, knowing that this was a memorable, special moment – a twenty-minute experience that would indelibly etch itself on my psyche.

Standing later before the tomb, I found myself saying unpremeditatedly, "*Well, I came back to see you, and I said I would*

265

do so", to Ibrahim the Patriarch, there in his tomb. I thought about that afterward and wondered what it actually meant. It was a statement from the soul. I had to sit down for a few minutes, quivering with the power of the place. The atmosphere was deep, charged and profound and I was thunderstruck, speechless, moved.

I understand why people fight over this place – it's not just superstition or overblown religiosity. This is a cherished, intensely *holy* site which inspires awe. You can feel the Power of the Presence. But wouldn't it be better to agree to share this place in peace, instead of polluting this Presence with rivalry, massacres and checkpoints? Has religion truly won here or has its antithesis – fearful, nervous aggression – prevailed?

Eventually we emerged from the mosque, sitting down between two of the checkpoints. A female Israeli soldier, machine gun hanging nonchalantly from her shoulder, hollered to a male soldier up the hill, also with machine gun, who looked like her boyfriend. They were having a laugh and Naima, who speaks Hebrew, chuckled at their joke. She genuinely treats Israelis as real humans, with no scorn or disdain. I was impressed with her neutrality and wit amongst these wildly paradoxical, rather painful scenes. But then she has to live with it on a daily basis and I guess the situation here presents a stark choice: you can eat your heart out over it or accept it as it is and make the best of the situation as it stands.

Half-way back through the souk, we sat on one of the arty EU-financed stone benches in a square, under the watchful eye of some armed IDF soldiers atop the buildings. Naima told me how much she missed her lover in Iraq, asking me whether I missed my loved ones in England.

I took her hand and said, "We both have a long wait ahead, Naima, to see our loved ones again, but your wait is longer than mine".

"You think I will *ever* live with him, Balden?".

"I pray that you will, for you deserve it. You're a good woman."

Her eyes were tearful. "We all must have *some* kind of pain, Balden". I looked into her eyes. A tear was making its way down my face too. Poor woman, like so many of her people, she cannot do much about her situation, but she channels it into peacemaking and raising a fine family. The acute experiential contrasts of a place like this, both tough and touching, bring out a breadth of feeling which, in the safe, switched-down emotional environment of my own country, is sorely lacking.

Six months later, I heard that Naima and her man had met up at last in Turkey, and were married. Then they went to Germany to meet her sons, returning to their respective countries to wait for the next time they could meet. Later on, they found a place to meet in Amman.

By the time we got back up to the centre of town, I was rather exhausted. I watched an officious PA policeman haranguing a bread trader for having an illegal stall.

"But that stall has been there all day, Naima."

"The policeman, he's just bossy. His wife probably nagged him this morning."

Today, with Naima's help, I'd fulfilled some sort of inner pact with my soul, on some deep level of being where the rational mind doesn't reach. She understood little of my soul-journey and my way of seeing things, but she was sensitive enough to be able to facilitate something deep in the energy-patterning of my life. Something had *happened* today – a connecting-up of hidden linkages, of something that can be sensed but not fully known. My tryst with Palestine, with its past and its future, was in some way sealed on this day. It felt as if there would be no going back.

Tomorrow, back to Bethlehem. A journey from Abraham's tomb to the birthplace of Jesus and King David – a further journey of the soul that cost eight shekels in a service taxi.

35 **Guardianship**
the Al Khader demolition threat

Why was I staying in this big, empty school on the edge of Bethlehem? This was a question I pondered. Yes, it allowed me to get on with work, but at times it was lonely. Then I had a revelation – one of those flashes where you suddenly see yourself playing a part in a larger chess-game.

Perhaps I was unwittingly acting as a guardian for the school and the hilltop. The teaching staff were off on holiday and the new centre in Deheisheh had drawn the admin staff there, leaving the school empty. Maybe I had been unknowingly requisitioned from Britain to look after the school? This became apparent only when the demolition threat arose.

The school was on the frontline and 25 houses around it had received pre-demolition notices. We fervently hoped this didn't apply to the school. An earlier demolition threat in 2004 had been seen off, after raising international support, but Israeli officials of that time had probably moved on and the new lot might not know we'd been through all this before. Either that, or they might be just plain persistent.

The Israeli authorities do not consider it mandatory to inform of intended demolition, so if you're not there to receive the papers, tough luck. If I was out or didn't hear anyone at the gate, no one would receive any papers. So we didn't quite know whether the bulldozers would come for the school – although Ibrahim suspected they wouldn't. Yet even if the school were left standing, demolition of the surrounding houses would undermine parents' trust – they wouldn't happily send their kids into an Israeli security zone. This could undermine the school's future, forcing it to move. Was that perhaps what the Israelis wanted?

So, in a *feng shui* sense, I started building up an energy-field, an exclusion zone around the vicinity. In esoteric jargon this is called 'psychic protection'. In my thoughts and meditations I worked at building and reinforcing a 'magic circle'. I took walks around the area, 'beating the bounds' and defining a protection zone. I visualised a dome of light over the hill, repeating a thought, a prayer, that only people with good intentions may enter and all others must stay away. I kept repeating this process day after day.

When Jane from England visited she reported that the atmosphere in the school seemed noticeably good and strong, implying that I had something to do with it. However, she pointed out an area of wasteland nearby which she felt was ignored and, as soon as she mentioned it, I knew she was right. So that patch soon received my attention.

The trick was also to disappear this area from the minds of those with acquisitive motives. This is *forgetfulness-induction*. Anyone over forty is, thankfully in this case, quite susceptible to it. I was extending a cloaking device over the area.

Some of you will think I'm losing my grip – you might be right. You probably wouldn't accept non-demolition to constitute proof of success. But compared to some of the madness that goes on in Israel and Palestine, this is peanuts. However, it's not all I was doing.

I busied myself sending out e-mails, photos and reports, posting information online and generally rousing support worldwide. It was poignant because settlement-expansion was hot news at the time, and settlement-expansion was precisely the issue here. It was hard work, yet the whole thing gathered steam.

We activated that ubiquitous yet rather negligent 'international community' – the one that issues declarations, makes resolutions and then conveniently forgets to go further. Well, it also has a sub-surface guilt complex and we tweaked it. To quote Hillary Clinton in 1997, "*The Hope Flowers School is a unique example of peaceful coexistence between Palestinian and Israelis*". Well, she had a wee bit of clout, and I pushed to have her memory jogged by American supporters who pulled strings through some State Department officials who had themselves visited the school.

In May 2005 eight members of US Congress had visited, and some British MPs and other worthies knew the school too. The British Consul General in Jerusalem had written in 1999: "*The British Government has expressed, both through the Embassy of Israel in London and to its Ministry of Foreign Affairs in Jerusalem, our view that the school's work should be encouraged*". One British MP specialising in Middle Eastern affairs heard of the current demolition threat and got straight on to the Israeli Foreign Ministry to ask questions – the Israelis now knew that the wider world knew.

The school had been visited by Euro-MPs and was recognised by UNESCO and the Swiss and German governments. Tony Blair, the Quartet High Representative, even offered to visit – in the end he didn't come. And an Amnesty International representative was to visit. Whether all this would make much difference was anybody's guess, but it was worth trying. For four days, in mid-thirties heat, I hammered away on my computer, firing off material and information, contacting politicians, diplomats and NGO staffers.

The Amnesty person arrived later with two sons in tow. I showed them all that was to be seen. The boys loved my guava juice and seemed fascinated to meet me. They gazed out over the panorama, one of them panning his video camera across the scene: there it was, the whole bizarre situation stretching before them – Palestinian farms, the wall, a settlement outpost, a military watchtower. They just couldn't believe that the houses around the school could be demolished. Their mum, a Jewish American and a rapporteur on justice issues for Amnesty, explained things patiently, and I added specifics. The boys were like magisterial investigators questioning us, taking video clips, extracting necessary details and noting them down on behalf of their justifiably proud mother. It was a fruitful visit, well worth the guava sacrifice.

Pictures of Palestine

The Israelis are good at creating 'facts on the ground'. They can come any day or night, demolishing buildings before anyone has a chance to stop it. Even by keeping us guessing they made life suitably difficult. Day by day we hung in there, getting on with work. But quietly, we waited to see whether the dozers would come.

I calculated it so that I could pack my bags and be out in fifteen minutes if necessary – but not without a few acts of peaceful resistance, such as photographic record-keeping and journalistic pretence. I hoped a rapid get-out wouldn't be necessary. Al Khader was truly not a security risk for the Israelis.

36 Hamas and Fateh
schism in the body politic

his chapter gets a bit political. It reveals another side to a story that Westerners have been told. Here's the key issue: *a momentous error was made in 2006 – and Israel and the West made it*. Its consequences have been unfolding ever since and they will continue for decades.

This was the Bush era, when the West, with its aversion to Muslim extremism, was busy 'not talking to terrorists'. The occasion was the Palestinian election of January 2006 in which Hamas won 60% of the vote – an election declared free, fair and exemplary in its execution by international observers.

But Israel and the West decided to have no truck with the newly-elected Hamas government – and this was the great mistake. Most aid was frozen in the months that followed and Hamas was labelled a terror organisation, deserving no recognition or support. The West failed to see that Hamas was also a social reform party with a history of charitable and welfare work – and this was precisely what Palestinians, particularly women, had voted for. Palestinians were disappointed with the compromises Fateh had made to please the West, pursuing policies with outcomes that often benefited the Fatah elite and its supporters. So people voted for Hamas, seeking democratic change.

Hamas had a militia and had backed suicide bombers back in the *intifada* and this made them 'Muslim terrorists' in the West's eyes. Founded in 1987, Hamas had risen to prominence in the first *intifada*, a party of resistance believing that the only way to deal with the Israelis was to match their intransigence and aggression. They went quieter in the 1990s as Fateh's negotiating strategy seemed to be getting somewhere, but as negotiations went amiss in the late 1990s, Hamas gathered steam again, to become prominent in the second *intifada*.

From about 2004, as the second *intifada* subsided, Hamas started transitioning towards democratic status but it needed time to get there, being a reform party with militants on its left wing and moderates at its centre. Yet the Israelis asserted that Hamas was a terror group and the West bought the story and set about shutting them down.

Hamas leaders were primarily doctors and engineers by origin – realists, interested in results more than fine politicians' words. This was why Palestinians liked them. Muslim beliefs formed the basis of Hamas' values – Islamism was a newer mindset which had superseded Arab socialist ideas of the 1950s to the 1970s. Palestinian Christians and seculars were accepted by Hamas, and the repression of women that Westerners shrieked about wasn't really a fact. Westerners conflated Palestinian Islamism with the extremism of Al Qa'eda and the conservatism of Iranian mullahs and Afghan *mujahedin*, failing to understand that Palestinians were not like this. Palestinians are pretty progressive, and they sought reform and modernisation without the whole Western capitalist package – in that package they saw community breakdown, inequality and subservience to Israel.

It wasn't specifically Muslim values that gained Hamas support. Most Hamas money went into schools and hospitals – this was popular. Also Hamas was uncorrupt, sticking by its principles in an increasingly unprincipled age. Its philosophy rested on the notion of the *umma*, of a community bound together by cooperation and solidarity – parallel to the idea of 'the working classes' which gave Western socialists their strength a century ago. Hamas was more meritocratic, egalitarian and transparent than Fateh: Fateh rested for much of its public support on preferential rewards, nepotism and

273

sinecures. Fateh had its good points and was respected, but it was tarnished by shady dealings in many Palestinians' eyes.

The philosophy of the *umma* works on the basis that community is the fairest form of social organisation, underpinned by a consensus of good behaviour, mutuality and shared destiny. Hamas was not like Al Qa'eda. Al Qa'eda lacked a popular constituency, set as it was on destroying the power of rich Saudi sheikhs and Americans, and led as it was by alienated and megalomanic Muslim radicals. Hamas was a popular movement speaking for large numbers of people. They sought Palestinian freedom, and were no threat to the established order of the Middle East or the wider world. It was also true that since the Israelis applied force and destruction, singling out Hamas for offensive action, Hamas answered back with force.

Many Palestinians were tired of corruption. Magnates in Fateh had lapsed into self-aggrandisement: patronage had been Arafat's way of rewarding loyalty. Understandable perhaps in the 1960s and 1970s, it had later become simply Fateh's way of staying in power. The West sent cash to fuel this patronage system and Fateh dished it out to its advantage.

After Hamas' 2006 electoral victory Palestine suffered an economic embargo from the West, experiencing severe hardship. An idea had arisen in the West: make Hamas unpopular by throttling Palestinians and then portray Fateh as saviours who could unlock the treasure chests. Some Palestinians did see things this way, and Hamas' reputation was weakened thereby. Hamas adhered to resisting Israel, a sentiment which had considerable support, particularly in besieged Gaza, but its 'blood, sweat and tears' approach was not as attractive to some people as foreign subsidy.

The Western media duly associated Hamas with Al Qa'eda and portrayed Hamas as a puppet of Iran. Yet Hamas had reservations about Iran, and the ayatollahs were Shi'as while Hamas were Sunni Muslims. Much of Hamas' money actually came from Qatar, but Westerners didn't dwell on that. Qatar was one of the

Gulf Emirates, the good guys, and Qatari support might reflect well on Hamas.

Hamas distrusted the Western media and was not good at PR. Its ethos of resistance was that of the freedom fighter fighting a local battle with Israel rather than that of the terrorist ranged against the West. Extremists across the Muslim world actually detested Hamas, turning against it for engaging in electoral democracy, and

Hamas disliked Al Qa'eda. Hamas advocated Muslim economics and social ideas, but it knew it had to carry the electorate along with it, so it had to be moderate and pragmatic, not extremist.

Regimes around the Middle East also disliked Hamas because it exposed their wealth and top-down power. Hamas represented a new kind of Middle East politics. They weren't angels, but they seemed like a new, cleaner force in politics.

As a resistance party, Hamas was bound to attract Western ire because historically the West had mainly taken Israel's side. Hamas' logic of resistance was rather Churchillian in that by 2006 many Palestinians had come to view negotiation as futile. Disappointment with Fateh abounded, and an urge to resist the Israelis hovered around.

Hamas militants advocated eliminating Israel but the party's centre accepted its existence: instead it wanted a return to the pre-1967 territory of Palestine with a capital in East Jerusalem, refusing to negotiate for anything less. It was willing to recognise an Israel which had withdrawn to the Green Line, but it would not recognise Israel unless that happened. Recognition of any other definition of Israel would amount to a capitulation of core Palestinian principles – and also of UN and international legal declarations of Israel's status as an occupier.

Israel repeated endlessly that Hamas was determined to eliminate Israel and this got stuck in a loop. Meanwhile Hamas needed time and peaceful conditions to calm its militants and bring them into a more moderate fold while Israeli tactics aimed at the elimination of Hamas through violence and propaganda. This irritated Hamas militants and other armed groups. The loop happened to favour Israel, giving credibility to right-wing Jewish militants, who tend to drive Israel's agenda.

The West meanwhile supplied arms, funds and military assistance to Fateh and in 2007 the Hamas government felt it was being unfairly treated and undermined. There was risk of a Fateh coup. Hamas MPs were arrested and imprisoned by Israel, removing its parliamentary majority and hobbling the Palestinian legislature. Things got nervy and a shoot-out started.

All this resulted in the cleavage of the Palestinian democratic spectrum. Hamas pre-empted a Fateh coup by seizing Gaza and fighting Fateh in the West Bank. Hamas lost in the West Bank, and Fateh lost in Gaza. Whether or not this cleavage reflected a master-plan of the Israelis and the West is open to debate – but the outcome was that the body politic of Palestine was now fatally split and this happened to benefit the Israelis.

The Palestinian public undermined itself by acquiescing in this political schism – though there wasn't much they could do once it started escalating. Democracy, which had looked so promising, died in 2007. After that the West Bank was ruled by Fateh which, while it had its virtues and its good people, was dominated by beneficiaries and appointees. One popular Fateh leader who could conceivably reform the party, Marwan Barghouti, a popular leader in the second *intifada*, had sat rotting in an Israeli jail since 2002. Paradoxically, Hamas supported his release, wanting him freed in return for Gilad Shalit, an Israeli soldier they had seized. They wanted Barghouti free because he could reform Fateh and help create a proper political dialogue in Palestine.

Meanwhile, in Gaza, Hamas, led by Ismael Haniyeh, doggedly resisted Israeli pressure. As a longterm strategy this might have succeeded if it could have constrained the restlessness of an imprisoned, deprived population, but Hamas' resistance strategy brought great suffering to Gazans, and its social reform ethos was weakened by security concerns and a creeping Hamas authoritarianism. This happened to favour Israel's agenda. Yet popular support for Hamas still remained solid, not least because Fateh still favoured its own oligarchy.

Politically, therefore, Palestine moved into a terrible situation, with both main political movements becoming authoritarian and undemocratic. The West's bias, its arm-twisting and military support, played a crucial role in this. Western taxpayers financed the situation and Israel gained from it, continuing its West Bank settlement-building, land acquisition, control of Palestinians and blockade of Gaza.

This put the West into an awkward position because things were tilting globally: the big money was now in the Gulf States and Asia and the West's preferment of Israel was becoming an embarrassment. But the West was weighed down by its vested interests, where the Israelis are influential. Something had to give. This was underlined during the Israeli bombardment of Gaza in early 2009, when world public opinion shifted against Israel while Western governments meanwhile shuffled their feet, omitting to criticise Israel. It happened again with the Freedom Flotilla in May 2010. Many international Jews sided against Israel, or at least its Zionist aspect. This lurking public antipathy has grown over time.

The West supported Israel and Fateh but was itself losing wealth and influence. Hence increasing pressure was asserted on Israel in 2010 by US President Obama to get a grip on settlement building and other excesses – the West needed to get itself out of a hole. It could not just abandon Israel as too many vested interests and shady issues would be exposed, but Israel was becoming a liability. An enormous mistake had clearly been made. Governments, Fateh and the PA were increasingly out of step with the public and something was bound to blow. The change came in the form of the Arab revolutions of 2011, loosening political gridlock in the Middle East. In Gaza and the West Bank, young demonstrators called for reunification of Palestine and restoration of democracy, without which dealing with Israel would be impossible.

There was a glimmer of light as well. Salam Fayyad, the PA prime minister, was an independent, non-Fateh politician, a former senior World Bank official – trusted, astute and rational. He took a line of stimulating economic development and establishing Palestinian 'facts on the ground', with a view to preparing it for independence and statehood. Some suspected him of being a Western placeman, but he was not corrupt and he favoured justice.

The West regarded him as a safe pair of hands, though there was some consternation over his idea of obliging the international community to recognise an independent Palestine within the pre-1967 boundaries, even though he was only calling the world to honour its existing obligations. His deadline was September 2011. The Israelis were anxious and the world was shifty over this. Coming in the same year as the Arab revolutions, a potent showdown reared its head. Israel was cornered: if it responded with military violence, the world would turn against it. But something else needed to happen too: the Palestinian 'body politic' needed to be healed. Gaza and the West Bank needed to be reunited.

The strange stalemate between Hamas and Fateh was upstaged by young Palestinian protesters. The two parties both embodied older generations and their failures, while younger people were seeing things with clearer eyes. The main answer was the reintegration of Hamas into the Palestinian political spectrum, since its moderate wing represented an ethos many Palestinians supported. Fateh would also need to clean up its act, restoring its avuncular nationalism and its principles.

This situation awaits an avalanche of events in which the tectonic plates of power shift wholesale and quick decisions will be needed. Aware of this, the Israelis have accelerated the judicisation of East Jerusalem and appropriation of West Bank land, with the aim of creating irreversible facts on the ground before such an avalanche gathers critical mass.

Muslim extremism is on the wane and a measured, modern, democratic orientation has again become the politics of the time. The Middle East is strong on youngsters. In Palestine the average age is around 21, while in the West it is around 45. The current generation of young adults is the globalised internet and mobile phone generation, lacking the fixed perspectives of its parents and grandparents. They look at the world differently. To younger people, Muslim fundamentalists are old-fashioned and Fateh represents their grandparents' generation while Hamas represents their parents' generation. If the pressure heats up, both parties risk irrelevance unless they deliver change.

Hamas is not *the answer* to everything and nothing is ever simple and black-and-white but, on a good day, Hamas seems closer to the answer than Fateh, unless Fateh reforms itself. But Fateh has its vested interests who want to retain power. Hamas represents decent leadership, social principles, human respect and an indigenous approach to Middle Eastern politics. It has a tendency toward gritty, spartan, authoritarian doggedness. In the longterm Hamas could achieve lasting peace since, unless something changes in Israel itself, Israel must be worn down through resistance. Israel, meanwhile, influenced by its own extremists and vested interests, digs itself into a hole while the West's influence is declining. A *situation* is gathering and a resolution of tensions is needed.

This might involve further violence in Palestine, a third *intifada*. One flashpoint is Jerusalem, another is land-seizures and settlement-building, and another is a possible Palestinian revolt against Fateh. It might be over water, it might be the restlessness of the young, or something else. Whatever is the trigger, the safety-catch is off.

Yet the majority of Palestinians and neighbouring Arabs seek no further conflict. Israel, dependent on having an enemy in Hamas, or in Hezbollah, or in Iran, needs to relax this historic obsession with enemies. But Arabs, while reluctant to re-enter conflict, are nevertheless unhappy with circumstances in the Middle East, and a tectonic shift just needs that trigger to start it. In Tunisia in early 2011, a desperate young man setting light to himself provided the spark that started the fire.

The Israeli people need to get a grip on the powers-that-be in their country. With or without further conflict, something on the Israeli side must give, as much for Israel's as Palestine's benefit. Something on the Palestinian side must shift too. Peace processes are a spent option. We're now down to *defining events* – decisive things that *just happen*. And there's always a chance of a miracle. After all, this *is* the Holy Land!

37 An Everyday Story of Peacemaking
humanitarian reality street

Humanitarian work isn't very often exciting and dynamic but there are highlights. One happened after a long day slogging at my computer and following a visit to the All Nations Café. The water was switched on.

Yes, this might sound strange, but it was a big event. Al Khader is supplied with water roughly once a month. Constant mains water exists only on the Israeli side of the separation wall, while Palestinians get rationed. There's no advance notice – the water just starts coming through the pipes and woe betide you if you miss it. Neighbourhoods receive water in rotation, the overall quantity supplied to Bethlehem being insufficient for constant supply to everyone. This overall amount is the crucial issue, and it is decided by the Israelis.

So everyone starts rushing around with hoses, pipes and spanners, making sure their domestic cistern – usually one or a few big tanks on the top of the house – gets filled before the water is cut off again. It's quite an occasion, a wee bit comical, with dads, uncles and sons running around fixing water pipes, excited kids running around getting in the way and mums setting their washing machines in motion, doing those extra jobs they'd saved for such a moment and generally reducing water pressure for everyone.

Al Khader was well-known throughout history as a water source, thanks to its local springs. The valley leading down to Irtas, the monastery village, was once green and fertile, but today the stream is dried up. The Israelis took control of the four springs that feed it and the water table sank, helped by diminished rains most likely due to climate change.

The three enormous ancient cisterns called Solomon's Pools were once fed by these springs. They are altogether seven acres in size, first built two millennia ago and expanded and improved since then. Now they are empty and dry: the water is piped to nearby Israeli settlements such as Gilo and Efrat, while some is graciously resold to the Palestinians at a high price, conveniently subsidising Israeli settler consumers.

Householders were running round sorting out their pipes when Ibrahim and I returned to the school. One flagged Ibrahim down as we drove along the road, saying we'd better get the school's water sorted out quickly. So Ibrahim and I ran around in the dark, sorting out stopcocks and connections. Eventually it was done and the school's tanks were left to fill until the water stopped. I ascended to the apartment and Ibrahim went home.

We had been to the All Nations Café over in Ein Haniya. Today's meeting hadn't been exceptional but it was pleasantly relaxing. Dhyan explained to Ibrahim, who had been trying to figure out what actually was happening, that the course of each meeting depended on who turned up and how they felt. Ibrahim had come half-expecting a serious conference but the meeting constituted just three Palestinians, two Jews and three Europeans. Nothing dramatic happened, yet Ibrahim and I both came back glowing – after all, an evening in good company sitting round a fire can be deeply soothing.

It's rare for Ibrahim to simply sit chatting and doing nothing, and I enjoyed seeing him there with a big smile on his face, joking and sharing tales. He chattered in Dutch with a woman from Holland and I saw in him a lightness of being, reconnecting him with his times in the Netherlands back in the 1990s before he returned to take on managing the school. Again I was reminded why I was here – to serve as a supportive soul-friend to Ibrahim and his family.

This was an unspoken addition to things I was actively doing such as, recently, working to stop the demolition. And that wasn't the only kind of burden-sharing – there's also the task of handling bad news. In this case, the news didn't impact directly on the school, but nevertheless it was dispiriting, affecting people's mood and hopes. It concerned the way in which the international community influences Palestine.

ICAHD, the Israeli Committee Against House Demolitions, which we asked for assistance with the demolition issue, had just had its EU funding withdrawn, so they couldn't help much. Worse, this would affect house demolitions across Palestine – just at a time when the Israelis were stepping up land-seizures and demolitions in East Jerusalem and the West Bank.

It was likely that the EU had given a few years' support to ICAHD and decided to stop, perhaps expecting the problem of house-demolition to be solved or believing ICAHD should find funding elsewhere. Or perhaps the Israeli government had quietly lobbied to have the funding withdrawn – which is not uncommon. This is a problematic flipside of finding a mother-lode of funding – it dries up when you're not looking, just when you need it to continue. Your work is suddenly judged, in some committee far away, to be no longer important, or the champion who supported your cause moves to another post, or someone raises awkward questions, or something else happens. It puts people in organisations such as ICAHD in a difficult position: do you stop work because the funding has dried up? If you're dedicated, the simple answer is, *no, you carry on* – but it gets more difficult.

War is funded on a different basis to peace. Peace-work must fulfil its aims in a few years and, if it doesn't, it gets the chop – if it doesn't work quickly, then it must be ineffective. But war-funding is less conditional, even when there's media grumbling or an economic crisis going on. Everyone accepts that war involves unknowns, but peace funding doesn't receive the same leeway. Peace organisations just get cut off: a letter arrives with the news, and that's it – no support even for scaling down operations, as one would have in a war. I was sad for ICAHD: they had done good work for many years and it's not their fault that demolitions continue and their work is unfinished.

War is an enormous business proposition, and peace is perceived to be less profitable. However, in 2009 the Institute for Economics and Peace in USA showed that pumping economies with military expenditure is no longer viable. In 2007, global military expenditure was $1.14 trillion, rising to $1.5 trillion by 2012. A trillion is a thousand thousand million – a lot of cornflakes. Something is out of step here, in these days of economic downturn. One cause

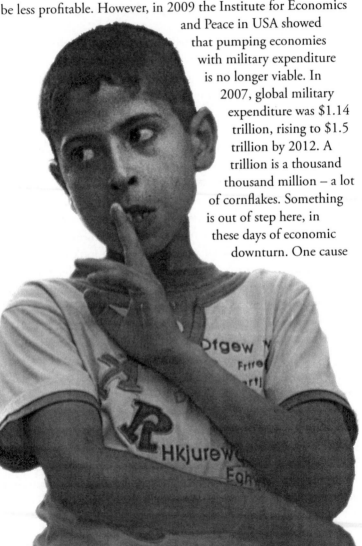

of the declining benefit of war is that a decreasing proportion of expenditure is made on wages for soldiers and more labour-intensive forms of arms production, while an increasing proportion goes on high-tech gizmos and corporate profits. This cuts the alleged 'trickle-down' economic effect of military expenditure.

But the economic outcomes of peace are greater and more widely distributed, benefiting particularly retail, finance, tourism, agriculture and insurance. Peace also removes the costs of war in terms of longterm resource, land and social damage, injury, pollution and loss of productivity. According to the Institute, the economic benefits of worldwide peace would have been $7.2 trillion in 2007. Yes, we need to put ICAHD out of a job, since conflict is undesirable, but only by properly ending conflict.

Then there was more news. In a week's time I was to have the company of up to fifty members of Fateh, who would be staying in the guest accommodation at the school while attending a party conference in Bethlehem. I was concerned about the effect it would have on my work. Jokingly, I told Ibrahim that I had better behave myself when they came. "No", he said, "It is *they* who had better behave themselves, and you must keep your eye on them! These people could wreck the place. But at least we'll make some money and contacts".

Then there was a question that was bugging me. The day before, in Bethlehem, I had met a Danish aid professional, a human rights lecturer who, after working in Bosnia and Eastern Europe, had discovered Palestine and fallen in love with it. The Danish Ministry of Foreign Affairs paid her an annual salary, with expenses and office support. She was one of a new generation of qualified professional aid workers who had superseded humanitarians like me, driven as we are more by conscience and compassion than by career-building considerations. The new guys are good at dishing up figures, securing grants and training selected locals to be tomorrow's top dogs, while we old hands are closer to the ground, better at getting our hands in the dirt, dealing with real humans and their needs. We both have our value, but the hands-on types are being replaced by the smart dudes parachuted in from head office, and something is being lost in the 'real life' department.

I wished I had her expense account! I was running close to the wind. How is it that a ground-level long-stay worker scrapes along on a wing and a prayer, while a professional, bless her, dropping in for a fortnight on a tight schedule, has an expense account and annual salary? I've never quite figured that out – perhaps I'm just missing something. She was a nice person and I invited her to visit the school but predictably she ran out of time. In doing so she missed an important factor in her fact-finding mission – Hope Flowers had big answers and lots of real-life experience that she needed to know about.

This support question nagged at me. I was beginning to feel exhausted. Looking after myself, managing many things, going at it from morning till night, by now half-way through my stay in Palestine, my endurance and clarity of purpose were drooping.

Next morning I awoke bolt upright with a burst of inspiration, brought on by our evening at the All Nations Café. It's funny what has to happen before you get one of these inspirational bubble-ups from the soul. Sometimes it seems to require a time of lostness, of drowning in the turgid complexities of life, no longer knowing why you're here or where you're heading. Then comes the clarity. Suddenly I had a clearer sense of what I yet had to do here in Bethlehem.

It was 1pm and I hadn't even had my breakfast, so invigorated was I with renewed purpose. I jotted down ideas and tasks and got down to it, firing off letters, e-mails, memos and notes. It was too much for one person to handle, but at least I had a renewed plan of attack. The others running the school had too much to handle too.

There was Ghada, the school administrator, pregnant with her third child. She needed time off but no one could take over her duties. A big grant application was under way, and two noble ladies in California had taken on the work, but they relied on Ghada to provide all the necessary information. There was Maram, who organised the courses at the community development centre, but she was weighed down with worry over her husband Ibrahim and his difficulties with the PA security men. She had gone down with a slipped disc – surely a symptom of carrying too many burdens – so she was out of action. They had three kids too.

Ibrahim was ricocheting from task to task – from political manoeuvring and financial management to sitting with a worried teacher counselling her over personal difficulties. I admired his resilience yet found myself in the awkward position of needing his assistance while not wanting to add to his pressures by demanding it. There was Hala, who led the teachers and took a salt-of-the-earth approach, admirably keeping her cool, but she was a mother and wife too, juggling a lot. Then there was Hind, mother to all of them and widow of the founder, who seemed to preside calmly over her flock, though I could see from her face that it was fortitude more than an easy life that made her appear like that.

I won't labour this point by mentioning other members of staff, all of them accomplished life-jugglers and situation-navigators too. Suffice it to say that, although this was the school vacation, life was still a high-pressure affair. This is how many Palestinians live. Life here cannot be organised and channelled in quite the way it works in the West. Everything is an uphill struggle with copious unknowns and sidetracks, not only because life is complex but because there's a killer factor: it's an occupied country where the occupiers enjoy making life difficult, as a strategy.

It all makes for a tricky environment to live and work in, and I'm full of admiration for those who do. I myself can leave and go home, but they cannot, for this is their home. Yet this is why, as the world tips into increasing chaos and hardship, Palestinians will become expert advisers to the wider world. They know what chaos is like and how to live with it.

Part Four:
We Shall Overcome, Perhaps

38 Output
computers, patience and reconciliation

When my last book *Healing the Hurts of Nations*, about international relations, came out in 2003, a friend asked, "But why didn't you write about the Israel-Palestine conflict?". Well, I wrote snippets about it but I found it difficult to do so, not only because the second *intifada* at that time left most observers stunned and clueless, but also because the prospect of writing about it had long daunted me. You can lose a lot of friends over it, and there's so much to get your head round and weigh up.

Problem is, you'll always displease *someone*, who will call you biased or wrong and discount or contradict what you say, often quite virulently. You have to be brave and take your chances when writing something that a wide variety of people – Westerners, Jews and Arabs, all with a variety of persuasions – are likely to read. This confusion makes neutrality and balance look like fish without water. Neutrality is a luxury which involves weeding out anything that is inconvenient. Many are the outsiders who come in with grand peace plans and ideas, only to find them clatter and shatter on the broken cobbles of Palestinian streets.

The two, or actually many, sides don't even participate in the same conflict. This is a fight between certainties that don't even respond to each other. It's about subjectivities, world-views, angles, facets of a diamond, the wholeness of which no one sees. Everyone is biased, including me. I sincerely hope God is an exception.

291

Pictures of Palestine

But, guess what? *I did it.* For three days I sat there sweating in the heat, with a big bottle of Jericho springwater to drink and a cloth to wipe my keyboard, banging away and finally coming up with an overview of the conflict. Too absorbed to think of food or distractions, with mobile phone switched off, I persevered relentlessly, my focus disturbed only by occasional visits from the school-cleaner's son, who hung around hoping to have a go on my computer or to purloin something to munch. Until I sent him away, cruel that I was.

My aim was to outline the Palestinian situation for the school website so that readers could understand the school's situation. The essay saw things from a Palestinian viewpoint, though still, I hope, presented reasonably. Previously I had been stymied by a vain wish to be objective and neutral. Taking a 'biased' viewpoint, I went into free-flow and it landed up far longer than intended. I'd waited fifteen years to write an account like this – and now it was too long. I decided to leave it for a fortnight to see whether I might be able to shorten it later. That was a fatuous hope. Now it constitutes the basis of five historical chapters in this book.

Of all the places I have sat at computers, Hope Flowers is one of the better locations. I worked at a table in the volunteers' apartment on the fourth floor, looking out over a view with both endearing and distasteful elements. The big, wide windows framed a vista containing many emblematic elements of the conflict.

This was the frontier, an illegal boundary dividing a land in two. It's a far more material boundary than many international frontiers since it is defined by a concrete and stone separation wall. Internationally, to some this wall is the internal affair of one country, Israel, and to others it's a matter of global significance. The whole sorry story was scenically arranged outside the window, as if this school had been located here to catch it in full technicolor panavision.

But the school was built here a decade before the wall, the watchtower and the Israeli settlement. I found myself wondering what impression the kids would be left with as they grew into adults, having lived with these symbols of war. They might perchance see the end of this sorry saga in their lifetimes: one day Palestinians of another generation will sit with Israelis wondering what it really had all been about. One day, all that concrete for the separation wall will be torn down and used for something else. But for now it's there, an abuse of architecture and landscaping, a manifestation of people's mutual antipathy.

Anyway, there was work to do. Back to the website. Next came a page about Bethlehem. Even here there was some explaining to do: why was this historic Christian town now 90% Muslim? Well, the short answer is that the town was flooded with Muslim refugees in 1948 and 1967, and then drained of Christians thanks to their emigration to far-off lands. The good news is that Muslims, appreciating Bethlehem's fame, support the town's Christian heritage. It gives them a sense of *being somewhere*. Folks in Yatta and Jenin don't have this privilege.

I had a classic webmaster's problem – extracting the necessary information for the website from my 'client', the school. Many clients tend unthinkingly to hope a website will appear by magic. Unfortunately they need to be good communicators with available time, providing text that lays out their stall, answering questions and giving details, and making executive decisions about overall design and presentation. But when they are involved up to their eyeballs with a project, it's difficult for them to step outside it all to figure out what outsiders need to read. It involves hours of thinking, writing and fine-tuning – and the best person to do it for the school was Ibrahim.

I could improvise some of the material, but I still needed him to provide information and send it over. "Yes, I'll do it tomorrow." He sincerely *meant* this, but something else would capture his attention each day. He's such a nice man, rather a saint really. Don't tell him that, because he'll laugh out loud, fiddle with his mobile phone and then change the subject. It was tricky nagging and pressurising him – he had so much on his plate.

Pictures of Palestine

Life in Palestine is an ongoing crisis-management routine where the issue that shouts loudest gets dealt with. It's not helped by the fact that everyone else, locked into the same juggling routine, butts in or rings up, demanding an instant solution before the next pressing issue comes along to overpower it. You'd be in the middle of a meeting and someone would burst in presenting an issue with little care for what they were disrupting. Disruption is standard, so the best thing to do is to out-disrupt other disruptions. I kept notes of dropped threads and unanswered questions because I was lapsing into the very same mentality. My polite British upbringing which had trained me to wait until others finished speaking got the better of me. I waited, made lists and sent reminders.

Patience. Do other things, *wait, wait.* I began fearing that my time in Bethlehem would draw to a close before things were ready. People probably believed my web-work involved a quick copy-paste job, but it involves meticulous editing, fact-checking, gap-filling, composing summaries and re-working text – and that's before you start actually building the web-page.

A conscientious webmaster can spend ages on one page, finessing text, processing and inserting pictures, testing for different screen-widths, browsers and computers, adjusting font-sizes and text-boxes until it's dead right. Sometimes it's like a battle – blood, sweat and tears.

In war, you enter the fray and do your best. The outcome is unknown until it all ends, and the aim is to minimise bloodshed

and maximise outcomes. This happens on the keyboard too, except the battle is with yourself and, figuratively speaking, the bloodshed is mostly your own. Actually, the sweat was for real, hot as it was, and I shed some tears too since I was churning my way through a gaggle of niggly personal issues grinding around in my psyche.

I was getting into rather a state, sitting there talking to myself too much. Everyone who mattered was too busy, or elsewhere. I was overdosing on life and its wrangles, with things going amiss and grinding half-worries that never got far. I missed my loved ones, wishing I could go home for a weekend. Even I, a meditator for decades, a counsellor and a source of insight for many people, was losing my way.

I was saved by a baby. She arrived to stay for a few days, adding her own tears to mine. She had had too much of life, needing to grizzle and complain for the first day of her stay. She cheered up afterwards and her newborn antics – those radiant smiles, those carefree flailings of arms and legs – were charming, a changer of moods and strong medicine for me. Suddenly I laughed at myself – here was a newborn counsellor reflecting my feelings back to me, and she made me chuckle. She had brought her parents with her from Germany, and they stayed with me for three nights, taking a break after a peacemaking conference near Beit Jala.

These conferences happen quite a lot. There are many peacemaking and reconciliation groups and gatherings and, if you're a conference and workshop junkie, you'd be fully occupied here. In the media you hear a lot about politicians in peace processes that never get anywhere but you rarely hear of these ground-level peace-building efforts. There's a constant stream of get-togethers, trainings and 'encounters' going on, where people enter into social bridge-building and conflict-transformation fry-ups, trying to forge some real-life truth and take steps toward mutual understanding. My visitors had been at one of these.

I liked them. She was German and he had escaped Afghanistan as a teenager in the early 1990s following the Soviet withdrawal, when warlords and *mujahedin* started battling it out to establish who was to be chief. As an Afghan, he had personal experience of many issues persisting in Palestine and, as a German, she had a parental heritage of warfare behind her from WW2 just as I did, as a Brit.

The wounded healer: painful experience becomes the compost in which a capacity for healing is germinated.

Both of them were open-minded and we had some fine discussions when baby had gone to sleep. These two helped me realise how much I had changed: in the 1980s and 1990s I had run many such gatherings in Britain, attempting to pressure-cook transformation amongst large groups of people, witnessing people's pain and dilemmas, hammering out issues to uncover resolution and breakthrough, and it had been a deep and rich experience.

But by the late 1990s, after fifteen years of hearing the personal stories of so many people – conflict victims, Holocaust survivors, victims of child abuse, family violence, social rejection and other human horrors – they all started melting into one and repeating themselves. I became rather jaded and realised that I needed to do something more tangible, to chip away at the factual, practical steps involved in building a new world instead of perpetually *processing issues*. I was now in Al Khader, not sure if I was cooking or being cooked, and losing my perspective in the process.

These Germans healed me, reminding me that I needed to remember what ultimately it is all for. I needed to regain perspective and keep things in focus. Twenty-five years older than they, I unwittingly gave them an insight too: that the path is long, things aren't quite so simple, and sometimes you lose your way. Sometimes you even wonder whether any progress has been made at all and you just feel like going home and giving up.

A Brit, a German and an Afghan happily sharing space, together with a baby – all of us in the peacemaking game. Now isn't that a sign that history moves on, that peace is possible, that nightmares end? Our parents and grandparents had been enemies and we were soul-friends, working on the very same side, the side which says *no to war*. Or should I say, *yes to peace*.

39 Back into the Future
Fateh and the Will of God

A few days later I woke up with more weighty concerns. Time was moving on and many things were not done. I was waiting for material, for further funding that didn't arrive, for a loan-repayment that never came and for a women's empowerment course that wouldn't start. There was more. Fateh was to have its conference in Bethlehem that weekend, with the fiftyish delegates staying at the school guesthouse downstairs. There was to be a security clampdown and I was to provide my passport and a picture to be given clearance to enter the school.

Fateh had also taken over the Hope Flowers Centre in Deheisheh. Ibrahim and the admin team had to move out for a week, vacating offices and meeting rooms for Fateh top-knobs. This was manageable since it was the summer vacation, though it gave Ibrahim yet another reason to get distracted.

So I felt restless. I had woken up with a rather lost and disoriented feeling – one of those where you can't retrieve your sense of time and place and you're not sure whether you're on the right planet. I resorted to a strategy of pottering around attending to small, spontaneously-arising things.

This approach has a well-worn Islamic equivalent, summed up in one word: *inshallah* – if it is the will of God, it will happen. If not, it won't. We Westerners find this notion difficult, being addicted to plans, timetables and control agendas. Many humanitarians come a cropper on this once we leave the developed world, plunging with the best intentions into a world that, apparently, is only *developing*.

Here, reality-as-it-is tends to override plans and expectations. The term *inshallah* highlights a key cultural contrast between Westerners and Muslims.

This is one reason why Israelis tend to beat Palestinians in conflict situations. Israelis think ahead and ring-fence Palestinians so that, by the time Palestinians address an issue, the Israelis have already got there. Many Israelis, if truth be known, would like Palestinians just to disappear. The vast majority would not wish to commit genocide or ethnic cleansing – they simply wish Palestinians would *evaporate*. This, of course, is not going according to plan, since those Palestinians are still there. So here, in this conflict, we see a cruel divergence between plans and realities.

Israelis can also be pretty unsystematic in their own way. They tend to see things very much from their own viewpoint only, believing fervently in its rightness and bulldozing it forward until reality moves over to accommodate it. *Chutzpah*, it's called. Except reality doesn't always move over.

Two French guests stayed for a night a few weeks earlier while travelling around the West Bank. They had tried to enter Nablus and, arriving at a checkpoint, their way was blocked, since internationals were, according to the IDF soldiers there, not permitted in Nablus. My French friends' Palestinian taxi-driver knew this wasn't true, but it's best not to get into a row with Israeli soldiers at checkpoints. So they retreated, went to another checkpoint and got in there. There are plenty of instances in Israel of an avidly-run security system which is quite arbitrarily applied, and the trick is to find out what's happening that day and to proceed along the path of least resistance. Palestinians are good at this, and this is how they confound the Israelis. It's a never-ending game.

To return to our philosophical point, there's a dialogue between the Western 'plans, principles, policies and procedures' method and the Arabic 'fate, firefighting and fudging it' method, and each is valid. Today's deflation of the West is difficult for it: the Western grand plan and the unfoldment of factual reality are diverging ominously. The Western mindset is in trouble.

There's an operational elegance to the *inshallah* method. When I visited Palestine in 2005 I came with eight tasks, set by my sponsors of that time. Toward the end of my visit I had completed just one of them and was worried. They naturally wished to see results and here I was, failing abysmally. I resigned myself to returning home empty-handed and somehow finding a way to explain myself. However, the next day, Ibrahim Abu el-Hawa, bless him, rolled up in a minibus carrying all of the people I needed to see. Within hours everything was resolved in one fell swoop. Magic, and a good learning experience.

The resolution of this paradox lies in the Sufi adage *trust in Allah and tether thy camel*. This means, rely on things unfolding as they will, but don't overlook obvious things that can save the day. So I chose to trust that there must be a good reason why things were not progressing with the website. But I still went downstairs to the school office to nag Ibrahim Issa. It was worth a try, and a few things did progress. I caught him at the right moment, he apologised for his distractedness, gave me the information I needed, I gave him a hug and all was well.

Similarly, the Fateh conference turned out to be a void concern as the full complement of Fateh guests didn't come to the school. Bizarrely, Hamas in Gaza fixed it, by stopping Gazan Fateh delegates from leaving Gaza for Bethlehem because Hamas was annoyed about its own members who had been jailed and mistreated in the West Bank. So, the Gaza delegates didn't turn up, an accommodation crisis was averted and Fateh members didn't in the end use the school, except for a few delegates for one night. It seems that the location, out at the far end of Bethlehem, was undesirable for status-conscious Fateh people, anxious not to be marginalised.

I have been rather critical of Fateh and I have my reasons. They have, I believe, allowed themselves to fall into a trap, due to lack of foresight concerning the right use of power. Israel and the

West laid this trap for them and they duly fell into it. The West offered them big money in return for a negotiated settlement and many Palestinians genuinely believed it was worth a try – except that it didn't work. In fact, in some ways it was a trick. By 2000, Palestinians were frustrated at the lack of progress and a window of opportunity for negotiation closed.

But by then, Fateh bigwigs had got used to their salaries and privileges, accustomed to using Euros and Dollars to placate the Palestinian people. When Arafat died in 2004, Abu Mazen, 'a man we can deal with', as the Israelis said, became

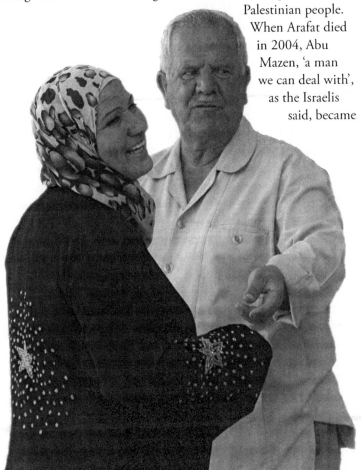

president, and Fateh was confident it would win the 2006 Palestinian elections. But Hamas won. Neither Fateh, the Israelis nor the West foresaw or accepted this and, after a sad internecine fight in 2007, Fateh ruled the West Bank and Hamas retreated to Gaza. The money decided it.

Fateh leaders sincerely believed that their *coup* was right and they did subsequently achieve some notable results, building up the West Bank's infrastructure and economy. But, to complicate things, Fateh itself was divided between contrasting schools of opinion vying for leverage and this compromised the efficient running of the Palestine Authority. Nevertheless, the money kept everyone together and made it expedient to keep Fateh in power. Palestinians were conflict-weary and needed stabilisation and regularity, and all this meant that many important issues got buried.

The consequences were now coming to a head at the 2009 Bethlehem conference. Truth-speaking was needed because many Palestinians were fed up with Fateh – honesty and integrity had not been its strong point. If debate was stifled at the conference, Fateh would dig itself deeper into a hole, eventually to be judged by their people to have betrayed them.

By *their people*, I mean the Palestinian people. This highlights the trap Fateh had fallen into – a conflict between party interests and those of Palestinians as a whole. Arafat, head of Fateh for decades, used rewards and hand-downs to get his way but, whatever his faults, he also had vision and principles which kept things in some proportion. He had a firm sense of what was right for Palestinians. If someone tried to bribe and cajole too much, he fiercely let them know, keeping his eyes on the main goal, the liberation of the Palestinian people.

Bill Clinton sustained a dose of Arafat's ferocity. Anxious to make his mark on history, in the late 1990s Clinton got the Israelis to make 'generous concessions', offering land in exchange for peace (though still only a paltry 18% of 'historic Palestine'). Clinton hooked development aid to this, thinking Arafat would say yes. But Clinton and Ehud Barak, the Israeli PM at the time, naively believed it would be okay to miss out concessions on East Jerusalem, the Palestinian capital. It wasn't okay. Arafat walked out, feeling tricked – and he *was* being tricked. Except that he simply refused to play. To this day, Western media and Israeli propagandists claim Arafat 'inexplicably nixed the deal, offering no counter-proposal'. Well, Jerusalem just *had* to be in the deal. It was obvious.

The key issue had been left out in an attempt to arm-twist Arafat into accepting an unacceptable deal, but he was having none of it. He stood by one of his people's key requirements: East Jerusalem as capital. He also stood by his covenant with Palestinians, for whom, if East Jerusalem and a decent deal on refugees are not on the negotiating table, there will be no deal, period. It would be like asking Churchill to sacrifice London for peace with Hitler, and to stop all British troops in WW2 from returning home – a proposition he *never* would have gone along with.

Arafat died and Abu Mazen came along, anxious to please the Americans, get the Euro-money and be seen to be reasonable with the Israelis. In the 1990s this was an understandable pitch, though by his time it was really outdated. Fateh made concessions to soften the Israelis but yet again the Israelis failed to match them, continuing to build walls and settlements. Fateh accepted funds from abroad, hoping Palestinians would make do with that.

But, as Ibrahim Issa sometimes says, this money was like morphine, not medicine, and an addiction set in. The doctors (Fateh) became beholden to the drug pushers (the West) and the patients (the Palestinians) grew increasingly grudging about the side-effects. Fateh members became accustomed to cushy lives and fat cheques, and Palestinians were reluctantly pacified by the spillage falling off the table, yet they were not happy.

Meanwhile, no one legitimately represented *all* Palestinians' wishes. Fateh, the political party, was almost the same thing as the PA, the governmental structure. Fateh was funded by the PA, which meant that, when Hamas gained power in 2006, things got awkward. Hamas would have to rid Fateh of its funding, to create a level democratic playing field, since its own funding was independent, and Western aid donors weren't falling over each other to fund Hamas. Fateh didn't want its funding to dry up, and the Israelis and the West saw an opportunity. They quietly urged Fateh to get rid of Hamas.

Hence the Fateh-Hamas conflict of 2007. It didn't work well for Fateh since Hamas struck first, seizing Gaza. Fateh and the PA took power in the West Bank while, constitutionally, Hamas remained the legitimate government. This confusion suited the Israelis, and the Palestinian people were the losers.

In Bethlehem in 2009 Fateh was now faced with a cruel choice. They might eventually become history, superseded by someone else more representative. To avoid this they had to stand up and say an emphatic *No* to the Israelis, thus risking loss of foreign support and certain in-fighting within Fateh. Many opinions ricocheted around. To quote Ali Jarbawi, a Fateh minister, the differences were "Geographic – West Bank, Gaza, north, south, inside, outside – then there's the young, the old, the left and the right within Fateh, those with Oslo and those against". What kept this lot together was a simple fact – leave Fateh and you sacrifice your income.

Then there was the question of resistance versus negotiation: at the Bethlehem conference Abu Mazen reasserted the value of negotiation but reserved Palestinians' right to resist. There was a problem with this. To quote Ali Jarbawi again: "You cannot have an Authority and an *intifada*. You can't have resistance to the occupation while you have an official Palestinian address on the ground [since the Israelis would simply bomb hell out of you]. It's either resistance without an Authority or an Authority without resistance".

Of course, the West and the Israelis preferred a divided, passive Palestine, though they wouldn't admit it. They wanted the PA to act like a franchise, handling policing and social affairs while remaining toothless. The Israelis had delegated their dirty work, management of the occupied territories, to Fateh.

Ibrahim Issa is a sincere, dedicated peace man and he doesn't advocate conflict. Politically, he's non-partisan, believing both Fateh and Hamas to have their assets and flaws – he's green-oriented and humanitarian in leaning. But one evening, we sat discussing things just before going to a cultural evening at Bethlehem University, and he answered my questions surprisingly straight, his opinions reflecting his frustration as a peacemaker and educator.

"We need some honesty," he said. "The PA ought to refuse *all* foreign money and stand up for Palestinians, exposing the true situation to the world. If necessary we should opt for short-term hardship, creating a humanitarian catastrophe. Truth and reality would at least emerge, ending this soporific nightmare. We are throttled and imprisoned, and the world should see this and apply the UN resolutions it has signed up to. We need to stand up for ourselves and tell the world to stop sending us morphine to quell the pain. We need to deal with the causes of the pain itself.

"Either this, or the Israelis should be honest. They want to dominate us and keep us down. So alternatively we should have one nation called Israel, with the Israelis in charge. Israelis should do the policing and security, run social services and face the full consequences of being an occupying power. They should rule over *all* the land and face the full cost. It might mean years of hardship for Palestinians, but the outcome will be truth and justice: the Israelis will not have a Jewish state with so many Palestinians amongst them. Truth will come.

"With the first option, the world will not be able to face what it has done, abandoning and betraying the Palestinians to an occupier. The world will have to force the occupier to face truth and give Palestinians a genuinely fair deal. With the second option, Israel as a nation will fail, because an Israeli minority cannot rule a Palestinian majority and also have a Jewish state with longterm security and peace. It will come to a showdown either way."

This is the father of three children talking, and it's their future he's gambling on. This is the director of a peace and democracy school. He is not a violent resistance man – he's just fed up. Ibrahim is right: we need honest truth. No more foreign complicity in an enormous crime. Yes, you taxpaying readers of this book unwittingly fund this crime.

This was the way it was going. In late 2009 Abu Mazen stated that he would not stand for re-election as president because negotiations had not worked and he was tired. Salam Fayyad, the prime minister, stated that, unless something changed by September 2011, Palestine would require the world to recognise it as a state within the pre-1967 borders, as legally defined under multiple UN resolutions. The Israelis retorted they would not accept this, though they didn't actually have a strong hand of cards to play, or any alternative strategy. The wider world would have to *do something*, or watch a very edgy situation, even a massacre, unfold.

The Palestinians did lay down the gauntlet in 2011 and many people cheered. The Palestinians took greater control of the agenda. As this book was being published, the world adopted a strategy of kicking Palestine's application for recognition by the UN into the long grass, to take the heat out of the situation. The matter will unfold. But something has shifted – and it results from the turning of a tide that took place at the Bethlehem conference of 2009.

Let's face it, the Israeli project has not really succeeded. Jews don't have a safe place to live and they have sacrificed their nation to a ruling clique which has wrecked their society and led them into an armed nightmare. Israel is ruled by a strange alliance of generals, Zionists, nationalists and Orthodox hotheads, an arrangement that's not even fair on most Israelis.

Israelis are slowly becoming a minority in this land. Most Jews in Europe, America and Russia feel they are getting on well enough where they are without needing to move to Israel. One third of the Russian Jews who migrated to Israel in the 1990s after the Soviet Union fell have returned to Russia. Many American immigrants retain dual nationality – a get-out strategy if needed. Some liberal-thinking Israelis have left. Israel is assertive but insecure, and a clock is ticking. It's tragic for the *sabras*, Jews born in Israel, for whom it is their only home. But then, Palestinians don't require Jews to leave – they just require an end to Zionism and occupation.

Pictures of Palestine

Israel has lost track of its national purpose and Israelis have omitted to realise that they have equal rights to Palestinians. They're a small nation, like Ireland or Finland. Sorry if I offend Irish, Finns or Israelis, but it's true! Global power and money come increasingly from the East, not the West. Israelis must live with Palestinians and Arabs in peace and mutual good-neighbourliness. That's the deal.

Fateh had fallen in with an enormous lie. It wasn't intentional: Abu Mazen tried his best, and there are many good people in

Fateh with sound principles. But they became puppets of foreign paymasters and as a result, there's a massive disjunction in Palestine. Another election, a third *intifada* or some other truth-moment will expose it. Fateh have got Palestinians into this situation and, unless they do something, a crunch will come and history will not stand on Fateh's side. This is why the Bethlehem Conference was crucial.

Poor old Ibrahim, meanwhile, had his school and centre requisitioned. There would have been no shortage of automatic

rifles at this peace school that week and the Israeli soldiers over the valley in their watchtower would have had a more interesting week than usual. So, perhaps, might I. Thanks to Hamas, none of this actually happened.

As for the cultural evening, it was delightful. A young dance troupe brought Palestinian tradition to life in full colour and vigour. *Debka* dance style is reminiscent of a previous occupying power, the Ottoman Turks, the movement and music being rather Caucasian or Cossack in flavour – though I almost got into trouble for saying so. One must never offend Palestinian national feeling. Thirty dancers dressed in fine costumes acted out a saga in song and dance which I didn't understand, but it ended in triumph and joy. The show reached several climaxes and the audience of hundreds rose to its feet each time, rapturously clapping and loudly singing along.

Despite the situation Palestinians find themselves in today, there is so much hope amongst the younger generation. This isn't escapist fantasy: they know in their bones that they have a future, despite everything. You can *see* it in them. Sometime, somehow, their day is coming. May God protect them. May we, as fellow humans, support them in making an honest national breakthrough. They deserve a change. Screw the politics – this concerns *people*, and when the people lead, leaders will follow. It will be a breakthrough for Israelis too, though I doubt many Israelis would believe me.

40 Diplomatic Initiatives and Ironing Boards

what early mornings can do

My mobile phone was ringing in the office. I raised my head, bleary-eyed after another late night. Half past six. Groan. Something in my brain calculated I wouldn't get to the phone before it stopped ringing, so I drifted back to sleep.

Bang, bang – someone was hammering on the door. This managed to raise me. It was the guy responsible for looking after the Fateh conference delegates. He spoke almost no English, and I almost no Arabic. Bemused, he looked at me standing there in my dark red *jalabiya* with gold embroidery down the front. I had got this three years before in Tunisia when my son and I had trekked in the Sahara with the Bedouin, who had said I looked like a caliph in it. This morning I didn't feel like a caliph. The man handed me his phone. It was Ibrahim.

"Balden, very sorry, can you find an ironing board and iron?" Blimey. I had wondered whether there was some sort of security alert, or the Israelis were coming, or whether I had done something disastrously wrong. When you're in a strange country there are things you expect not to understand, or bloopers you half-expect to be caught making. But no, an ironing board. Right... an ironing board. Umm... Miraculously I soon found one that I didn't know was there: my intuitions were clearly more awake than my thinking brain. Iron? Well, that hadn't been there either until I found it!

Problem solved, now back to bed. Not a chance. Energetic Arabic music was coming in through the window from a neighbour's garden and I realised this was going to be one of those long, strange days that unfolds elastically after a short night and a weird start. I gave in to it. By the time I was on my second cup of tea, my brains were more or less what my son, when he was young, had innocently called 'compost mentis'.

The Fateh people had arrived late the previous night, Tuesday – they were supposed to arrive Sunday night. I had been talking to a friend on Skype, and heard noises. Strange, as this vast building was usually empty apart from me. I was scantily clad, it being a hot night, and I had expected no more company than that of my shy gecko who wouldn't, I calculated, really mind. Somehow I doubted that geckos possessed morally conservative values. But no, when I went out to check, someone was walking along the corridor, mercifully with their back to me. Fateh was here. Ooops.

Now my brains still weren't fully cranked up that morning and I seemed to have started blogging without having much to say. A spark suddenly came up and I launched into telling my readers of a visionary explosion I had had a few days before. It was an unfinished bundle of formative ideas – what I call a 'download'. A brainstorm. I get these every now and then. People think I'm nuts when I tell them the results, uttering expletive responses like 'ridiculous' or 'impossible' and sometimes they indeed are right. But sometimes they turn out to be wrong.

This was the 'download': *A 2024 Plan for Palestine*. It arose out of my earlier discussion with Ibrahim when he had expressed frustration over the corrosive stalemate reached by Palestine and Israel. The latest round of this sorry drama involved Israel conducting settlement expansion in a most aggressive way, inciting clashes with Muslims on Haram al Sharif in Jerusalem's Old City and forcing evictions in East Jerusalem. The residents were branded illegal occupants, having been there only fiftyish years, and Jewish settlers walked straight into their houses, taking over. In response had come the customary disapproving reactions from abroad, then nothing.

In my jottings I wrote down the bare bones of *A 2024 Plan for Palestine*. Don't ask me why 2024 – it just sounded right. I've learned not to interfere with 'downloads' like these. Whenever I've got into trouble with them, it has been because my brain has stepped in, trying to impose interpretative logic on them. This is perhaps why Allah woke me up early this morning, through the agency of Fateh and its ironing-board needs, to keep me from getting logical. After all, it was full moon, and reality bends and twists at such times, even for dedicated reality-conservationists.

There had been an incident the evening before, when I was down in a grocery store in Al Khader. The guy who ran it speaks passable English and we were chatting when suddenly, outside, there was the blare of sirens. A powerful black pickup truck raced dramatically up the main street, bouncing crazily over the speed bumps, with eight or so security men in the back, hanging on for dear life, dressed in dark blue uniforms, brandishing sub-machine guns and seemingly on full alert, ready for a shoot-out. Everyone stopped and stared, notably unmoved.

Then, as the din receded, the shopkeeper wryly said, "They say they guard our security, *hamdillah*, but in real life they're busy hunting dangerous bananas". He might be right.

41 A 2024 Plan for Palestine
peaceful war, wealthy poor

Ishall now submit to you my series of crazy ideas – mainly just to ventilate some possibilities. It's an exercise in blue-sky thinking. It starts here: Ibrahim reckons that the only way to break the Israeli logjam is for Palestine to place its cards on the table and play for high stakes. Several options are available.

Option one: Israel should shoulder its responsibilities as an occupying power, the PA dissolving itself to cease being an overblown municipality doing Israel's dirty work, and the world should stop dishing out the 'morphine' of aid-and-development funding, financing Israel's occupation by taking on social costs that Israelis would otherwise have to pay. This option would expose Palestine's true situation, kill many illusions and precipitate matters. It would hurt, but it could improve on the current stymied situation where Palestinians are held in limbo with a non-solution in which they are losers.

Option two: Palestine could invite Jordan to re-occupy the West Bank and Egypt to re-occupy Gaza, then dissolve itself, annulling the Oslo agreements and returning to its pre-1967 status until such time as it could be independent, or something else happens. Israel wouldn't accept this, since Jordan and Egypt would probably have to invade the territories. I don't get the feeling these governments would want to do that, so this option isn't a goer, but it's worth mentioning.

Option three: Salam Fayyad's 2009 suggestion was to build up national infrastructure and oblige the international community to recognise Palestine as an independent country with borders at the Green Line. This would require the world to fulfil its existing obligations arising from UN resolutions and court judgements made over the decades, deeming the occupation of Palestine to be illegal. This strategy relies on UN member states actually fulfilling their promises – something they're not good at doing. But it is faintly viable. The alternative, doing nothing, probably charges a higher price.

In response to Palestine's UN application the Americans threatened to withdraw aid funding. This suggests a fourth option for Palestine, requiring great courage: refuse all foreign funding. This would remove the disempowering leverage that the wider world – Europe and America particularly – exercises over Palestine. It would create a national crisis. It would undermine Fateh's power unless Fateh changed radically. It would oblige donor countries to change the nature of aid funding, if they so chose, or it would tip Palestine into a crisis and reorientation of its national economy.

This would require strong leadership in Palestine, either of an inspirational or a forceful kind. But in the long term it could correct many things. To some extent this is where Hamas might have headed, had it remained in government from 2007 on. A wide range of outcomes could emerge from it, some very painful, ranging from destitution and breakdown to disaster relief, to a reinvasion of OPT by the Israelis or to a national Palestinian mobilisation of great proportions. But it could also end many ills – aid dependency, corruption and ill-distribution of wealth and power in Palestine. It is unlikely.

These hypothetical options aren't the main point here, yet they all point in one direction. For decades we have lived with a myth that a negotiated peace will come, Palestine will achieve nation status and Israel will pull back. This myth has been played out without substantive progress for over twenty years, giving Israel cover for saying one thing (negotiating for peace) and doing another (taking land and throttling the Palestinians).

Pictures of Palestine

But *Palestine remains an occupied country.* That's a fact. Peace processes have achieved little, so we need to get real and move on. The Israelis like to do the deciding, yet it will be the Palestinians who will judge whether and when peace and justice have genuinely arrived. This judgement will be based on facts on the ground, not lofty words and sweeping diplomatic deals.

As Ibrahim says, whatever happens, it could take 25 years for a full, final solution to come. But here comes the important bit: *any sacrifices made would probably be only as bad as those already being made*, so they might be worth making.

Palestine has little to lose except its current ambiguous, hand-tied oppression – a situation to which it has become terribly accustomed. People have already died, lost their homes and lands; Israeli walls and settlements have already been built; Palestinians control their lives only to an extent and, as things stand, their prospects are poor. This puts Palestine in a perverse position of power: *it has less to lose than Israel.* Israel has prosperity, influence, military security and international standing to lose. This gives it greater vulnerability to change. It has less of a free hand, stuck as it is with the consequences of its actions over time. There is a fifth option too. Palestine could wait until Israel, which regularly shoots itself in the foot, blows its feet right off. This might take time and it requires patience and fortitude. Of which Palestinians possess quite a lot. Meanwhile, there are things that can be done by Fateh and Hamas, together or separately.

Palestine needs to steal Israel's initiative, and it is perhaps already beginning to do so. For too long, Israel has been the initiator and Palestine the responder. The strategic trick here is to re-position yourself so that you name the terms of the game, so that the other guys are reduced to responding – and then keep piling it on. Dear old Mark Regev, the smooth-talking Australian Israeli government spokesman we've heard so often in the media, is good at this PR technique. He makes outrageous things sound reasonable.

So it's necessary to snatch the initiative and change the game – end the sleepwalking, shift the facts and get people moving. Armed resistance doesn't work: if it did, Palestine would be free of occupation. Negotiation doesn't work: if it did, results would already be visible. Israel has been running the agenda since 1948, endlessly repeating to the world that Israelis are victims protecting themselves. Yet it is Palestinians who, on balance, are the victims. So let's indulge in some strategic, historic-scale thinking, jumping ahead. For the key issue is not independence, it's *what happens afterwards*.

First, let's make some assumptions about the world of the coming twenty years. Let's assume that the West, a major player in this conflict, subsides still further in its global influence. Let's assume that world climatic and environmental conditions get worse and that global resource and commodity supply problems and prices escalate, forcing change in many arenas. Let's assume that nations will be less able or willing to invest in military hardware, preparedness and adventures – including the United States' military support of Israel. Let's imagine that the world's emerging multi-polar power geometry could bring new forms of diplomatic confusion and possible gridlock to Palestine's case, since there are more independent-thinking players in the game than there were in former decades.

These are reasonable assumptions. What does Palestine do in such circumstances?

Well, it could do three main things. *First, seize the diplomatic initiative and precipitate radical moves.* Palestine needs to force the issue in new ways. Various of the strategies mentioned above could be utilised, mostly leading to serious crises for Palestinians, yet they are all based on a recognition of failure. To recognise and act on failure is a sign of strength – better than wallowing in it – and it's better to be the first to do so.

Salam Fayyad's strategy of state-building and seeking independence from the UN could be a runner. If Fayyad gains sufficient international backing, then an Israeli military intervention or other repressive measures to block it would definitely put the cat amongst the pigeons, obliging the wider world either to accept Israel's will or to intervene definitively – either way, greater truth will prevail. If Fayyad achieves nothing, a likely outcome is a new *intifada* – or some other reaction. Something has to move, and movement would start a momentum which would sooner or later have to progress to a solution – acceptable particularly to Palestinians. The onus is on the relationship between Palestine and the international community. Israel meanwhile has already overplayed its hand in the last sixty years and it has few strong cards to play, few new tricks or solutions.

Yet another alternative is to play a bigger game. Palestine could jump over the search for independence and propose a macro-solution affecting the whole region, encouraging the formation of something like a Middle Eastern Union. Its seeds exist already in the Gulf Cooperation Council, a common market of the Gulf States and now Jordan. In our new, multi-polar world, big players like China, India, Russia, America and Europe will increasingly call the shots and small nations risk being nudged aside, so this isn't too radical a proposition.

Pictures of Palestine

Forming incrementally like the EU did, a Middle Eastern union would surround Israel, obliging it to come to some sort of deal. Throughout history, the Middle East has mostly been united, so reintegration is not an exceptional task. Such a move would change the context of Palestine's situation. It would take years, but this conflict has already taken years, and if this strategy became the only viable alternative, it could be worth trying.

Palestine is a decisively catalytic country, a thorn in the sides of many countries, so it can afford to be proactive. The governments of Palestine and Israel have a shared problem: if they don't *do something* then the Palestinian people, and Israeli settlers too, are likely to take action themselves. But violence is not the only option: there has in recent years been a growing non-violence movement amongst Palestinians, though large-scale non-violent actions haven't yet been tried. After all, there are five million Palestinians in 'historic Palestine' and five million in the diaspora. If things grew desperate and 10% or half a million of them started walking, in, out or anywhere, we have a very potent situation. If things get desperate, this too is an option.

To gain the diplomatic initiative, Palestine can lay further issues on the table. It can, for example, agitate for denuclearisation, even demilitarisation in the Middle East – an idea needing a true champion. This is a national security issue for Palestine. Israel's main nuclear facility, Dimona, near Bethlehem and Hebron – and a prime target – poses a health and security risk to Palestinians, but it affects Israelis too because the country is so small. In truth, Palestine would do Israel a favour by promoting the idea of denuclearisation – though only a few Israelis would currently agree.

In the long term, demilitarisation would be one of the greatest solutions the Middle East could give itself. This sounds idealistic, yet it is one of the clearer political aspects of the largely non-violent Arab Spring revolutions of 2011 – it has quite quickly become more doable. Except the Middle East's current regimes rely on military strength to maintain their positions. But it is foreseeable that, within a decade or two, a movement this way is possible.

Pictures of Palestine

On many big questions such as water resources, ecology and climate, refugees, economics and the impending decline of the oil trade, Middle Eastern cooperation is urgent and Palestinians stand in a strong position to encourage it. Not because Palestine is a state, but because it is a volatile millstone around Middle Eastern necks unless its problem is solved.

Finally, as mentioned earlier, Palestine could play for high stakes and reject all financial aid offered on existing terms. This would cause a humanitarian crisis and oblige Palestinians to think afresh about the welfare of their families and communities. This isn't new, since Palestine has experience in raw survival. Such an action would hurt and shake things around, but here's the nub: things might not be worse than they now are – and this leads us to another point.

Here's a proposal that few have thought about: *Palestine could declare itself an experimental hothouse, a prototype nation trying out new forms of staying alive.* This sounds fanciful, but Palestine is already in trouble, so this strategy might not be as bad as it looks. The people of Gaza, with little external support, are already experts in making do with extreme conditions and scant resources.

Such an experimental strategy would give Palestinians a national project and a cause to mobilise for survival and reconstruction. One experiment could even involve living without government – not a new thing, since Palestine had no proper government between 1967 and the mid-1990s. It stimulated a localised consensual system of social operation based on tribes, families and communities which worked quite well, under the circumstances. This proposition may sound ridiculous, even ruinous, but remember: we're already in a ridiculous, ruinous situation.

Here's a second proposal: *look at what strengths the nation has, and make use of them.* What are Palestine's strengths? Well, it is close to rock bottom and things can't get much worse. *That's a strength.* It gives the nation resilience at a time when many nations are shaky, themselves facing sovereign bankruptcy. Palestinians are accustomed to hardship and survival. I don't advocate hardship lightly, yet continuing with today's formula is a hardship too, wrecking and dividing Palestinian society.

What Palestine lacks is a national project. It seeks independence but it has no clear picture of what to do with it. It has no oil, no great locational advantages except its holy sites and few promising industries with which to prosper. Besides, the purpose of a nation isn't to buy cars and drive around in them, or to serve the designs of a rich elite – there's more to life than this. Palestine has a literate, active, brainy, growing population, and it has a body of unique national experience that many populations lack. Living without effective government and on a low budget has yielded a relatively strong society which, with or without nationhood, is asset-rich in 'the human factor'.

Half of the Palestinian population is spread worldwide in a diaspora. As Israelis have drawn on the Jewish diaspora, so can Palestine draw on its exiles. Diaspora Palestinians complain of a creeping sense of disconnection from their homeland, yet they hold a key. I don't mean financial remittances: I mean know-how, ideas and initiatives, connections and available hands. Palestine is, in a sense, a nation without borders, located everywhere that Palestinians live. If it fails to gain nationhood, its strong national identity endows it with a diaspora which gives it outreach and resources beyond that of many nations.

With or without nationhood, Palestine can engage its population in a nation-building project using hands, energy and brains – none of which it lacks. It can strive for agricultural autonomy, industrial self-sufficiency and community resilience. That is, mobilise Palestinians in land-improvement, sustainable reconstruction and social infrastructure-building for survival, developing mechanisms to meet its people's needs. Palestinians know how to get through enormous problems despite everything. Do you hear of mass-starvation and cholera in Gaza? No, life is tough, but they survive despite everything. The key is to mobilise what the nation *does* have. Many countries need the social resources Palestinians possess.

Pictures of Palestine

Palestine can thus engage its brains and available hands in building resilience, reducing dependence on outside help, capturing available energy and resources, bypassing Israeli obstructionism, reactivating the land and providing a new sense of direction for its people. This sounds idealistic until you remember that the rest of the world might also have to do similar things in coming years. Palestine could, in this context, run ahead of the game. This is a 'war effort' without the shooting, and Palestinians know how to do it.

A third proposal: *look to the genuine needs of the Palestinian people and of the land.* Don't emulate the wider world in the way that it ruins its societies and wrecks the land, all for the dubious privilege of sitting in traffic jams, consuming branded corporate products, creating enormous waste and letting some people grow fat while others pay them to do so. Do something different. Hamas has proposed elements of this, a new system based on the *umma*, the human community, though it could go further. The *umma* doesn't have to be religiously based – it can be based on an ethos of mutual human care, cooperation and whatever it takes to make that community work. Palestine needs to go beyond what Hamas proposes.

This is a fifty-year strategy, but the desecration of Palestine has been going on for sixty-plus years, so long term thinking is worth it.

We need to look at forestry, agriculture and replanting the soil to shade and nourish it, to conserve water, raise water tables and encourage rain, also feeding and employing people. This concerns capital pools, bartering systems, microfinance and community resource-sharing. It involves education for a new, peaceful world – Hope Flowers already treads this path and such knowledge does not need to be imported. Guns can turn into ploughshares and rubble into resources; townspeople and country folk can help each other. New community initiatives are needed and medical, agricultural and engineering practices can be redefined. Social mobilisation awakens the inherent power within a people, and Palestinians are closer to succeeding in this than many other peoples.

Pictures of Palestine

This is not about party politics: it concerns inventorising a people's survival capacity, its needs, its strong and weak points, its available resources. It rests on cooperation in the face of crisis. Palestine is surrounded by walls and checkpoints, throttled and squeezed, existing in a simmering crisis where things can easily get worse. The option lies between making a proactive choice or passively muddling through – and the latter has been the main option thus far. A nation finds solutions quicker if it seeks them willingly, if it determines its destiny, if it conducts a national effort to survive and prevail. If Palestine seeks independence, it needs to *adopt* and incorporate independence, utilising what it already has.

Yes, I'm an interfering foreigner offering easy-sounding solutions while not having to suffer the consequences. I might be oversimplifying things, but look at the core issues here. The aid that Palestine needs is not Euros and Dollars – Ibrahim's morphine. The true medicine is ideas, potentials, initiatives and the stuff of humanity, including mobilisation and effort. It involves raising the spirits of a people and setting about a national project – something that people *can do*, on the strength of what they *already have*.

This would make Palestine more immune to the pressures it has suffered. The economic embargo imposed from abroad in 2006 and 2007 was tantamount to a *coup d'état*, a foreign intervention causing untold hardship. Palestine was vulnerable to it because of its dependency on foreign aid. So perhaps we need to cut the loop.

If anyone has better ideas, go tell the PA – you'll find them in Ramallah and it's not a large town. Carrying on without a strategic change is not an option for much longer. Palestine's situation is dreadful, and things don't look good. The wider world is changing and it's time to explore some wild ideas. Palestine is already quarantined, already in trouble, and it doesn't have as much to lose as most countries. In 20-30 years it could be a world leader in taking its national life in its own hands. But this depends on making a big decision.

These ideas raise many questions and they have holes, but consider the options. If Palestine doesn't adopt a radical national project, only a few possibilities remain. One is more of the same. But the wider world is changing, and Palestine risks becoming a victim of such changes. One is a third *intifada*, possibly achieving little except suffering and loss. Another is UN intervention which, if Cambodia and Kosovo are anything to go by, would be unsatisfactory, ineffective and corrosive. Another is Israeli prevalence in the West Bank and continued quarantine for Gaza, dragging on for decades – but does even Israel really want this to go on indefinitely? Another is to wait for Israel to undermine its best interests and go into self-imposed crisis – but even then, Palestine needs a plan to work by. Palestinians might even find themselves rescuing Israelis from their own fate – a cruel irony.

The worst option is that nothing progresses except climate change and general deterioration. No, Palestine can do better than any of these.

42 Form-filling for Peace
grants and learning-difficulties

My fingers were getting a lot of exercise. I'd been working on a grant proposal with two ladies in California, communicating with them online, and now I had to cut down and improve the text – as a book-editor it's in my scope. The aim of the project was to spread Hope Flowers' experience in learning-difficulties education to other schools in Palestine and adjacent countries.

The plan involved running a teacher training course for teachers from Jordan and the Gulf States, setting up an online knowledge bank, compiling a training manual, organising a conference and setting up a resource website for the wider Arabic-speaking world. The manual would be translated into English for distribution worldwide, especially in conflict zones.

It was pioneering stuff and Hope Flowers had various strong points to back this application. With over 25 years of experience, its vision, principles and know-how were sound. As a refugee, Hussein Issa had set up the kind of school he himself had needed when he was young. His widow Hind, daughter Ghada and son Ibrahim had carried it through the hard times of the second *intifada*. The pressure of need, the sheer dedication of staff and the support of parents, grant-makers, volunteers, trustees and others meant that the school has developed remarkable methods – all on a minimal budget. The low budget bit is significant: a quarter century's progress had cost less than two attack helicopters, and arguably brought infinitely greater long term benefit.

Pictures of Palestine

Since government in Palestine was weak and ineffective in the 1980s and 1990s, the school experienced hardly any interference from the authorities as it evolved its methods. If you listen to teachers in the West, one of their great complaints is educational politicisation and the effect of schemes, directives and regulations cascading down from government, impeding the inherent gifts and hands-on knowledge of teachers, stunting their initiative and encouraging the departure of many talented professionals. Hope Flowers had been free of this and so it developed solutions aimed at creating real results, rather than pleasing school inspectors. The children and parents were the school's inspectors.

During the two *intifadas* the school had evolved effective methods for dealing with war-trauma. Then, after 2004, the mayhem in Bethlehem subsided and life returned to a form of normality (relatively speaking). The emphasis shifted toward handling learning difficulties arising in families suffering poverty and the damaging after-effects of conflict. Parents unconsciously passed on their own difficulties and stress to their kids.

Pictures of Palestine

So the school increasingly worked with children's families and the wider community, not just in trauma-recovery but also with family counselling and empowerment, helping them to restructure their lives, develop their livelihoods and deal with the daily facts of family life. Some Palestinian kids can be unruly, and understandably so, since they have few privileges or prospects and life is quite pressured and deprived. Families had experienced things no humans should.

Swimming pools, parks to play in, freedom to go to the beach? These hardly exist here. Kids are out on the streets – and there are loads of kids. This street life is also quite nice, providing children with a life-based education, helping them develop social and survival skills many Western kids nowadays lack. I remember seeing five boys playing in the street for hours with a pile of cardboard boxes – who needs costly toys? Children have a prominent place in Palestinian society and its large families give a sound social structure within which kids grow up. Older kids play a role in younger kids' lives too – and so do old people and relatives. Many family homes are gathered in gaggles, where branches of an extended family live alongside one another as a community of many people.

So Hope Flowers, through pressure of circumstance, has become a centre of excellence in working with the psycho-social effects of conflict. Psychological pain and agitation are major root-causes of conflict: children born around the first *intifada*, raised under curfew with tanks in the streets and fathers and uncles carted off to jail, were teenagers in the second *intifada* – at stone-throwing and mayhem-raising age. Nowadays they are parental age. Meanwhile, babies and toddlers of the second *intifada* are now teenagers. If this cycle is not stopped, another uprising is due as a new generation grows up and seeks a future.

Here I was, slogging through the grant application. We spent ages on it. We sought $118,000 from an American peace foundation, the outcome being that 300-500 teachers could be trained within one year. Thousands of children would thus be affected, and many more would benefit indirectly since, within a few years, learning-difficulties education would have been instituted throughout the Middle East.

Having started out in my peace-building career with Vietnam and Ulster forty years ago, it is the *causes* of conflict that matter to me, and this form-filling was the kind of work I felt right doing, in order to help fund the addressing of those causes. As the English language point-man for the school, I had two ambitions: to raise the school's international profile to make it better known and supported, and to do the necessary groundwork to secure consistent, ample financing so that the school could escape the constant, dreary worry of funding its survival.

This was no joke. The school was at the time heading for difficulties paying teachers' wages – and they were trying hard not to panic. They went from grant to grant and if an application was rejected or they didn't have time for the lengthy application procedures, or if Western funders' own funds dwindled – as they were doing – basic necessities like teachers' wages suffered. Also, many funders preferred to allocate budgets to more exciting things than wages. These teachers earned $250 per month, $350 in good times. To give a comparison, a British teacher earned about $1,500-4,000 per month and some British head teachers actually earned half of Hope Flowers' total annual turnover.

Fundraising was a constant burden. Donors' confidence risked being undermined by issues such as the demolition threat, still ongoing, since the school's work could be hampered if neighbouring houses fell under the bulldozer. And everything had to be explained, justified, detailed and costed. The added challenge was that wider events in Palestine and their effect on the school were unpredictable – an issue which again needed explaining to funding bodies, who could easily draw the conclusion that, if aims and outcomes didn't end up matching, funds must have been misappropriated.

43 Bedouin Holding Court
peace and justice on Manger Square

On Monday a guest turned up. This was refreshing; alone in my penthouse pad, I talked to myself more than was good for me. Sanha was twentyish and from Korea. An intelligent and pleasant character, she had been travelling in Tanzania, Europe and the Middle East. Israel was her last stop, and she had found herself crossing into Palestine and liking what she found. I shall always remember the graceful Korean bow she would give in the mornings or before bed, or whenever she wished to give thanks – and I would bow back, to her initial surprise. We need more of that in this world.

After taking her to see some remedial classes downstairs at the school, I took her into Bethlehem for a wander around the Old Town. People are interested in foreigners but a good many of them, especially children, stared at Sanha, transfixed – they don't usually see Asians close-up, since most come as Christian pilgrims in crowds, avoiding personal contact. Also, Palestine's isolation behind walls and security controls doesn't give its people much experience of foreigners. Sanha was not unused to being stared at and lots of people we talked to wanted to ask her questions.

I could see a quizzical look in some people's faces. "Who's he got with him this time?" I'd had a half-black Brit, an Indian and a variety of European women with me, and now here was a Korean! Be it noted, readers – especially those who labour under the illusion that visiting Palestine is dangerous – that a large proportion of visitors here are women, and they're probably safer in Palestine than in most other countries. The streets of the West Bank are generally safe for women to walk alone.

We wandered down to Adnan's near Manger Square to find a surprising event in progress. A circle of chairs was arranged outside his shop and occupying them was a collection of venerable Bedouin. It turned out that this was a clan court. There had been trouble in Adnan's clan: someone had got angry and slugged another clan member who slugged him back, and a feud had started. Violence

is unusual in Arabic society (this may surprise you) and it was a
serious matter. So the family heads put a stop to it immediately and
arranged this meeting.

Adnan's clan has 80,000 members in three countries once
united under the Ottomans – Palestine, Jordan and Saudi Arabia.
His father is a local headman. In instances like this, people may
choose between recourse to law or to traditional clan mechanisms.
The latter had been chosen in this case, not least because there is

a certain slow, expensive randomness to legal process. This is an age-old procedure where family heads get together, talk the matter through and reach a judgement. Much of it, interestingly, involved sitting silently.

There was a grave authority, solemnity and quietness to the group. Someone would come along, sit down with the three elders, discuss things, then leave, and there would be another thoughtful silence. Occasional words would be exchanged. Then someone else would arrive and the same would happen. The elders were taking evidence and opinions.

Numbers would grow and shrink and still the old gentlemen sat there, mint tea occasionally served from a family-run café just down the road. A car would stop, the driver would emerge, shake hands, exchange some words and drive away. This went on for some time. Clearly no hurry.

There was a tremendous feeling of occasion, mutuality, listening, respect and gravitas to the proceedings. I felt honoured to sit on the side of it. Adnan would buzz around making sure everyone was serviced, barking orders to his sons to go fetch things or sort something out. This was a human convocation of deep tradition yet tremendous functionality. It felt to me that, if ever I were in trouble, I might choose to accept the judgement of a court like this even if it went against me, since the degree of serious consideration of the issues was remarkable.

The clan is a survival mechanism binding Palestinians. Westerners have to resort to banks to borrow, to construction companies to build our houses, to strangers to give us a job, to law to resolve disputes, to childminders to care for our kids, to residential homes for our aged parents, and we generally have to struggle on alone through life to make our way. Palestinians have each other. Capital, expertise, second opinions, connections, manpower and wisdom are all available within the family. Duties and obligations, hassles and stresses are too, of course.

The Bedouin have a certain status and respect, an aura of specialness. They are a kind of humble aristocracy, highly regarded among Arabs because they live a life of relative simplicity, traditionally being desert nomads. The desert is the spiritual home of the Arabic people, and the Bedouin are its guardians – even though most are settled in houses now. Bedouin have a recognised neutrality and autonomy, and they are sometimes called on by Arabs to be adjudicators. Their Islam is rather different too – they have a magical aura, an instinctive connection with their roots and a noticeable intuitive side. If you're sensible, you don't mess with them.

Yet for Israelis, hooked into Western sedentary notions of property, registration, taxpaying and urbanity, the Bedouin stand at the bottom of the pile, and many of their villages and ranging grounds are unrecognised by the Israeli government. So they get booted around too.

I took my telephoto and wandered a respectful distance down the street, to see if I could inconspicuously take some photos of this scene. Then I became aware that I might have been noticed, for as soon as I levelled my camera, one of the younger men beckoned. *Oh dear, I hope I'm not offending anyone.*

"They want you to photograph them, brother, and please give brother Adnan the pictures." All of the old gentlemen looked at me intently. Inspired by Sanha, I bowed to them in an Asian way, and they graciously nodded back. I was thereby granted authority to record the event.

So I took pictures. This was a great honour and I gave them to Adnan a few days later on a disk. In my time I have been honoured to photograph many special subjects, from golden eagles, tall ships and Druid ceremonies to Tibetan Lamas, ancient beeches and moonbows, but this crowned the lot.

44 Moses on the Prowl
an interfaith encounter in Beit Jala

Shortly after the Bedouin clan gathering, I found myself at an interfaith encounter above Beit Jala at the Everest Hotel, which lies on the boundary between the Jewish and Muslim sides of this crazily divided land. The event was organised by an Israeli reconciliation group called Interfaith Encounter and it concerned Moses or, to Muslims, Abu Musa.

Moses was the chosen theme around which to air our respective ways of seeing things, on the basis that a conflict roots itself in *beliefs*, and faiths are the most deeply-rooted of beliefs. We were encouraged to speak out, unafraid, while also being mindful of the *way* we presented our truths, so as not to cloud the discussions with undue upsets.

Moses is a patriarch of the Jews and Christians and one of the prophets of Islam. He was one of history's notable leaders and lawgivers and a water dowser, magician and politician to boot. Jews trace their identity back to him since tradition has it he extracted them from Egypt, taking them through profound formative experiences and to the threshold of the Promised Land. Then his juniors, Joshua and his gang, decided to wrest the land from the Canaanites while Moses departed into the wilderness to end his days in Jordan, the Judean Desert or, Kashmiris say, in Kashmir.

We were fiftyish people, sitting in a circle. Most of the Muslims were in their thirties and forties while most Jews were in their fifties and sixties – all sincere and likeable people, the majority of whom had never met each other before. We each took our turn to speak, then we divided into groups to discuss things, reconvening later. Some contributors were relatively doctrinal, quoting the stated line on Moses from the *Torah* or the *Qur'an*, while others raised their own ideas.

One American Jew, who happened to live in the settlement of Efrat just over the wall from Hope Flowers, had a profound knowledge of Kabbalah, rattling off significances and numerological interpretations from the scriptures in an erudite and utterly unrememberable way.

I was surprised at two young Muslims who ran a plastics factory in Hebron, who looked like guys you'd meet downtown partying late into the night. They had remarkable knowledge of the scriptures – not just the *Qur'an* but the Jewish and Christian scriptures too. Then there was my garrulous friend Fareed, who did much of the Arabic-English translation, loving to talk at length and having very wide-ranging, free-thinking views. People took it all seriously, and the proceedings were interesting.

They were also having fun, this assemblage, and the dialogue session went well. Really, it was just an excuse to bring people together to bond with each other, forging personal links across the great divide, and in this it was successful.

Pictures of Palestine

While everyone was socialising in the evening, Ibrahim dropped by to see me. He was off early next morning to Tel Aviv to meet someone from the Belgian government, who had suddenly got cold feet about funding his planned radio station project. Ibrahim, as previously mentioned, had been accused of being an Israeli collaborator because he did bridge-building work between the two sides. Someone in the Palestinian hierarchy hadn't liked it and word got around. To satisfy his accusers and protect his family, Ibrahim had had to dissociate from organisations promoting contact between Arabs and Israelis. He had to erase many of his Jewish contacts too. This had been difficult, though expedient.

Hearing about this, the Belgians decided that Ibrahim was no longer a peacemaker, since peacemakers are supposed to work on both sides. According to this logic, he was now ineligible to receive funding. In case there was trouble getting through the Gilo checkpoint, he had to leave very early in the morning for the meeting in Tel Aviv, to persuade them otherwise.

Europeans, from our detached vantage point, can have very fixed conceptions of what peacework is all about. The Belgians probably didn't realise that Ibrahim had adopted this withdrawal strategy to save his life and to keep his family out of trouble. So now, he had to go to Tel Aviv to persuade the Belgians to stay on board. I wished him well and returned to the proceedings.

Everyone was having a fine time. My Hebron soul-sister Naima was there. She didn't contribute much because she isn't a heady sort, but she had a magnanimous matriarchal presence which soothed all stresses. She sat there beaming, silently presiding. There was a genial and interesting Jewish professor of anthropology from Tel Aviv with whom I connected well, plus a Muslim head teacher of a secondary school in Hebron who struck me as a solid type I could trust in an all-out crisis. They all seemed to rather like their British interloper.

Then came the tricky bit. All sorts of people invited me to visit them in the coming weeks, yet I was running out of time and still had mountains of work to do. It's not cool to turn down people's invitations, so I muttered pleasantries and left it at that. Right now I wasn't worried. I joined some of the Muslims smoking *shisha*, much to the interest of many of the Jews, some of whom, I suspected, wanted to join in. They possibly thought the water-pipe contained drugs, but Palestinians smoke only apple, cherry or herb-flavoured tobaccos, and they're most particular about avoiding intoxicants. Water pipes are a social, sharing thing.

Next day, the guest rabbi was late. He was to teach us the Jewish angle on Moses. We hung around waiting, so Yehuda, the convener, suggested we launch into discussions on Abu Musa and this we did. One interesting slip Muslims made during the discussions was to talk of the *Ten Commitments* which, to me, is a far richer term than Ten Commandments. This highlights a deep difference between Islamic and Judaeo-Christian thinking. Contrary to Western perceptions, Islam involves a lot of individual spiritual choice-making, partially because there isn't an authoritative priesthood to define things and partially because Islam involves a very personal act of faith and understanding of spirituality and scripture. So the notion of making a commitment rather than being commanded is rather neat, methinks.

Islam is seen by Muslims as a reformed faith, an upgrade of foregoing faiths, incorporating many elements from Judaism and Christianity. The five greatest Muslim prophets are Noah, Abraham, Moses, Jesus and Mohammed. Where I personally diverge from Islam is that I don't really see why the reforms stop with Mohammed. As a Sixties veteran, and having been part of a wave of spiritual reform in modern times, this mattered to me.

There were a few ruffles at various points. An English Christian, David, the retired doctor I'd met in Jerusalem a month earlier, volunteered that Palestinians were born to suffer. A charming gent, he wouldn't harm a fly, but some took his statement to be racist or condescending. He meant that, on some level, Palestinians had collectively chosen a path of suffering as a way to truth. I mentioned the Buddhist Sanskrit term *dukkha*, usually translated as 'suffering', which really means *predicamentality*, the experience of 'sitting between a rock and a hard place'. Buddha taught that

335

life is an experience of ongoing dilemmas and it hurts, but the hurt generates the urge to develop spiritually. This elicited a few nods of understanding and the matter moved on. Phew.

But the key issue here was that someone asked David, "Where did you get this from?" presuming that David knew something scriptural that the questioner didn't. David was nonplussed at this stage, being elderly and a bit absentminded, so I interjected, "It's David's observation, not scriptural". At this point there was agreement with David from about half of the Muslims, while the Jews stayed diplomatically quiet and other Muslims asserted that if it wasn't written in scripture, David had no authority to say it, and therefore he wasn't right.

Interestingly, all this brought out a divide not between Muslims, Jews or Christians but between autonomous thinkers, who practice what Muslims call *ijtihad* or independent thinking, and those who follow the guidance of scriptures and orthodox interpretations. The question came up again when, once the rabbi arrived, he talked about Moses meeting and talking with God in the burning bush. One Muslim asked, "How did Moses talk with God?" Rabbi Sylvester didn't really answer this, saying that only the prophets could talk with God, as if they had mysterious powers we do not, and such direct communication has not been done since their time.

Sorry, I don't quite agree. As one who has had plenty of profound revelations, 'downloads' and flashes, I believe revelation to be an ongoing process of immense value – as long as people aren't too dogmatic or naive about it. But I decided not to push this point because there was a lot of competition for airspace right then and it would be a delicate matter. If I'd talked about my own experiences it could sound as if I were making big claims, or it could be interpreted as blasphemy. So I dropped it. To handle potential heated situations, sometimes you have to concede a point even when you don't want to.

But the discussion spotlighted something important to me, something that drives me to mix with all these doctrinal God-freaks in the Middle East: I enjoy being stretched by people's perceptions and understandings and contributing to stretching theirs. I appreciate the interchange. While subscribing to a deeply personal sense of morality and conscience, I don't follow moral rules. One of my pet sayings is, 'There's no right or wrong, there are simply outcomes'. Question is, what outcomes do you want to live with? This can be interpreted as amoral yet, in my experience, it prompts a sense of continual moral self-examination which demands ongoing awareness and review – something that prescribed rules of morality do not.

Sadly, I missed the Islamic section of the conference that afternoon, in which an imam gave the Muslim rendering of the Moses story. Ibrahim rolled up at the hotel in Beit Jala bringing an expat Englishwoman, Marianne, with whom he was planning his radio station. She worked for a Swiss foundation promoting 'media for peace and human dignity'. Starting a radio station is a complex matter; it needs serious funding and delicate setup. Ibrahim and Marianne had just discovered at their meeting with the Belgians that they were competing for funds with an upmarket NGO proposing a public service TV station in Palestine.

We spent a long time talking. Marianne was open-minded, experienced in media matters and in running radio stations in Congo and Rwanda, but inexperienced with Palestine and its intricacies. So, over multiple cups of coffee, Ibrahim and I explained things and she took them in with interest. A former news reporter, she was inculcated with Western media slants on Palestine, riddled with misconceptions – that Hamas is just a terrorist group, that Western funding does only good for countries like Palestine, that democracy is the best form of governance, that cultivating 'moderate Muslims' is the best way to counteract 'extremists', or that Palestinians ought to disarm to gain peace. Well, it doesn't look like that from the inside, and the West badly needs to get some binoculars.

So I missed the concluding part of the conference. When Naima and Fareed came in to say goodbye, I felt I had missed something. I hope Moses didn't mind. One cannot do everything.

45 The Power and the Glory
*tension in Al Khader,
tranquillity in Mar Saba*

Late one afternoon, the power went off all over Al Khader. Apparently it wasn't the Israelis; probably crummy old transmission equipment. I spent the evening by candlelight, wore down my laptop battery and then read a book – Ariel Sharon's autobiography, as it happens, just to stretch myself. It was rather self-justificatory, considering the sheer number of people who have suffered and died because of him.

A consequence of the power cut was that the internet router downstairs wouldn't fire up when the power returned next day, so I didn't have internet access. I asked Ibrahim for the manual so I could fiddle with the settings. No manual. I would have to wait until he searched around at home, *if* he remembered. Or perhaps I should improvise and experiment. But I didn't have time. Oh, and I forgot, this was supposed to be my first day off for weeks.

This was *just typical*. Everything was complex, convoluted and time-consuming, and I was beginning to chase my tail. I needed to fulfil a promise to Amnesty International to photograph a few of the Israeli court orders threatening demolition of Palestinian houses, so I asked Ibrahim to explain to a neighbour what I needed and why.

I was invited down the hill, theoretically for twenty minutes. The guy didn't have his court order right then, and could I come back tomorrow evening? It would have been easier if he had simply referred me to a neighbour to look at theirs but, no, it had to be he who helped me, and I would have to wait. Then I was obliged to sit there for two hours drinking lemon juice and politely listening to another neighbour telling me (yet again) how hard life was for Palestinians. It's necessary to do the listening, because 'bearing witness' is important. If Palestinians feel *someone understands*, it really helps them.

His story went like this. "We don't care about talking and peace processes any more. I am forty and time runs away. My children might never see better times. I have seen no improvement in my lifetime. The Israelis, they threaten to come, to knock down my dream: I saved for my house and built it with my own hands, and they say they will knock it down. What will my children think? Why should they believe in peace if they see our home being destroyed in one hour by a bulldozer? Why should they listen to this talk of peace?"

I bore witness to his anguish. But it was supposed to be my day off and I genuinely needed a break. I escaped, managing to get an hour lying on the flat roof of the school, soaking up the sun and reading. Then back to work.

I was rapidly losing my cool. It was that grant application: our American partners needed it done by the following day, since they had other things happening and, as they were volunteers, we couldn't really insist that they wait for us. I had laboured hard through the figures, text and guidelines, but I was stressed out and couldn't concentrate. I was progressing too slowly. I worked on but, by late afternoon, the power went off again. I won't repeat the unholy expletives I uttered. The current revision of the application was not even half done. I gave up. Then Ibrahim rang, inviting me out. Now that's a good idea – let's get outa here.

Ibrahim took Marianne and me to Mar Saba. Through Bethlehem and down through Beit Sahour we drove, out into the country, through Al Haddadiya, Al Hujeila and Dar Salah. Then we turned off onto a winding road into the desert. Up and down switchbacks we went, through an empty landscape with high hills and deep wadis, distant hilltop villages, striated rock formations, caves and dramatic views. On and on through the dusky desert we went until, at the end of the road, we reached the Greek Orthodox monastery of Mar Saba.

It was *so quiet*. Dead still. The silence amongst the rocky desert mountains was deafening. Something in me opened out and released a deep sigh of relief. I shed a few tears. In the West Bank, one gets too accustomed to being in a densely-populated, hyperactive built-up area, hemmed in by security walls with the spare space filled with Israeli settlements. But here there was real space, an almost booming tranquillity.

Dug into the side of the mountain was the Byzantine monastery, with its domes, thick stone walls, its small, deep windows and an air of timeless silence and solidity. On the other side of the deep-sunk gorge, over which the monastery perched, was a steep cliff with caves once occupied by early Christian hermits in the centuries following Jesus' time. It reeked of history, stark desert beauty and the soul-presences of ancient saints long departed.

Down below in the canyon was a rushing river. Its size surprised me, this being a desert landscape, and I commented on it to Ibrahim. In a matter of fact voice he said, "Oh, that's not natural.

Pictures of Palestine

That's the waste water that comes from Ma'ale Adumim" – one of the largest Israeli settlements, northeast of here. It has 33,000 inhabitants, and it was started in 1975. Eighty-six percent of its land was once privately owned Palestinian land, and it had been home to the Jahalin Bedouin. Now it's a modern commuter settlement, a West Bank suburb of Jerusalem.

This is the town's effluent, rushing downriver past this 1,600 year old monastery – and the river empties into the Dead Sea. From the Dead Sea there is no way out since it is the lowest point on Earth, so the effluent presumably concentrates there. If you buy 'healthy' Dead Sea mineral products – soaps and skin conditioners – they have extra added flavour from Ma'ale Adumim. This country has atrocious environmental standards.

While at Mar Saba, soaking up the voidsome tranquillity, I reflected on the crush of tasks I had before me and the tense state I had got myself into. I offered up a prayer for a solution and breathed in the warm evening air, consciously letting go of my tensions. As I sat there quietly on a rock, within twenty minutes a solution suddenly came up, out of the blue – it all spontaneously slotted into place.

The top priority was to get the grant application right, to do the best possible job with it. We needed that money: the training course *just had to happen*. It was more important to get this application *dead right* than to beat ourselves up trying to keep to a tight schedule – we actually had a month before it should be submitted. I'd have to clear this with the American ladies we were working with – except the internet was down. But somehow I knew it would work out – it had to. This relaxation of urgency meant that I could have a day off on the next day, to clear my head. That was the most important thing right now. Ah, relief!

That was the gift I received at Mar Saba. Sounds simple, but when you get locked into stress, clarity gets lost and solutions distance themselves as fast as you reach for them. In gratitude, I put my forehead to the ground in prayer, shed a few more tears and gave thanks to the spirits of the saints in this eerily quiet place.

Pictures of Palestine

We drove back through the advancing darkness and, when I got back to the school, the power was still off. Next day I was still trying to fire up the internet router, without success. So I could not talk with our Californian friends to explain the revised plan.

One needs a lot of patience in Palestine. Things just don't work as expected. Partly this is a side-effect of the occupation, partly it reflects the fact that reality just doesn't bend to suit Westerners and our urgencies – reality does its own thing. Yet magic happens in other ways. When the power went off, another power took its place: a power of truth and reality.

When eventually I contacted the Americans, the delay was perfectly alright. I was learning so much from being here.

46 Trauma Recovery
children of the intifada

Khaled forgot. I had rung him for a taxi and, there I was, roasting in the sun, waiting. He's a lovely chap, useful to know – he'll fix things, find things and rescue you if you need it. Once, he visited England after falling in love with an Englishwoman from the thoroughly provincial small town of Minehead. But he failed in his hopes of a future with her and a residence permit to go with it, returning in due course to Palestine. He talked fondly of the consolation prize he gained from all this, seeing Manchester United. Some Palestinian men look on Trafford Park, the team's home ground, as devout Christians look on the Church of the Nativity. Visiting it was one of the memorable achievements of Khaled's life. But that day he forgot to pick me up.

It's something you have to get used to, part of the psychology of a nation which has had its life completely, repeatedly ruined. Plans evaporate and an organised sense of order in life becomes a distant fantasy – something they do in places like England or Germany. I myself had been developing a crisis with this mindset – my patience, perseverance and perspective had eroded away. Some plans were scrapped, some were indefinitely postponed, other unforeseens landed on my plate, things went wrong, some things couldn't be done until another was done first, which itself was dependent on something else... and, before long, I was stymied, tense and wondering what to do. Then the power went off again, and the internet too. That had finished me off.

Pictures of Palestine

My psyche had been jammed, clogged and knotted. Even when meditating, my brains boomed and a mosquito irritated me. I was in a mess. I had lost track of what I had been thinking, exploded as it was in a paroxysm of tangled dilemmas. I had landed up in a heap on the floor, with a few ants examining my suitability as dinner. Well, metaphorically, at least.

Then came the visit to Mar Saba. There I gave myself permission to relax and take a day off and, the day after resting, I looked at the logjam of outstanding issues, shrugged my shoulders and got on with the first thing that came up. I had finally joined the Palestinian mindset. I still felt lost but more pleasantly so than before, having accepted my lot.

So there was I, standing by the Hebron road, late for my appointment to meet Fatima and her husband Mohammed. I had rung her to say I was running late, but now I was *very* late. There weren't any service taxis – Ramadan, a month-long religious go-slow, was starting.

The phone rang. Fatima. "Where are you, Balden?"

"Still on the Hebron Road at Al Khader, Fatima."

"We come and pick up you. You wait there." The phone went dead.

Then it rang again. This time it was Khaled, apologetic – no, mortified – over having forgotten me. Obviously he'd been hit with a case of absent-mindedness, which people can get while they're fasting from dawn till dusk for Ramadan. I assured him it was okay, that things were sorting themselves out. He was anxious that I might think badly of him. Poor man, shame is such a strong force in the Palestinian psyche. Eventually he rang off.

Then a taxi stopped, peeping its horn, the driver bearing that look of anticipatory expectancy: he wanted my business and, as a rich Westerner, I was honour-bound to give it. *No thanks, I'm okay.* As they do, he looked bewildered – why should this foreigner want to stand by the side of the road? His English didn't stretch to understanding my explanation. He saw my demonstrative hand-signals and drove off shrugging, just then seeing an old wreck of a car drive up with a smiling couple in it, both calling to me. It was Mohammed and Fatima.

As I got in, I was half-expecting them to take me to Deheisheh where they lived but, no, they had other ideas. I had been looking forward to visiting Deheisheh, but I needed an insider to accompany me because in places like that it's not cool to barge in on people's world with a big camera. Some people there don't want the Israelis or the PA to see photos of them. So I needed an insider's company and Fatima had offered it, or so I had thought. But no, they were taking me on a tour of Bethlehem instead. They figured that, as a photographer, I should get some good shots, but not in Deheisheh. Alright, change of plan. Off we went – first stop Irtas.

Irtas is just down the valley, an old monastery village spread across the side of a valley filled with market gardens. It's a calm, benign village, presided over by the monastery and a big statue of the Virgin and Child. Ironically, the mosque dominated the proceedings as we arrived: the calling to prayers boomed out across the valley, joined later by the contrapuntal disharmonics of another mosque further down the valley, calling its own flock.

I wandered around capturing shots while Fatima and Mohammed loitered in the shade of a tree, trying not to look like conspicuous Muslims trespassing on Christian ground – the monks and nuns here are respected and slightly feared. It's a lovely place, a haven of homely tranquillity. Except for one thing: up the valley on the hill looms part of the Israeli settlement of Efrat, glowering over Irtas to remind its inhabitants who's boss around here. Such are the stark contrasts of this land. After a while we were off to another part of the village, to a memorial to Yasser Arafat.

"What does it say, Fatima?"

"It says he was killed by the Israelis, that he's a martyr of the Palestinian people."

She wanted me to note this: she's one of those who believe that Arafat was poisoned. Just recently one of the top people in Fateh had thrown a fit, accusing Abu Mazen and some PA men of getting

rid of Arafat on behalf of the Israelis, and more than a few Palestinians agreed. Whether or not that was true, it's certainly the case that Arafat was worn out and in ill-health by the end of his life. His long years of fighting, exile, wrangling, hardship, threats to his life and, at the end, confinement in his Ramallah HQ during the *intifada*... all these factors killed him. We might never find out whether or not he was poisoned – Muslims bury their dead too quickly for autopsies. But his death marked the end of an era, and the Israelis definitely gained from it. The great heroic champion of the Palestinian cause had gone to Allah.

Instead, the Israelis had the sedate Abu Mazen to deal with, a gentleman more willing than Arafat to compromise and bend. Some Palestinians were quietly relieved because they still believed that, if only they continued playing the negotiation game, something would be gained. It took a few more years to find out this was not to be the case.

Arafat knew Zionism well. He started his life as a fighter aiming to eliminate Israel, and he understood the mentality of elimination that Zionists themselves suffer. Arafat stalwartly stood up against Zionism, but toward the end of his life he grew tired, wanting to achieve a semblance of his dream of a revived Palestine, even if much diminished from the one he first dreamt of.

So in the 1990s he chose to trust the Israelis and the Oslo process by making deals, accepting a modest prospective Palestinian state and hoping for improvements later on. The state didn't happen and no improvements came. Thus the second *intifada* in 2000. The Israelis used the Madrid conference and the Oslo process of the 1990s as cover, continuing to build facts on the ground – West Bank settlements, settler by-pass roads, checkpoints, controls and 680km of planned separation walls. When international bodies passed judgement on the legality or wisdom of this, Israelis simply accused them of anti-Israeli bias and carried on.

Fatima and Mohammed wanted to show me this by bringing me to Arafat's memorial. As twentysomethings, they had been teenagers in the second *intifada* and toddlers in the first, growing up when hopes were rising, only to see them dashed. They were not angry, just resigned and factual. The Palestinians had lost, and that was that.

They put great energy into their jobs – he a medical engineer and she an occupational therapist at Hope Flowers. They both kept a bright countenance but I knew they privately wondered whether anything would change or whether it might be better to move abroad. They wanted to stay here, have children, get a house, but perhaps it was still worth cultivating foreign friends like me, just in case.

Next they took me to a high-point at the Palestine University, perched atop a hill overlooking Deheisheh and Duha. Ibrahim once told me, slightly scathingly, that this private university was for the richer beneficiaries of the Palestinian dispensation – students with money but neither the brains nor the qualifications to go to Bethlehem or Bir Zeit, Palestine's top universities. Whatever is the case, Palestine University is superbly located on its hill, and my hosts got me past the guards to take photos. You could see a princely panorama with the ancient Herodeon to the south, Bethlehem and Jerusalem to the east and Beit Jala to the north.

Then we visited a vantage point overlooking Deheisheh refugee camp, a higgledy-piggledy area of buildings clinging to the hillside, where everyone is relatively poor and knows everyone else. It's an urban village where the disadvantaged, with few prospects, no capital and reduced rights, can live. Many are refugees or their descendants, but others simply lack money or resources. UNRWA provides social services to the area, its Bethlehem HQ adjoining the camp. What's notable though is that Deheisheh is remarkably well cared for by its inhabitants – it is tidier and more organised than many other parts of Bethlehem.

The issue here is a mindset, a psychological state. Ibrahim Issa grew up in Deheisheh, and his father Hussein grew up in a tent here in the 1950s, when it genuinely was a camp. But they escaped that mindset and, comprehending it, created a school where the mindset could be transformed in others – a majority of the kids being descended from refugees. This transformation involves healing the emotional and mental damage that is brought about by violence, injustice, horror and hardship. The damage becomes a psychological loop, passed down the generations and interlocking with social disadvantage to become an all-pervasive syndrome from which escape requires supreme effort.

Fatima said that Deheisheh is a friendly, neighbourly community. When they were married a year earlier and she moved into the area, everyone knew who she was before she knew who they were. She spoke with pride and affection for the place, but she and Mohammed didn't want to be seen with a Westerner looking like a journalist, to be seen to be *different*, well-connected, for they relied as a young couple on the people of Deheisheh and their neighbourly solidarity.

After Deheisheh they took me to the Church of the Nativity. There was something touching and significant about two Muslims taking me to this Christian shrine. Nevertheless, though it is historic and holy, the atmosphere there smelt somewhat of 'moneychangers in the temple', its sanctity drowned out by flashing tourist cameras. Today it was crawling with Italian visitors, happily snapping on their digitals as if God was busy elsewhere and it hardly mattered. I loitered in a corner, futilely trying to imbibe a sense of the holiness of the place.

But then came the real purpose of our visit: my hosts showed me where forty fighters had died during the *intifada* in 2002, having taken refuge in the church. The Israelis laid siege and placed snipers on the roof, picking off Palestinians one by one until starvation and destitution plus international intervention led to a negotiated end to the ordeal. This was an act of heroism and resistance that many Palestinians see as a critical point in their recent history, a final dramatic act of resistance before giving up the fighting.

We then went down to Beit Sahour, the quaint centre of which is Christian and, this being Sunday, closed and quiet. The shops were shuttered and the streets empty except for cats, who seemed to have deduced the advantages of staging feline tactical operations on holy days. Beit Sahour is where the shepherds watched their flocks by night, as the legend goes.

We drove up to Beit Jala, then off on a side-road and around the hill behind the town to the grounds of the Cremisan monastery, famous for its wines. The pinewoods and greenery here were lovely. But our destination was further along the hill – a vista overlooking Jerusalem and, on the neighbouring hill, the glaringly modern Israeli hilltop settlement of Gilo. Mohammed showed me the empty, tree-clad land below us, where Palestinians without passes can smuggle themselves into Israel, dodging IDF soldiers. The security wall had not yet been built here so, with some nifty footwork, it was still possible to get into Jerusalem illegally, bypassing the checkpoints.

Close by, an old Bedouin was sitting on a rock. He was quiet and still. Watching him for a while, I realised from the way he was sitting that he sat there a lot, presumably waiting for someone to come up the hill, smuggling themselves back out of Jerusalem. I longed to photograph him but something in me didn't want to steal his space and secrecy, so I refrained. This old man had seen the long saga of the conflict unfold throughout his life, and now he was reduced to sitting patiently, waiting, perhaps for a son or relative. There are significant numbers of wanted men in Palestine – wanted by the Israelis, Hamas, Fateh or disparate factions. When you meet them, they're friendly until you ask a personal question or wish to take a photograph, and then they look stern, say No and start disappearing, fast.

Finally Fatima and Mohammed took me to a high point above Beit Jala where, on a clear day, you can see the Dead Sea valley eastwards and the Mediterranean westwards. It wasn't clear that day. This place is significant to Palestinians because they are penned up, with zero chance of visiting the Mediterranean or the Red Sea and only a slightly better chance of relaxing by the Dead Sea. My friends showed me a panorama of their land, a land that isn't theirs, where they are indigenous yet treated almost as aliens.

They were bright and optimistic, yet there was a resigned helplessness in them too. In the car, I interviewed them for a podcast. On some questions they shrugged their shoulders: they didn't know what would happen next, what the future would bring. They both did the best they could with each day. They talked of having children and progressing in life; Fatima had a dream of opening a school for disabled children. I wondered what lay ahead for them.

This is what happens to the psyche of a Palestinian: attending to whatever comes next, you hope that the rest will work out. You go forward more with faith than with realism, because realism gets you down. You stay as happy as you can, hoping things will get no worse. Someone expressed the downside of this to me: *it's not a matter of good days and bad days, but bad days and worse days.* So staying happy is a survival strategy for dealing with perpetual uncertainty and adversity. Yet strangely, Palestine is an uncannily happy place. This is a perverse crisis-managing happiness, an insecure, volatile cheerfulness that can plummet or turn ugly if Israeli soldiers appear over the hill.

This psychology also means that you drop having ambitions, you cease cleaving to an aspiration of hope. Yet Palestine is a well-behaved place with near-zero crime, good behaviour and friendliness in the streets, so this firefighting mentality has its virtues.

But nevertheless, Khaled, bless him, had forgotten to pick me up – a classic example of this syndrome. Forty-five minutes had elapsed between my call to him and the arranged pickup, several things had happened in the meantime and it had slipped his mind. But it all worked out well anyway, as it does, if you let it: Mohammed and Fatima showed me their world, giving me a glimpse of life through their eyes, and I was deeply grateful to them for that. I just wished I could magic them up a new car.

47 **Harvesting Organs**
the international community strikes again

I t could be true. The allegations made in the Swedish newspaper *Aftonbladet* in late August 2009, rigorously denied by the Israeli government, had a ring of truth, though such reports would no doubt be fought all the way. A truth-deficiency is not unique to Israelis but Israel still has a big reputation for half-truth, untruth and denial.

The Israel-Palestine conflict is a microcosmic reflection of the state of the world, a concentrated dose of what's happening all over, as though the world has unconsciously dumped its garbage here. Or the inhabitants of this place have unconsciously taken on a larger than normal load of the world's reservoir of gunk, guilt, fear, shame and horror. This is how we do it nowadays, in our remote-controlled, imaginalised, media-pervaded world: instead of doing wrong and carrying the responsibility ourselves, we devolve and outsource crimes and wrongs to others to do on our behalf – and we're hardly aware of it happening.

The *Aftonbladet* report revealed that transplant organs had been harvested from young Palestinians who had met their death in clashes with Israeli troops in the 1990s. It implied that this had been official Israeli policy. Unlikely, surely – but nonetheless somebody found a gruesome way of profiting from conflict. Organs harvested by the KLA in Kosovo in the 1990s happened to find a market in Israel too. Things like this happen in hardened cultures such as the Israeli army, which habitually turns a blind eye to atrocities it is implicated in. For Israelis, turning a blind eye is a survival mechanism. Don't look and you won't see it, don't see it and it's not there.

We humans get terribly accustomed to crimes and atrocities recounted daily on the news. Once something bad is done, a precedent is established so that doing it a second time becomes a bit easier, so if we can get away with it, we do it again. The long term costs come later – and perhaps it doesn't matter. We *all* do it. We buy coffee without considering the true costs it might levy on the world – it's *only* coffee and I'm *only* one person, so what difference does it make? But a billion people buying coffee makes a planetary problem.

We also give implicit permission for things to happen by simply *allowing* them to happen. In the Israel-Palestine conflict, the world periodically registers its disapproval of house-demolitions, bombardments, atrocities and injustices, yet little more is done and so it is *permitted*. It is legalised by dint of the fact that we didn't actually stop it.

Many Israelis simply haven't seen themselves as committing atrocities against their fellow humans. They started out in the 1940s seeking to establish a nation for themselves against the backdrop of incredible atrocities levelled against them in Europe and now Israeli society and authorities work hard to shield people from seeing what their country is doing. They believe they're defending themselves against cruel, heartless Arab terrorists, out to get them and kill their children, yet the danger is strategically exaggerated.

When these 'terrorists' are dehumanised, it's okay to kill them and violate other people in the process. In actuality, people identified as terrorists are often the vulnerable, feelingful sons and daughters of caring mothers and fathers, frequently just standing in the wrong place at the wrong time. Or perhaps they're young people confused about life and the standards we should live by. Or perhaps they're pushing an agenda and fighting for a cause they genuinely see to be legitimate – or a mixture of all of these. So there they are, thirteen years old, throwing stones and rocks at Israeli soldiers who are taking the land of their grandparents and then they get arrested.

Pictures of Palestine

Young Israeli soldiers see a teenage Palestinian under arrest, blindfolded and handcuffed, and naturally they believe he has done something wrong – otherwise he wouldn't have been arrested. So they kick, punch and make fun of him and are given implicit consent to do so not only by their officers, whose hearts have been hardened by years of this stuff, but also by the cultural rationale with which they have been brought up. Anything Israel does is right, and everyone else is wrong – this is the mentality of Zionism.

Thus, another atrocity noted in the news at that time, of soldiers mistreating Palestinian teenagers – raiding their houses, seizing them in the middle of the night, binding them, throwing them in jail and hitting, kicking and mistreating them – becomes normalised, excused. The more these young Arabs cry and scream, the more they must be learning a lesson, so the soldiers kick them some more. That particular news item was provoked by ex-IDF soldiers speaking out after completing their national service. But they, of course, were called deranged cowards, traitors, self-hating Jews, thereby themselves being dehumanised. Clearly they were fabricating such allegations. Except that they weren't.

Take this one step further. A 'bad apple' in the IDF knows that someone will pay serious money for transplant organs. Doctors don't question how organs got there as long as they function – they're medical organs, items for use – so this bad apple gets a few conscripted medical students on his side and they start a discreet, profitable business selling organs. They are protected by army routines, whereby a dead body is returned to its Arab parents with some excuse and the distressed Palestinian parents, glad to retrieve the body, bury it as fast as possible, as is the Muslim custom. So no one finds out and there is no autopsy or investigation – and even if they do find out, it is deniable and vehemently denied.

This is another habit that Israelis – and all of us – have fallen into. If you deny and cover up something strongly and artfully enough, you can get away with it, even sincerely believing the untruths yourself. You can even turn the argument around and make the accuser look bad; thus, the Swedish newspaper reporters were clearly

anti-Semitic. Avigdor Lieberman, the Israeli foreign minister of
the time, even dragged up the Swedish record from WW2, seventy
years earlier, when the Swedes turned away many, but not all, Jews
who sought refuge in Sweden from Hitler. He gave it as
evidence of Swedish anti-Semitism. He's from Lithuania,
a neighbouring country to Sweden and formerly part of
USSR, and some older Lithuanians resented Sweden's
success as an independent, neutral country. So the
accusation was bounced back – Swedes are anti-
Semitic – and a dishonesty was reinforced. The Israelis
implied that the accusations of organ-harvesting
clearly could not be true because the Swedes clearly
had an anti-Israeli agenda. In other words, it's okay for
soldiers to harvest organs from prisoners and 'enemy
dead', and we'll protect them if they do. This wasn't
stated, but such a conclusion was nevertheless implied.

So such a crime is permitted to continue, and the world shiftily accepts it. Why? Because the world as a whole is complicit. After all, USA has given more than $43bn to Israel since 1993, and it doesn't want to be seen to have bet on a bad cookie. Germany has paid billions of Deutschmarks and Euros in Holocaust reparation, and doesn't want to be seen to be anti-Semitic. Britain has exported armaments to India, which re-exports them to Israel to be used against the people of Gaza – so let's just forget it and hope nobody makes a fuss. If someone does make a fuss, we'll simply have to deal with them – it's just a PR issue.

The world is stacked up like this. An enormous truth-and-reality process is needed to unravel this vast, intricate, global web of untruths, deceits and indifference built up over decades and centuries. To cover its complicity, society likes to single out and blame perpetrators, as bankers were blamed for the 2008 banking crisis. But while bankers were crucially responsible, the public permitted the situation to develop and bought into it – so they were responsible too. Similarly, it's *Israeli soldiers* doing this, not me. *They* should answer for what they have done, there ought to be an independent enquiry.

So the Israelis staged an enquiry that took nine months to report, by which time most people had forgotten about it, apart from a few human-rights campaigners who, let's face it, will make a big fuss about *anything*, won't they? The report raps one or two people over the knuckles and says that, really, most of it was empty allegations. The world's media duly reported this, and there it was, sewn up. If anyone makes a fuss, well, they're just extremists or soft-hearted liberals.

So, we read of the atrocity, we suitably disapproved and the matter was dealt with. Or something else diverted our attention, so we forgot and the matter was buried. If Israel refused to mete out justice, or if the culprit was court-martialled but quietly released a few months later, well, there's nothing much we could do – that was Israel's internal affair. Information overload and the perpetual rush of news reinforces this process of public and institutional indifference.

The matter would pass. After all, people had made their money – the criminals from selling organs, the medical establishment from saving lives and the media people from reporting such sensational news. Everyone's point had been proven – that Israelis are bad guys (while *we* of course are good) or, to Israelis, that the world unfairly stands against them. So everybody felt justified in taking the positions taken.

Except for one thing: months later, evidence quietly surfaced that this crime of organ-extraction actually did take place. Few noticed. But even if it hadn't taken place, the furore had shifted the lines of moral acceptability one more centimetre in favour of indifference and they got away with it. Even if organ theft is stopped, the next time a similar atrocity comes along, the world will be a tad less interested, so they'll get away with that too. We're all too busy, really, to do anything much – so, if a Palestinian house is demolished or another IDF soldier makes a confession, well, with regret, I haven't got time.

This is how things go. But there's a problem – or a glimmer of light, depending on your viewpoint – because this house of cards, this mountain of interwoven lies, is unsound. A big truth-process is building up pressure in our time. It might not happen as a result of human conscience, enquiry or truth-seeking, since we're all so very embedded in the mountain of untruth to dig ourselves out and the media, managing our thoughts and beliefs, are very sophisticated. But somehow it will leak out anyway.

What's the glimmer of light? Well, *reality prevails*. Revelatory events happen whether or not we like it and elaborately dishonest constructions are never earthquake-proof. Something is unravelling, and there will come a critical point where the whole tangled tapestry starts coming apart – no longer limited to bad dictators, horrible bankers or corrupt politicians, but implicating all of us, for the part we have played in it.

The claim that Israeli soldiers were harvesting organs from their victims just scratched the surface. There's more underneath. The whole Israel-Palestine conflict, which should have ended ages ago, is riddled with it. But we must be careful not just to heap opprobrium on Israelis. They do what we *all* do, each in our way, to greater or lesser degrees. It's just that it seems to be more intense here.

Pictures of Palestine

This is a veritable Holy Land, where frontline human issues get stuck in front of our faces. In the modern context, that's *holy* – it's revelatory, apocalyptic. It's a cruel world, and the cruelties here are more blatant and exaggerated than in many places – though there's fierce competition for the brutality top-spot in a variety of countries, or even concealed in hidden recesses just down the road from you and me.

Palestinians aren't perfect. They've gone off violence, but they are a damaged people who have experienced more than their fair share of human cruelty, so they're both sensitised and hardened. When they blithely chuck a chocolate wrapper on the land, saying that they have more pressing problems to worry about than litter, they too demonstrate a disregard that we humans have made a habit of. They too are storing up a problem that, while not as bloody as their conflict with the Israelis, is nevertheless just as big.

We're *criminals*, we humans. I might be a tree-hugging, effeminate, idealistic fuss-maker who ought to get real, but I'm also one of those who lifts the carpet and looks underneath. What's there is an enormous, festering, fermenting mass of gloop, waiting to erupt. This is why my view about the extracted organs headlines seems a bit scathing. For if you think *that's* a big outrage, just wait – *there's more*!

The *Aftonbladet* allegations struck a raw nerve. We know that this stuff does happen, so why all the fuss? Why don't we just land troops in Israel to stop this carnage? Because we're all a little bit afraid of what might happen if we lift the lid, setting in motion an explosive truth process. We could be exposed ourselves, we'd have to take risks, we might not survive. So, it's better that it happens *over there* in Israel and Palestine, out of harm's way.

Perhaps this is why conflict-zones are often called 'theatres of war', places where humanity's horrors are acted out under media spotlights so that we can watch from a distance. This is why I invite you to take some risks in your life and come and bear witness in a place like Palestine. It sorts out something in your heart and mind – and that can only be good.

48 Proportionality
soft power and foreign relations

Can Israel learn to practice a little humility? What's going on at a deeper level? These were the questions I reflected on in the aftermath of that spat of venom between Israel and Sweden over the Swedish newspaper allegations of the Israeli army trading in transplant organs extracted from dead Palestinians. It's one issue of many that came and went, but they keep on coming, and they all add up.

Israel needs Sweden more than Sweden needs Israel. Closing IKEA in Israel, as PM Netanyahu boldly threatened after the organ harvesting affair, would cause IKEA to rise in the esteem of millions of consumers worldwide – another own-goal for Israel. Israel is a small country, and its people pay a price for this bluster.

Clearly the Swedish tabloid newspaper struck a nerve, yet in Israel, at the time, there was little discussion of the allegations themselves and whether they actually needed investigation. The reaction was largely affront at the very expression of the allegations. Heinous and offensive accusations were thrown back at Sweden by Netanyahu and Lieberman, the foreign minister, who behaved like snarling dogs.

This resentful reaction exposed Israel: if it reacts this way, it *must* have something to hide – this is a conclusion many people will quietly form. By levelling 'anti-Semitism' at Sweden it also weakens the notion of anti-Semitism itself, abusing it. Israel cries 'wolf', but Sweden is no wolf, it's a husky-dog – reliable, perceptive, sniffing around, susceptible at worst to digging occasional holes in the snow.

Pictures of Palestine

The claim of unfair treatment does not remove the possibility that there was organ-harvesting. Israel loses not only fairweather friends over matters like this – as it did with Turkey when it killed nine Turks during its assault of the Gaza-bound Freedom Flotilla in 2010. It also embarrasses staunch allies such as the Americans. After Abu Ghraib and Guantanamo, Americans would think, well, if these things happen for America, they can happen for Israel, so why doesn't it own up?

Eruptions like this really need to calm down before they cause too much damage and if truths are to be spoken, they shouldn't come in the form of accusations followed by angry responses. This betrays something deeper on both sides, a clash of two countries with contrasting ethics and views: Sweden, twice a warrior nation in the Viking period and the 1600s, has pacified itself, while Israel, in history a victim nation, pushes its weight around. In eyeballing each other they each see a mirror image of themselves.

Each country feels confident in its rightness: Sweden feels quietly right and Israel assertively right. Sweden sees itself as a haven of justice and reason, and Israel sees itself as an embodiment of revived Jewish destiny. Neither can quite own

up to the other side of things, so they accidentally locked horns. Unconscious issues play a big role in geopolitics: perhaps Sweden needs to be more pushy, and perhaps Israel needs to be more pacific.

From the Swedish viewpoint it is of course correct that such a matter as organ harvesting needs investigation; this conforms with Swedes' sense of justice and systematic application of law and principle. From an Israeli viewpoint, whatever the veracity of the claim, the Swedes must be rapped on the knuckles for daring to snoop into another country's affairs. Both nations have contrasting complexes which clashed.

And yet, there's a problem. As mentioned before, Israel needs Sweden more than Sweden needs Israel and there will be more people worldwide cheering for Sweden than for Israel, in this instance, thanks to stored-up feelings about Israel's actions in recent decades. So Israel risks an avalanche of ill-feeling against it unless its bombast is tempered.

Some basic issues have also been confused with bigger issues. In Europe, a picture had been building up of a barbaric and insensitive Israel, especially after the Gaza bombardment of 2008-09, and the organ-harvesting allegation fitted that one nicely. Then some Israelis had residual feelings about what happened in Europe 60-80 years ago: the Swedish saga in WW2 is something Swedes feel shame about – they turned away Jews seeking refuge, to avoid incurring trouble with Hitler. Yet one of Sweden's national heroes from WW2, Raoul Wallenberg, was a famous Jew-rescuer in Hungary whom Swedes see as a national hero. So a lot of conflicting stuff was stirred up.

As great ruminators, Swedes respond to events with the haste of a lumbering old elk. They might have their prejudices, but they're one of this world's less troublesome peoples. It's an open question whether Israelis will examine what has been thrown at them from the Nordic direction. To bluster back rather than acknowledge errors might cover one's tracks in the short term, but people get wise to it.

Pictures of Palestine

Israel's doggedness served it well during its early struggle for survival up to the 1967 Six Day War, but it then failed to notice that things were beginning to change. Time has moved on, and people worldwide, including 400 million Arabs, now see things differently. They see Israel as an oppressor, not a victim. In such a climate, it is better for Israel to step back rather than lash out – this isn't a war situation, and Sweden was not setting out to crush Israel as Israel seemed to feel.

A naked truth leaked out in a far-off place and, in its reaction, Israel became once again its own worst enemy. Whatever legitimacy there was to Israel's war on Hezbollah in Lebanon in 2006 and on Hamas in Gaza in early 2009, its case then was lost through overkill and disproportionality. Whatever its argument for continuing to build settlements in the West Bank, the sumtotal of what Israel has done to Palestinians over the years has morally weakened its position. In forcing issues, Israel undermines its long term, wider interests.

A friendly, cooperative, less strident Israel is what the world seeks; things can be done another way. Britain discovered this: it lost its greatness fifty years ago and at times risked isolation by pushing its point too hard. Brits gradually learned the value of stepping back when necessary but Britain, though it has ten times Israel's Jewish population, is still only a medium-sized country. It had to learn to respect the bigger guys, even learning to kowtow to China – which, a century ago, it had tried taking over.

There are advantages to being nicer – people do you favours, think leniently of you. If they're bigger than you, this matters. When people build up a wave of antipathy against you, it's often because they are not feeling *heard*. The organ-trading allegation reflected a European feeling that its warning signals to Israel had not been heeded – Europe was feeling increasingly unhappy over Israeli behaviour. So perhaps the Swedes were a good sparring partner for Israel because, whatever their faults, Swedes are pretty reasonable and they don't throw bombs around.

Israel needed to step back and this would have created helpful dialogue. Israelis and Swedes have a lot to teach each other, especially as Sweden has what Israel needs – it's a diplomatic, reliable, respected country. A big wave is stacking up against Israel, and it weakens its best longterm interests by omitting to be congenial.

Another Jew-rescuer of history, the medieval Kurdish sultan Salah-ad-Din, used to say that *every drop of blood spilled charges a price*. This is a 'soft power' issue: Swedish fighter jets aren't bad, but Swedes don't use them much because they have plenty of soft power – IKEA, Volvos and Nobel prizes. Soft power decides many things and Israelis should get wise to it. This is the age of majorities, and many Chinese cities have bigger populations than Israel.

49 Monday, and it's Ramadan
life-improvement

The phone was ringing in the early morning yet again! I had been up working late and staggered out sleepily. It was Ibrahim, announcing that the women's empowerment course was starting at the Hope Flowers Centre in half an hour. Ah, I had forgotten – it was one of those arrangements that should have happened a month ago and had been pushed to the side of my mind, crowded out by other imperatives.

Then, the rub – Ibrahim was busy and couldn't take me. This was problematic; it wasn't just about a lift to the centre, it concerned giving a proper explanation of my presence as a photographer to the women on the course. I needed a key person in Hope Flowers to translate for me as I explained to the women why I needed to take photos, since last time they had refused to let me. By hearing the sound of my voice, I hoped the women would be convinced. If not, I wouldn't get the photos.

Many disadvantaged people in Palestine are 'persons of interest' either to Israeli or Palestinian security services, for a variety of reasons. Poor people tend to support Hamas or other radical or religious groups, and these are out of favour with Fateh. Palestine isn't exactly a one-party state (or two, actually), but it is in danger of heading that way, with Fateh in the West Bank and Hamas in Gaza. Also, a proportion of religious people don't like being photographed, especially during Holy Ramadan, which had just started.

Pictures of Palestine

This is why I needed this photographic session to be set up properly. I needed to explain that it wasn't Western prurience or intelligence-gathering for the authorities. Photos were necessary for publicising Hope Flowers and its work and, without photos, raising money to support further courses would be more difficult.

The people funding these women's empowerment courses were Quakers in Britain with a genuinely enlightened interest in supporting the courses. They supported women's projects across the Muslim world and they were interested in tracking the true value of the course to Palestinian women, so they needed photos and a report from me.

This may seem simple but the course should have started earlier, the delay needed explanation and I was up against a classic Palestine problem. I knew that the funders needed to feel that good outcomes were arising from the five-figure sum they had given – and that was perfectly reasonable – but things don't quite go according to plan here in Palestine.

There were two problem issues. The first was that disadvantaged women often need persuasion that such a course will bring them benefit and that it's worthwhile prioritising it in their lives, as they are accustomed to being dumped on and lied to. With these streetwise ladies the proof lies in the pudding, so you've got to create some happy customers first to persuade the rest. There had been a false start where, in a course for 25 participants, six turned up to the second meeting, so the course was postponed.

The second issue was selection. Hope Flowers had asked UNRWA to select participants, but overworked UNRWA officials had been insufficiently clear about Hope Flowers' educational intentions. Some women they selected were of the go-getting kind, already blessed with social and educational advantages – and they were not the people Hope Flowers was seeking. Hope Flowers sought women from the 'sink areas' of Palestinian society, who could not usually help themselves.

This reveals a social divide in Palestine between those who are set on a course of self-improvement and those who stay in the traditional mould. It's not that veil-wearing traditionalists are wrong, for self-improvement can involve waving goodbye to many of the secure ways of the extended family and the community and it demands confidence and momentum, perhaps some money and certainly a resolve to make an extra effort. It also concerns perceptions: some people genuinely believe that staying in their peer group is safer than striking out, and in many cases this is true since, once you strike out, you're on your own.

Refugees and the dispossessed bond with one another in ways that people living modern, prosperous lifestyles have lost or turned away from. They stick together when there is little else to rely on; they raise a large family which becomes a security system and pension-provider; they tend their social roles, crops or herds, playing a part in their community, as their security mechanism, and thereby they maintain their security.

Then there's UNRWA where, thanks to the economic downturn, staff were cut. The money-boys at HQ determined this and Westerners demanded it, calling it 'accountability', 'transparency', 'efficiency' and 'delivery'. You have to retain those who inspect, verify and write reports, otherwise funding can be withdrawn. The staff who do the *real* business, the people on the ground, are more expendable. The people who file the reports and figures matter most – and their accountability is to head office, not to the people on the ground.

The outcome was that overworked UNRWA social workers had taken shortcuts and selected women who weren't quite the intended beneficiaries, so Hope Flowers had to start again, ferreting out participants one by one through the grapevine. The upshot was that the course was delayed, I didn't have the necessary photos and my report was behind schedule. But today the course was finally starting so I had my breakfast, got ready, phoned Khaled the taxi-man and arrived at last at the centre, thinking I was late.

But no, people were milling around, nothing had started and Maram was looking flustered – many women had not come. It was Ramadan and people were going slow, unhurried. I don't blame them, since Palestinians are usually busy from dawn till night, putting Europeans to shame with the intensity of their work, family lives and full-on lifestyle. Not only were many women absent, but those who were present didn't want to be photographed. "Sorry, Balden, I'll ring you another day", said Maram.

It was yet another exercise in acceptance but this was getting urgent: I was soon leaving Palestine and needed the stuff. I sat down at a desk to do some other work and suddenly Maram came into the office. More women had arrived and it was okay to take photos, so off I went, camera in hand. An explanation was given to the women and this time they recognised me, gave me the nod and even some warm smiles. They accepted Maram's assurances, scanned me for my human qualities and said Yes.

As I lurked at the back of the room, waiting for the right shots to emerge, I was the subject of rapt attention from five young children who had come with their mothers. This Westerner with his big camera made a seductive noise when he pressed the button, and his camera had all sorts of buttons and knobs he fiddled with.

Pictures of Palestine

I got my photos and snuck out to continue writing. Later, Maram came to tell me even more women had arrived, so I went in again and the course was now in full swing. The teacher, Ibrahim Afaneh, a food-science professor, was good and the women were visibly enjoying it, asking questions and making points – not a yawn or sullen look in sight. This course was interesting and relevant, and they were not being *lectured at* but talked to. We had lift-off – the feeling was palpable.

When word got around afterwards, these courses would be flooded with applicants. This was new stuff and it had to overcome the scepticism barrier. Once Hope Flowers had a quorum of satisfied customers, and once friends and neighbours saw how these women were progressing, they'd want to join too.

What were the women learning? Well, it was knowledge about improving one's life, about running a small business, working in cooperatives, craft standards, food hygiene, money-management, computer use, finding your market, dealing with family issues and talking over the matter of changing one's life.

It involved personal counselling and sharing groups: the women had a hard life, brought up in tough circumstances where rights, opportunities and progress were things that happened only to other people. Their husbands and brothers had sometimes been carted off, they had little education, they had parents, kin and children to look after and hassles to face. They were poor: indeed they *survived*, but they had none of the advantages that stimulate progress, and they needed willpower to help themselves advance. That's why Hope Flowers ran these courses, and why a Quaker trust in UK financed them – this way, conflict was transformed and human development set in motion.

Later, the women emerged for a break and there was much excited chattering in the hallway. I felt privileged to sit there at my desk with half an ear listening to their voices, hearing how this course was lighting them up. It was pioneering stuff and I was happy to be here, playing a part.

Part Five:
Salam's Express

50 The Enemy Within
a third intifada?

I was two weeks from leaving and getting out of Israel was a looming challenge – when you leave, you may be subject to interrogations. I planned to set off for Amman two days before my flight to London so that, if a problem arose at the Allenby Bridge, I wouldn't miss the plane. There's an unsettling tension when in Palestine because, although the West Bank itself is safe and friendly, entry and departure are controlled by the Israelis, who sometimes regard internationals as a potential threat. Yeah, me, a tofu terrorist.

I think it's connected with the tectonic grating of two contrasting mindsets. One says 'You're with us or you're against us' and the other says 'We're all in this together'. Unless proven otherwise, the first presumes threat and the second presumes trust – and each encounters problems when it meets the other. Israel generally suffers the former and, if you're not Jewish, it's commonly assumed you're a possible threat unless you prove not to be. Palestine suffers the latter, and if you're judged 'a good person' it doesn't matter greatly about your nationality, faith or ethnicity, but it can lead Palestinians to make acts of trust not always in their best interest.

It's strange, the inherent Israeli trust of fellow Jews and their distrust of *goyim*, non-Jews. This book might be judged by some people as anti-Israeli, but if I were Jewish its contents would be more allowable and I would probably express more vehement criticism of Israel too. I'm a polite Brit with clipped passions and, while I disagree with many things Israel does, I'm not inherently anti-Israeli, yet that distinction is difficult for some people to understand.

I read an interview with Dr Uri Davis, a Jewish resident of Arab East Jerusalem. He's a pro-Palestinian and anti-Zionist Israeli, married to a Palestinian Muslim. This is something definitely not done, though such mixed marriages do exist, more commonly a few decades ago than now. The non-Jewish partner as well as shared children frequently have difficulties, access and rights problems in Israel, and some couples have to live separated by the wall.

This can happen in Palestine too. A popular theatre-director in Jenin, Juliano Mer-Khamis, born of a Jewish mother and a Palestinian Christian father, who worked for Palestinian rights, was gunned down in 2011 by a Muslim fighter – not least because he worked to bring terrorists to peace.

Amazingly, in 2009 Davis was elected to the Revolutionary Council of Fateh, its policymaking body. His election was sensational and, I guess, risky for him. I wrote to a friend saying that I hoped this man lives to see old age. Dedicated as he is to opposing Zionism, he could be regarded as a traitor in Israel, risking finding himself in someone's crosshairs, but he seems to be safe, respected and welcome amongst Palestinians.

The problem with the threat mindset is that mere suspicion implies guilt and there is little defence once suspected; this became Mer-Khamis' problem. Forty years ago student anti-war protesters like me were branded Communist sympathisers and traitors, which we weren't, and it was equally bizarre around 1989 when this mindset became obsolete, when 'Commies' were suddenly re-humanised and forgiven their sins. I hope Davis lives to see a day when similar forgiveness happens to him, as a supposed traitor to the Jewish people, for this will symbolise a wider healing of the conflict, not just a relief for him.

However, he might get away with serving in Fateh. Being Jewish he's a special case, sitting within the Israeli concept of 'us', even if he straddles the divide by working with 'them'. Between Jews, disagreement is acceptable, if not normal. But if you're *goyim* it's different: non-Jews have less right to disagree, liable to be labelled anti-Semitic and blacklisted.

Davis said in his interview that the only difference between South African and Israeli *apartheid* was that Israeli *apartheid* is better disguised. Israel claims to be the sole democracy in the Middle East – not true since, whatever their failings, Jordan, Turkey, Iraq, Kuwait and Lebanon, and now Tunisia and Egypt are variously democratic. Besides, democracy is not itself a panacea: many democracies worldwide have serious democratic deficiencies, including those in Europe and America which regard themselves as upholders of democratic standards. In Israel, over a million Arab Israelis have far less democratic clout than much smaller Jewish minority groups numbering just thousands, which dominate the country and its political agenda. South Africa was a democracy – for whites. Israel claims that the rule of law is safe and well within its borders, yet this is true only for Jews, and this claim is judged by Israeli rather than international standards.

Davis might be alright initially, but what happens if the political temperature rises and polarisation increases, or if there is a return to conflict? He's brave to stand up for his principles, as do a number of courageous Israeli souls for whom I have great respect. Opposing the government is not uncommon amongst Israelis, but joining the 'enemy' government is something different; but then, differentness or exceptionalism is a very Israeli characteristic so, in a way, he's operating true to form.

In the global media there's never-ending talk of 'peace processes' and 'progress in talks' but frankly this is something between obfuscation and outright deception. Negotiations serve as cover for Israel's warlike acts and for international complicity in them. Guns might not largely be firing, but land is being taken, an occupying force maintains an iron grip, families are chucked out of homes, people are arrested, Gazans are bombed and Palestinians are jailed and still dying, today. IDF weapons fire somewhere pretty much every day. That's not a peace process – it's more like a mounting pile of precursors to the next outbreak of conflict. So, are Westerners' hopes of peace in vain? Are they deluding themselves, lulled into false hopes, or naively manipulated? Yes, to all of these.

It is because of all this that both Palestinians and seasoned international observers hold little faith in peace processes – not least because the customary mediator, USA, has for long supported one side, and the vetoing power of USA in international forums has protected Israel for decades. The futile negotiations of 2010, under Barak Obama's auspices, once again demonstrated that America's position and the value of peace processes have dwindled.

The legitimacy of all three negotiating parties – the Israelis, the PA and Hamas – has been seriously eroded, as shown in the 'Palestine Papers' leaked by Al Jazeera in early 2011. These papers, covering the peace negotiations around 2008, showed how much the talks were weighted against the Palestinians, how Israel, US and UK wanted to destroy Hamas and engage Fateh's support in doing so, how far Fateh went in making concessions and how little Israel matched these concessions – overall, they showed how much the peace process was being angled into the form of a capitulation by the Palestinians.

The final determinants of peace are the Palestinian people themselves, not just in a referendum, which was promised, but on the street. Sustained acceptance of a peace treaty and compliance with it by ordinary Palestinians, particularly the young, is needed, and this will happen only when they see Israelis – especially settlers, nationalists and the IDF – demonstrate their own acceptance and compliance. Palestinians do have a certain mature wisdom or perhaps weariness – they know they won't get everything they seek – but they do need sufficient restitution to make them truly feel safe and bury the hatchet.

They don't expect this to happen soon, yet there is still a collective intuition amongst Palestinians that peace will indeed come one day – perhaps not as a treaty but as a reality-shift rendering conflict obsolete. Perhaps they are waiting for Israel to shoot itself in the foot to the extent that it becomes an equal partner in conciliation; perhaps they await the international community following up its legal decisions and UN resolutions with firm action; perhaps they await the full fruition of changes being brought by the Arab Spring; or perhaps they just pray to Allah for his grace and mercy.

A treaty follows public consensus and the arising of genuine peace on the ground, otherwise conflict or post-conflict problems will sooner or later arise. In Northern Ireland, peace came in the 1990s because ordinary people, weary, drew a firm line, applying personal pressure on combatants and agitators, enabling politicians and secretive organisations such as the Orange Lodges and IRA to step back from their own provocative roles. Even then, renegade terrorists have still tried to break the peace, but without success, since that peace is thorough, consensual and popularly reinforced.

But the waiting nibbles away at Palestinians' patience and tolerance. They try to be optimistic, yet hope leads to an accumulation of emotional pressure which, if heated sufficiently by adverse events and circumstances, can explode and go crazy. Palestinians don't *want* things to be like this. Most try to get on with life, maintaining a good mood, but the Israelis thoughtlessly eat away at Palestinian sensitivities, patience, tolerance, rights and daily lives. In 2009, the time covered in this book, the hottest issues were Jewish settler infiltration in East Jerusalem and into Haram al Sharif, the Muslim holy precinct in Jerusalem's Old City – but land-appropriation, settlement-building, ethnic cleansing in the Jordan valley and other frictions also added fuel to smouldering embers.

Incursions into Haram al Sharif, the site of the Dome of the Rock and Al Aqsa, were troublesome because the Jordanians are still its official protectors. This led to an awkward diplomatic situation above and beyond the emotional and religious issues involved. Yes, historically this is the site of the Jewish Temple Mount of two millennia ago, but it's a crucially delicate matter, and Israeli incursions are the worst way to approach any possibility of sharing this holy space. It's like pagans in Europe threatening to invade Christian cathedrals located on pre-Christian sacred sites – Gothic cathedrals are themselves heritage sites and not up for demolition, whatever lies underneath them.

Pictures of Palestine

Besides, Jews are not traditionally concerned about holy sites – this is a modern Zionist preoccupation, a response to Muslims' and Christians' concern for holy places. Ideological Orthodox settlers dream of rebuilding the Temple of Jerusalem, but this would involve demolishing the Dome of the Rock and Al Aqsa, on a UNESCO World Heritage Site.

Settlers attempted to enter Haram al Sharif and Israeli archaeologists dug under Al Aqsa, seeking evidence of the Temple and, in the process, causing structural damage to the mosque. This made Muslims nervy – the second *intifada* had ignited over Ariel Sharon's bold army-backed incursion into Haram al Sharif in 2000 – and if Israelis genuinely believed in peace they would not carry out such provocations. In 2009, Israeli government *hasbarah* asserted that these invaders were actually foreign tourists and that Muslims had mistakenly identified them as Jewish settlers. Everyone shook their heads in dismay and incredulity.

These were not outright confrontations but merely acts of erosion, framed to eat away at Muslim confidence to a point where Palestinians break out into violence and mayhem, thereby justifying the sending in of Israeli troops 'to keep the peace' and thus neatly transferring blame for violence onto Palestinians. This is a standard tactic.

In East Jerusalem, many are the stories of properties bought from Palestinians then being resold or transferred to Jews, or of Palestinians being told that they were living illegally in properties that they had occupied for decades. They were turfed out on the street only to watch Israeli settlers moving in on the spot.

My friend Ibrahim Abu el-Hawa, who isn't good at paying his bills, was taken to court and fined 1.2 million shekels (about $300,000) for non-payment. This sum was impossibly large, way beyond the value of his house and it could permit the Israeli authorities to evict him. Located in dense Palestinian housing on the Mount of Olives, his house would give settlers a foothold from which to expand. They would immediately be in there, financed by American money and backed by Israeli troops. American money, both private and governmental, is behind much of the trouble in East Jerusalem.

This slow accretion keeps such acts of war below the radar of the international media and diplomatic community. A trickle of events is insufficiently sensational to generate headlines, and global complacency permits minor acts of war to take place, inch by inch, month by month. The PA complains, but the most it can do is refuse to participate in peace talks. So talks don't work, which suits the Israelis, who blame the Palestinians; it's a clever trap, except that this *hasbarah* now wears thin.

These are ingredients of the next outbreak of violence. Palestinians' suppressed frustration is such that the next *intifada*, should it happen, might turn against not only the Israelis but the PA too, since the PA's credibility is in question. Both Fateh and Hamas risk becoming irrelevant, outpaced by developments across the Middle East – it's a daunting prospect and potentially a sorry sight. The main counterbalance is Israel's vulnerability to international pressure as well as serious disquiet within its own society. Many Israelis are pretty fed up with aggressive settlers. They don't like it when, travelling abroad and being asked where they come from, they are met by an awkward silence when they say 'Israel'.

This is Israel's secret enemy: *guilt*. Beneath their intransigence, bluster and apparent certainty, Israelis are not so sure of Israel's course. The wider world also has a mound of accumulated guilt about its acquiescence over Palestine, a creeping sense of culpability which is surreptitiously turning opinions against Israel. Quietly complicit for so long, the world could be obliged by circumstances to *actually do something*.

Israel pushes its case hard, but nowadays its hand of cards is weak and it has become a sad thing to witness such hubris. The only way to stop this drift is a change of behaviour on Israel's part, to which everyone else would respond positively. But the Palestinians might need to set the change in motion by shifting their own position: it always takes two to tango, and the tango changes when one partner starts dancing to a different tune. Bizarrely, Palestine nowadays has more freedom of action than Israel.

51 Tide Turning
a new soul-sister

My phone announced the arrival of a text from my brother in England. My mother had gone into hospital and our nonagenarian parents needed extra care. My brother had valiantly managed the situation thus far but he was now asking me to go straight to my parents' house to look after them on my return to Britain.

Well, yes, of course – but I had planned a break to decompress from Palestine. It's important to transition properly on return because one needs to get over 'Palestine syndrome' – otherwise one can be oversensitive and reactive, making bad judgements and feeling rather lost. I still had loads to do in Palestine, and time was running out. Suddenly, thanks to all this, I was knocked off balance, my capacity to think went awry and I melted into tangled overload.

Don't panic, Palden: where's the silver lining? Soon, the gift arrived, on the 21 bus. Sahera was a young British woman who had volunteered to work at the school. I had briefed her by e-mail. She seemed both excited and nervous about coming – nervous particularly over whether the officials at Ben Gurion airport would admit a Brit with a Muslim name. As it happened, her entry was straightforward – unlike some American supporters of the school who had been sent back to the States just a month earlier, blacklisted and in a state of shock.

I went down to Bab al-Zqaq to fetch her, first visiting Adnan to sort out details about his website. He was seriously upset about his business – he hadn't had any sales for two weeks and was broke. So today I bought a dress from him for one of my daughters and discreetly donated toward his son's school uniform too. This was tricky because he felt ashamed to receive donations, but when he went out on an errand, I slipped a 200 shekel note into the hand of his helper, saying "Just say it's a gift from Allah". Then I went off down the street, up the steps past the persuasive sweet seller who yet again managed to get me to buy some almond cakes, through the Christian Quarter and down to Bab al-Zqaq.

Would I find Sahera easily? The 21 bus had just arrived. Out of the bus emerged a young woman with some bags and, as she turned, it was it was like something from a film: a long, slow-motion moment of silent recognition. We took a taxi back to the school and I showed her around.

So a 59-year old white Brit was meeting a 26-year old British-Kashmiri Muslim, neither of us Christian, in the town of Jesus' birth. Something deep had called us both to this place and now here we were, two strangers who seemed to know each other uncannily well.

I was born in the shadow of WW2 and brought up in the Cold War; she was born in the shadow of the Kashmiri conflict and brought up in a time when Muslims in the West were increasingly looked on as alien and dangerous. The Kashmir conflict had begun in the late 1940s at the same time as Palestine's, when her parents were children – and both conflicts had flared up as a result of negligent British decolonialisation. Her parents had migrated to Birmingham, England, in the 1960s, just when I was taking LSD and going through my awakening in Liverpool. Sahera was born in 1980s Birmingham in the very year that I, then a thirtysomething, started a series of pioneering community-building events in England. We were very different yet our motives for being here at Hope Flowers somehow intersected. A Sixties veteran and a young British Muslim, we both came from misunderstood minorities – hers was an ethnic and mine an ethical community, both of us feeling marginalised as Brits.

Pictures of Palestine

This journey was like a pilgrimage for her: Palestine is significant for Muslims everywhere and as a British passport-holder she was, unlike many Muslims, able to visit Palestine. Although Muslim, she was also part of a hip-hop culture – she'd done all-nighters, reiki and world music; she was fasting for Ramadan but wore no headscarf. She was searching for a new path in life, just as I had done when younger, and we had both made a deep choice to carve our own paths through life, to break out of the pot we were planted in.

That evening I'd been invited to Adnan's family home, and Sahera came along for *iftar*, the Ramadan fast-breaking evening meal. By now I was accustomed to Palestine and the way it looks but, as we careered along a twisty road in Adnan's car, I saw afresh the hilly landscape, dotted with houses and villages, through the eyes of an outsider.

As we sat in a circle on the floor with the men and boys around an enormous tray loaded with food, Sahera was the only woman present – the women and girls ate separately in another room. This was incongruous but, wisely, Sahera took it as it presented itself. She was a vegetarian like me, oddly for a Muslim, and this was a

by-product of her Britishness. We avoided the chicken legs and ate only the rice, lentils and veggies. Adnan's family was concerned that we might somehow die of undernourishment and plied us with extras, but Palestinians know well that Westerners can be weird, so it wasn't too much trouble.

Later we sat out on the rooftop in a circle with the men and boys as they discussed family matters in Arabic, at times heatedly. One of the grandfathers I'd seen at the clan court in Bethlehem was there, presiding. Adnan was under pressure: years ago he had gone his own way, attending university and then starting a souvenir shop instead of joining the family business, but his enterprise had done badly, thanks to the building of the separation wall and the decline of tourism. They pressured him to close his shop and join them, and doggedly he refused. Watching the dynamics was fascinating; I understood little except the tone of the conversation, but the feeling of family, with both its inclusivity and its tensions, was strong.

Before being driven back to Bethlehem, Sahera and I insisted on meeting the lady of the house – not usually done, but we exercised our prerogative as Westerners. She was reluctant but we gently obliged her to emerge from the back of the house, shook her hand and thanked her for the food. We were grateful for sharing this Bedouin family occasion.

On our return to Manger Square, the square was filled with men at prayer – a moving moment for Sahera. In England, Muslim prayer is discreetly hidden away in unobtrusive mosques, often converted from houses and old churches, but here were hundreds of people, young and old, out in the square, heads to the ground, rising up, hands out to open the heart and receive Allah's blessing, bowing, rising again and sinking down, all together. I've never managed to figure out how Muslims manage to form such straight lines and move in such unison during their prayer-making sessions, but they do. We stood watching, both deeply stirred, each for different reasons. I was soon to leave Palestine, feeling a wrenching sense of impending departure, and she had just arrived, taking in this new reality afresh.

Pictures of Palestine

We met an Arab Israeli couple from Nazareth, which is in Israel, asking them why they had come all the way to Bethlehem. "People are friendly here", said the man. "In Galilee we are like guests in our own land, we must obey the rules of another people." He sunk his neck into his shoulders, furtively looking around, to demonstrate. "We are not happy. We hurry between houses, stay out of trouble. That's why we come here. Here we feel safe and welcome. I'm Muslim, my wife is Christian, and we like to visit here – we feel at home."

"Do you want to move here?"

Hands splayed, shoulders shrugging: "I'm a doctor, I have patients, and we have family... Marta, she has her old mother to look after... How can we?".

I pulled him up and gave him a hug. "If I could, I'd move here too, my friend. But I can't, so I know the feeling." I have family and involvements in Britain and, being *goyim*, the Israelis wouldn't give me a residence visa.

In the following days, Sahera and I shared some fine moments. To be with a culturally-sensitive Englishman who respected her Ramadan practises and cooked a vegetarian *iftar* for her was a surprise relief, allowing her British and Muslim aspects to coexist happily. To have her company at the school – someone to talk to – rounded out the long, quiet days of my stay.

Fasting for Ramadan, acclimatising to Palestine and waiting to be allotted tasks by Ibrahim, Sahera rested in the afternoons while I performed my customary keyboard-slavery. At times we did our own thing, and on other occasions we went out or had long discussions. I introduced her to Fatima, asking Fatima to keep her eye on Sahera after I left Bethlehem.

But the best moment of all came with my customary Sunday evening meditation. I had informed Sahera about it in advance, expecting her to wander off and do something else, as most of my friends and family do. But she hung around as I settled, cross-legged, breathing myself down into a deep state and disappearing off with the angels. She was still there when I surfaced forty minutes later. A silent sharing of spirit had taken place – and spirit speaks a language that words cannot contain.

52 Hope Starts Flowering
school cranks up

The school was a hive of activity as teachers and staff received parents seeking to register their children and workmen put finishing touches to repairs. Suddenly it was all happening. Sahera had come to work for some months, to replace me after my departure. She possessed the demure quietness of a Muslim woman along with the bolder confidence of a modern Brit, each characteristic emerging at different times. This trip was a big jump, her first time alone in a Muslim country, yet Palestinians were not her own people and, like me, she was a foreigner. Palestine stands on the frontline of the tricky cultural interaction between the Islamic world and the West and this awkward paradox was also encapsulated in her own life and upbringing as a Muslim in a Western country.

She embodied the boundary-pushing role that Western Muslims play in updating Islamic culture. Muslims no longer adopt, accept and defer to Western ways as they might have done in the past: it's now a filtration process where the best of the West and the best of Islamic culture are accepted and the rest is modified or ditched. This means reviewing both Islamic traditions and Western ways, and their relevance in a globalised world. Somehow, modern Muslims are leapfrogging directly from past to future across the broken glass of the present.

The Majority World now increasingly sets the global agenda and the West has been caught talking to itself, its time of pre-eminence passing. On some semi-conscious level Sahera, like me, was working with the soul of our country and its light and shadow, with the effects of Britain's historic role in establishing the global village. Part English, part Welsh, I had the imperialist and the colonised in me, and she, Kashmiri British, was one of the colonised, absorbing the worldview of the former imperialists.

This globalised intercultural friction comes to a cruxpoint in Palestine, at this very school. Located as it is at the edge of Bethlehem, contrasting cultures meet, or fail to meet, here – colonists and colonised are separated by a high wall. Looking out from the school we see Palestinian smallholdings in the valley, and behind them the separation wall and the Israeli settlement of Efrat, creeping towards us year by year. The fault line of this friction is *right here*. Middle East meets West on the edge of Al Khader.

Hope Flowers, a Palestinian school in an occupied country, emphasises cultural transparency and understanding. In the 1980s and 1990s Jews and Christians attended the school but now, each for their own reasons, they're gone. The school emphasises spirituality and ethics and the art of being a good human, rather than religion and moral traditions. Here lies the heart of the matter: good behaviour, tolerance and honouring the boundaries where contrasting societies meet. Except at present they cannot meet – the separation wall is a rift in humanity's psyche. Yet the school reminds the children that things will one day change and it prepares them for that change.

There was another person who arrived at the school. Kurt from the Netherlands was a Transcendental Meditation teacher and would be teaching TM to teachers and children, to help them develop inner calm, cultivating a simple relationship with the spirit without squeezing it into the confines of doctrinal faith. A few months later Kurt had to leave, the school was told, because the Israelis rejected his application for a visa extension. However, in the coming year or two we were to discover that a hidden agenda was going on, of which he was a part, and dramatic challenges were brewing. But that is a story for another book.

Pictures of Palestine

The children are also taught Compassionate Listening – sitting in a circle and lending complete attention to each other's stories, bearing witness to each other's experience. It gives them ways of stretching their experience and understanding themselves beyond the framework of their own little worlds; would that more schools engaged in such work. Compassion isn't about feeling sorry or even agreeing with others – it's simply the art of *witnessing*, seeing what life looks like from the other side. If we humans allowed ourselves to do it more than we do, this alone would quickly resolve many of the world's ills.

The kids were returning to school the next day and it would be a big change after the quiet summer months. There was drilling and banging, coming and going, the hubbub of people and the sound of teachers preparing classrooms and having meetings. The geckos were probably wondering what was happening.

They're lovely people, the teachers – impressive as humans, though they wouldn't think themselves to be so. They were led by Hind Issa, the then educational director, and Hala her daughter, who headed the teaching team. Hind was a respectable, judicious, good-hearted, steady lady, who served as the mother-figure of the school – she had been with the school from the very beginning. She has a sweet smile when her face lights up, but she's the kind of person you shouldn't cross with; she'd probably scare the pants off an Israeli officer if he did the wrong thing. In some ways she's quite traditional, in other ways globalised and modern. Later she retired from her major duties at the school – she'd been at it a long time.

Hala was cuddly, busy, a mother-hen type. The teachers really liked her and her eyes and ears were everywhere. In Britain she'd be a popular deputy headteacher on £40,000 in a top-rated comprehensive school, where those tricksy 15-year olds would go quiet and hide their cigarettes when she breezed through, but then, just before leaving, she'd turn and say with a grin, "Got one for me?", then "It's okay, only joking!". The following year she emigrated to Canada, after an application to migrate that she'd made five whole years earlier suddenly turned up trumps. The school lost her.

The Issa family had assembled a fine team, dedicated to the school's aims and approach. They were certainly not in it for the money – the wages were poor and sometimes they had to hold their breath and rely on their wider families' support, but if you wanted to be a true teacher, this was the best place to be. Sure, like any teachers they get ratty and tired, but they know their stuff and they really care and they also get through to the kids. In the morning when the kids lined up in the schoolyard, a teacher would lead them in their exercises and the kids were right with it, arms out, arms forward, knees bend – this wasn't discipline, it was *focus* and togetherness. The kids could get unruly like any kids, but these teachers genuinely elicited their will to learn and when the kids were beyond learning, they let them play.

I was impressed with the teachers. Their hearts were in the right place and the training they had received and experience they'd accumulated at Hope Flowers made them leaders in their field.

Pictures of Palestine

They weren't really aware of the broader significance of this school – they just did their best to do their jobs well, not seeing themselves as pioneers. Neither did the other staff at Hope Flowers, except perhaps for the Issa family – but even they were so caught up in day-to-day issues that only sometimes could they stand back to glimpse what they were truly achieving.

One new teaching assistant faced an interesting challenge – apart from Ibrahim, he was the only male in a henhouse of females! A nice chap, young, anxious to please, he faced a situation many Western males have faced in recent decades, but one new to Palestine: how to be a man in a female-majority work situation. I clapped him on the back and gave him words of encouragement. Poor guy, I hoped his colleagues would be gentle with him! He stood on the gender revolution frontline, a sensitive male teaching young kids – and in Palestine a ground-breaker, though it probably didn't feel like that to him.

I interviewed the school psychologist for a podcast. Shirouk joined classes to observe the kids and identify those with learning or behavioural difficulties, or simply kids who were having a down day. Teachers are trained in dealing with this and referring cases to her. When kids facing problems were identified, Shirouk quietly buttonholed them, gained their trust, counselled them, visited their parents, led courses for parents and dealt with knotty cases. The school also called in members of a team of specialists when necessary.

Each child was individually monitored – and, dare I say, *loved*. Here they didn't take a disciplinary, psycho-pharmaceutical or finger-wagging approach to misfits and problem cases. Children weren't socialised and educated to become producer-consumers in a machine, but to become whole humans capable of exploring their full potential and making their contribution to society, something that Western schools try but often fail to do. Teachers strove to get inside the psyches of the kids, to heal and help them *be themselves*. Shirouk was a key person in Hope Flowers' educational strategy, though the whole teaching team was involved and they worked as a family – I was impressed with the friendship and cooperation between members of staff.

My stay at the school was coming to a close and I was sad to be leaving. I had just over a week to complete too many tasks, see a lot of people and wrench myself out of this scene. There was a lot to digest – and a lot to get ready for in Britain.

As for the demolition threat mentioned earlier, nothing happened. Well, not at first, and not as expected. At the time of publication, the smallholdings, the houses and the school are all still there. But something else happened instead – something far more complex and devious, a disguised attempted takeover of the area, unfolding during 2011. This rather fantastic story will be told in another book.

Meanwhile, I needed to complete the grant application and ensure that it was meticulously written, with rationales, explanations and figures, for the funding committee in Washington DC. But the thing I admired so much about this school was this: *whether or not the funding came, they'd somehow do it anyway.* But funding makes an enormous difference.

I've always been like this myself, one of those heroic fools who does things because they *need* doing, whether or not there is backing. In the longterm it's very wearing, involving an ongoing process of begging, hard work, letdowns and few rights and entitlements. But it's possible to achieve momentous things *anyway*, often on a shoestring, and rewards come to heart and soul. Older now, I'm glad I've followed this path, though the price has at times been high. There are still people back in Britain who think I ought to get a 'proper job'.

By the way, six months later we discovered that our grant application was rejected; too many applicants had applied for too few funds. And Palestine, well, it's a high-risk investment, isn't it, and how can someone in Washington DC really know whether the funds are used well, or whether they'd secretly be invested in terrorism?

53 Back to School
education for peace

I seemed to have developed a habit of being rudely awoken from sleep by the phone – it's the price of blogging late into the night. Tumbling out of bed, I slipped on my *jalabiya* and dashed for the phone. It was Hala; she was standing at the gate outside and they'd forgotten the keys. I looked out of the window and there were Hala, Hind and a vanload of teachers. "I'll be down – just a minute!"

I dashed into my room. Off went the *jalabiya*, on went the trousers and shirt, and I stumbled blearily down four flights of stairs, straightening my hair, struggling with that errant lock on the bottom door and stepping out into the sun to admit the waiting ladies. More were arriving and I mumbled greetings in Arabic and English and retreated back upstairs.

My blood hadn't started circulating properly yet, so my customary anti-gravitational stair-climbing act didn't quite work this morning. I went for a cold shower – the sun hadn't yet moved around to warm the solar heating system. Aaah, that did it. On went the kettle for the customary morning tea ceremony and Sahera emerged from her room.

Then a glorious pandemonium started up. Kids poured into the playground and teachers milled around, gravitating into the playground with the kids. A lovely scene unfolded as I gazed out from the top floor, photographing the scene below. Kids ran up to teachers to shake hands or give them a hug, boys screeched past on scampering trajectories, waving at the teachers or skimping their skirts while the teachers giggled and chattered between themselves and with kids. Everyone gathered in groups and teenagers lurked together in a corner, as they do; eight-year old girls discussed things earnestly with friends and boys kicked footballs around. A window in the watchtower over the valley opened and a pair of binoculars pointed our way. Good morning! The soldiers were slow on the uptake this morning.

It was a grand reunion as parents wandered around saying hello, then went off home, and the numbers of kids gradually grew. This went on for half an hour as the yellow school bus disgorged a gaggle of youngsters and disappeared for another load from another area.

I had worked with this school for some years but I had never been here during term time. Now here were the kids for whom I'd been doing all this. Tears came to my eyes – a connective, full-circle sense of completion was taking place deep down. All that work, those late nights, the heartache of things going wrong, the complexities, the e-mails flying back and forth and then Pam Perry dying. But today these were tears of joy, tears of humility, tears from the small child within me. *This is what it's all about.* Pam probably nodded, upstairs in heaven; she had spent the last seven years of her life disabled and

stuck in her house in England, unable to visit the school for which she worked so hard.

I thought of England. My former partner had been a college teacher and was now an educational coordinator and trainer of school governors, implementing education policy. From her I learned some of the inside secrets of the educational world in Britain. Teachers could not touch or show affection to the kids, for fear of attracting accusations of paedophilia, favouritism, unprofessional behaviour or a host of regulatory and social strictures, yet here at Hope Flowers affection is central to the educational ethos. Closeness, trust and emotional sensitivity are crucial to working with traumatised children.

In my country we wonder why young people are disaffected, why there are behavioural issues at schools, why academic standards keep on slipping, and why the media bleat about everything falling apart in schools no matter how much money is thrown at them, no matter how many commissions of enquiry are held. You don't really need a doctorate to understand why: it's all about the love in a society, about caring, tenderness, mutuality. That's what binds a society and awakens children's inherent sense of care and responsibility for their world, what stimulates young people to grow toward their full potential, giving sensitive humans a ground to stand on. It also gives insensitive and damaged humans a way of healing themselves and reaching out to others.

In Britain there are plenty of good teachers with fine motivation, but many are constrained by the education system and the politicised values driving it. Here in this school, where government intervention had for so long been slim – Israeli army intervention being a far greater issue – teachers could shine as humans and *truly teach*, vocationally. There was little status in this playground: the teachers were in amongst the kids, all friends, all part of the Hope Flowers brood. Such was my impression, but there is a qualification that I must honestly insert here: later, downstairs in the office, I talked with Ghada, who said, yes, it's lovely on the first day of term, but later on, well, it's not quite the same...

Pictures of Palestine

However, I still knew that, due to the approach of the school, things were very different here from Britain. Hope Flowers respects the inner sensitivities and subjectivities of children and it draws in parents and the wider community on a personal, friendship basis. Its aim is to remove the causes of violence from children and families living in a country where hardship levels are high, where tough stuff happened not many years ago.

During the last decade, tanks had ground along the road leading to the school. In 2002 the school was engulfed in a gun-battle and, when Ibrahim eventually got through on the phone to the Israeli commander, insisting on evacuation, the school was given twenty minutes to get the kids out. They just about managed, with two available vans for the whole lot.

But now there was a magic sparkle in this playground, a feeling of lightness and *presence*. Life and activity had returned to Hope Flowers after the summer vacation and I was reminded that this is a blessed project, not just for locals in Bethlehem but globally, serving as an incubator of new ideas and possibilities. Those who run the school have a protective, nurturing, human approach toward education and caring for the kids, which creates a strong energy-resonance and atmosphere. It *zingles*, it generates light.

Poignant too is the location of the school right by the separation wall, on the boundary of the West Bank – a wall between the distinct worlds that are Palestine and Israel. The contrast in social atmosphere is stark; geographically they are close and adjacent, squeezed into such a small land, but psycho-socially they could be on opposite sides of the planet – and if they were, they might not be in conflict.

54 God's Friend
return to Al Khalil

In Arabic Hebron is known as *Al Khalil*, the Friend, after Ibrahim al Khalil, or Abraham, God's Friend. It lies 3,000ft (930m) up in the southern West Bank highlands and has a strongly Palestinian character, yet traditional and modern elements rub along closely: there, on a street, are thoroughly modern plate-glass shops typical of any city and going along the street is an old man on a donkey cart carrying a load of pomegranates.

Hebron is a city of contradictions in a country of paradoxes. Its population is over 95% Palestinian, though Israelis control about 20% of it. Some Palestinians remain in the Jewish enclave, doggedly holding on to their houses, running the gauntlet of sometimes fierce humiliation and pressures, living a life of checkpoints and harassments that people in the Muslim sector don't generally experience.

Hebron's ancient Jewish heritage dates back some 4,000 years to Abraham himself and there was a Jewish presence here with few problems until the 1930s. *Misrahi* Jews have always been part of the Middle Eastern mosaic, only distantly related to the European Ashkenazi majority who now dominate Israel. The problem for Palestinians started when Ashkenazim immigrated in growing numbers after WW1, increasingly changing the face of Palestine and making it a westernised colony. Many indigenous Jews shared reservations with Palestinians about the incoming migrants, with whom they did not identify and from whom they saw trouble looming.

Pictures of Palestine

Not that the incoming Jews set out to be troublemakers – they were traumatised by persecution and violence in Europe. Many Arabs had some sympathy for them, but they didn't see why they should bear the brunt of problems that came with the Jews, or suffer quite the takeover they discovered was taking place. Immigration on this scale caused immense concern since land was being lost, frictions were brewing and the newcomers were changing everything. Revolts started across Palestine.

It overboiled as a massacre in Hebron in 1929, cranked up by the British with their divide-and-rule policies. Many Jews died, though there were also stories of Arabs sheltering Jews since they had long been friends. This massacre – a grave mistake – set a trend for events to come: in scenes like this the ensuing conflict took root. Two threatened peoples overreacted to each other and the British fanned the flames – it was a tragic situation.

The British moved the remaining Jews to Jerusalem in the 1930s. From a colonial ruler's viewpoint this might have seemed sensible, but it was unwise as a longterm strategy, increasing the separation of the two peoples. Hebron became thoroughly Palestinian and after the 1948 war it came under Jordanian rule. Then came the 1967

war when Israel occupied the West Bank and soon after this, the Jewish settlers descended on Hebron. But these were different Jews from those who had left decades earlier – they were recent immigrants with a strong agenda, led by Rabbi Levinger, a man with a mission to reclaim Hebron. Another mistake. Hebron has since then attracted very assertive settlers, supported by soldiers to protect them and, although only a few hundred live in the city, they control a substantial chunk of it.

I returned to Hebron on my birthday, together with Sahera, and we stayed a night with Naima and her family. We went down to the Old City, walking through the souk, which was far more crowded than the previous time I came. This time the centre of town and the souk were heaving with Muslims for Ramadan.

We navigated the narrow, winding streets intending to visit the Ibrahimi Mosque but, not being a Muslim, this time I wasn't allowed in because of Ramadan, though no law or custom expressly forbade it. Bizarrely, it was the Israeli troops manning the checkpoints on the approach to the mosque who barred me from entering. Naima tried inveigling me in, using her charm and asserting that I was a Muslim, but the Israeli soldiers were having none of it – they could see I was a Westerner.

So I sat on a stool by the main entrance to the mosque under the watchful eyes of the Israeli soldiers, as hundreds of Muslims streamed in and out. Folding my hands on my lap, I went into meditation and found myself going quite deep. I had come to talk again with Abraham – or at least with his ancient abiding spirit. While unable to enter the mosque, I was actually physically quite close to the Cave of the Patriarch under the mosque, traditionally regarded as Abraham's home when he lived here.

Sahera went in with Naima and Yaqub and I was happy for her because she considered it important. The night before she had visited a friend in Jerusalem and they had gone to pray in the Dome of the Rock – a rather crowded and stuffy experience, she reported. Today she was praying at the Ibrahimi Mosque, so she was doing two major sites in two days – pretty good going for a British Muslim brought up in a country lacking Islamic holy places.

Not that Sahera was exactly a devout Muslim – she was more a young truth-seeker, revisiting the Muslim faith from her own British perspective. As with many of her age and kind, she experienced a deep inner debate as to how much she was a modern Brit and how much a Muslim, and how these two identities interact. It was meaningful to her to come to Palestine, to be surrounded by Muslims during Ramadan.

But the Islam she saw here was different. Here, people wander in and out during prayers, some fall asleep in the mosque and there's a general hubbub going on. In Britain they all arrive and leave on time and it's tidy and disciplined, Islam being an alien faith in a British context, with no local heritage. This was a journey of discovery for her.

Meditating and centring myself quietly amidst the Ramadan pandemonium, I attuned to Abraham's presence and the ancient sanctity of the place. Before it was a mosque, synagogue or church, each of which it had been at different times, over three millennia ago it had been a Canaanite and Hittite holy place. Abraham came here because it already was a sacred place, just as Jesus was born in Bethlehem, an ancient site of many thousand years' antiquity, even in his own time.

I was 'gone' for quite a while, only distantly aware of the activity around me, off on another planet, in a timeless place. Eventually I slowly surfaced and opened my eyes, readjusting to the notion that I was sitting outside the Ibrahimi Mosque in an Arabic street-maelstrom. Naima was standing directly before me, searching my eyes as if thinking, "Wonder where he's gone?". Opening my eyelids, a bit like a newly-landed ET, I smiled beatifically, noticing Yaqub and Sahera too. They seemed ready to go, but I was rather 'out of it', once-removed, not quite ready to jump up and go back through the checkpoints.

But, realising they were itching to leave, I managed to instruct my legs to engage in pedestrian activity, got vertical and started rolling down the hill. The Israeli officer who had rejected my entry into the mosque had clearly been watching me with some bequizzlement.

Hardly a terrorist threat, I smiled at him and he managed an uncomfortable smirk back.

He had assumed I was a Christian. "I'm not a Christian, y'know. But while you successfully stopped me entering the mosque, I got exactly what I needed from this visit, in ways you'll probably never understand. So thanks for watching over me. God bless you. *Shalom*!" He fiddled his fingers and in that moment of stillness his gun, his stripes, his uniform held no power. I nodded goodbye to him and wandered off, down through the lower checkpoint, following Naima and company into the milling souk, where we came upon a showdown.

A group of Orthodox Jews had descended into the souk, presumably to assert their assumed right to be there. They were protected by gun-toting, helmeted young Israeli troops, nervously fingering triggers. A crowd of Palestinians fresh from Ramadan prayers surrounded and boxed them in, quietly and in an orderly fashion, so the Israelis were outnumbered. No violence was going to break out, at least from the Palestinian side, but the atmosphere was dead serious, stern and tense and I wondered whether the Israelis might panic. It was silently being made clear to the Israelis they were out of order being there. The shutter on my camera seemed loud in the pregnant silence of this intense standoff.

No Palestinians broke ranks, even the kids: they stood firm, quietly confining and facing down the settlers until they moved on through the souk, led and followed by the soldiers, pointing their guns nervously at the crowd as if an attack were imminent. It was a well-contained piece of conflict-management, and the Israelis did the right thing by not letting their nervousness take over. As soon as they left, there was consternation in people's talk, with much vexed shaking of heads, but they went their ways and the matter evaporated.

The binding effect of sheer, ongoing hardship gives Palestinians a capacity to handle this kind of peaceful facedown. Palestinian society has made a deep moral choice to hold together under strain, although if Israelis are over-zealous in their actions, or an informer is found, people can sometimes go nuts. I once met a former informant who, poor chap, had done it to get a permit to pay for a hospital operation for his sister. He wasn't happy about it, having made himself an outsider in his own society which, in Palestine, leads to an immense sense of loss.

On the whole, Palestinian families are integrated, protective and wholesome and there's something in their psychology that enables them to work together very much as one. It's by no means perfect but, overall, people get on and cooperate, as exemplified in Naima's family: they all cooked, cleaned and ran the house with rarely a maternal instruction and no nagging. It was a mutually-supportive household – five of them in three rooms. I stayed with 'the boys', four of us in one room, and Sahera slept in Naima's bed while Naima slept on the sofa. There was no visible interpersonal stress, though I'm sure they have their moments. Life isn't easy, but holding together is, for them, a source of strength and survival.

We had seen this togetherness in the souk and the crowds at the Ibrahimi Mosque. The Israeli officer had initially derived some gratification peeling me off from the group I was with, but in myself I didn't let his action get to me and, straight in front of him, I sat in peace. An American who had adopted Israel, his psychology was one of separateness, lacking that deeper sense of belonging that people have when they're born and bred in a place. Perhaps he needed to separate us out to reinforce separation as the norm. Perhaps he needed to assert his power, to help himself feel as if this land is *his* home more than theirs, where his rules held sway – just like the settlers in the souk, pushing themselves on others to make their point. All of them are deeply scared. *If you can't join them, beat them.* It's very sad.

The love these relative newcomers, the Jews, feel for their adopted land is admirable, but it doesn't override the love that existing inhabitants have. If newcomers' behaviour lacks care and respect for land and people, they need to review their situation. Actually, we all need to review our situation – wrecking, exploiting and stomping over the Earth is a thing of the past. It's good behaviour amongst all of us, without exception, that will decide our future.

55 Human Rights and Wrongs
shekel shekel

In Palestine, the flipside of family and collective togetherness is *clannishness* – our lot against yours. Palestine had little proper governance other than military rule from 1967 until the 1990s, so the clans and neighbourhoods of Palestine kept the nation rolling, maintaining social support systems and community order through two *intifadas*, building an underlying consensus on behaviour which carried them through difficult times. Clannishness is the reverse of this solidarity. It doesn't have to be so but, when a population is under duress, things can swing quickly from solidarity to divisiveness.

The body politic of Palestine suffered a serious schism in 2007, sorely undermining the collective interests of the people. The 2006 election had genuinely demonstrated electoral free choice – it was an exemplary election for the Middle East. A 60% majority voted for Hamas and the surprise result was clear and decisive: Fateh had expected to win but lost.

In a healthy democracy, the losers know that their time can come again, so they defer to the winning majority and accept the reasons for their loss, but this didn't happen. The propagandists and manipulators who refused to accept the outcome set about fostering division and rivalry, even despite the views of wiser heads in Fateh. A key person in this was Mohammed Dahlan, Fateh's security chief in Gaza. A troublesome man backed by the Israelis and the Bush regime, he made sure Hamas was portrayed as a terrorist organisation.

Pictures of Palestine

In the end, money and Fateh won, but the political spectrum of Palestine was sundered and hobbled and a healing will take a long time. Palestinians scuppered their future by permitting it to happen – though many feel they had little choice and that foreign intervention caused it. Still, the error of Palestinians was a lapse into clannishness, a dearth of dialogue.

Palestinians have another quality that can lead either to weakness or strength – the grief and anguish that lie buried deep in their hearts, often revealed only when they are hard-pushed. I saw this when talking to Fareed, who visited us at Naima's house. He is normally cheerful and chatty but his car had been stolen a week or two before, causing him real problems, and he showed an angst I'd never seen in him, complaining that to survive and pay his way, he had to work seven days a week. To add to his troubles, the Israelis had issued a demolition threat to his house some months previously. He had gone into debt to pay for house improvements and the enormous property-registration fee – all because his house was suddenly deemed illegal in Israeli law and this, plus the loss of his car, put him under financial and psychological strain that clearly showed when we met him.

This man runs a peace society, promoting dialogue and cooperation between professionals on both sides of the conflict – engineers, planners, doctors, teachers. If the Israelis genuinely believed in peace, surely they would leave Fareed alone – he helps ease the conflict. I couldn't help but observe in Fareed's case that, as in my own country, one of the best ways to hobble the activities of change-bringers and social activists, by design or not, is to give them big bills to pay.

Palestinians can be philosophical and easygoing about life's travails but, when their bravado breaks down, they can become emotional and impulsive, desperate to *do anything* to break the spell or remove the problem. Although generally firm under duress, when they lose their cool, they can start firing indiscriminately in any direction – emotionally, politically or, in former years, with bullets. This creates social, military and diplomatic problems by making a lot of noise with only marginal real effect, lacking any strategy. It is demonstrated in the rocket-firing from Gaza of recent years: Qassam rockets unsettle the Israelis on whom they rain down, but the actual military outcome is marginal. It causes the Israelis to bombard and lay siege to Gaza, at immense cost to the Gazan people. But does it achieve much for the Palestinian cause?

Hezbollah in Lebanon demonstrated a contrasting sense of focused strategy in their 2006 war against the Israelis. They operated a disciplined, effective and coordinated campaign for a distinct period of time and, although far outgunned, they made a big psychological impact on Israelis – and in war, this matters. This arose from sound leadership, clear motivation and tactics, but Palestinians tend to be more chaotic and impulsive.

Their innate character and the disturbing effects of generations of conflict has made Palestinians live for today. Certainly this enables them to survive and keep their spirits up, but it also leads to perpetual crisis-management, with no overall plan; they seek independence without having a clear idea of the shape and purpose of an independent Palestine. It unifies Palestinians against the Israelis, but what would happen if the Israelis suddenly stopped being a problem? Palestinians would likely suffer the same problem that Israelis seem to suffer – a strange psychological dependency on opposition. If the external threat disappears, they risk fighting amongst themselves.

This issue is typified in the Palestinian demand for the right of return of refugees. It's legitimate and a fundamental right – or at least, it was so years ago, and it should have been sorted out back then. Diaspora Jews are permitted to migrate to Israel without hindrance, solely on the basis of Jewish descent. Not so for diaspora Palestinians, who have no hope.

The problem is that the Palestinian right of return might be practically unworkable – although this is a pretty taboo thing to say. Exiled Palestinians have grown vastly in number, to five million, since 1948 and 1967 and the return of even half a million exiled refugees, 10% of them, could cause tremendous issues, affecting the fortunes of existing residents and returnees alike. There isn't a vastness of space, water and resources. Under current conditions, reclaiming property and migrating into Palestine in large numbers could be problematic.

It's a tragic dilemma that demands serious, objective thinking, the brave opening of a can of worms. Many exiled refugees are stateless and disadvantaged and, return or not, they need justice and support, for the sake of fairness and restitution. But in practical terms a major repatriation of Palestinian refugees could make this land an overcrowded nightmare facing enormous problems. Jewish immigration itself is accommodated by the settler colonisation of the West Bank, so that Israelis foist the problems of immigration – population density, rising property prices, quality of life issues – on Palestinians, creating an enormous problem for future resolution. This expansionist option isn't available to Palestinians.

The idea of Palestinian refugees returning to their ancestors' places of origin in Israel, or moving to Gaza and the West Bank in large numbers, is a recipe for heartache, whatever one feels about it, and there is no easy solution. Someone will need to set the levels of return, and I would prefer not to be at the meeting that decides it. The right of return is a question which won't go away, and it eats at the emotions of the Palestinian people – who is to make the historic decision about who is in or out?

Another critical issue is self-interest versus social and national interest; people err toward self-interest for good reasons, but the scale and proportion counts. In the PA, the business and the NGO worlds, a privileged minority of Palestinians earn good incomes and perks, and there is resentment among those who don't benefit from this patronage and privilege system. Many thus regard Fateh as a party of self-interested empire-builders. Self-interest crucially undermines the fabric of the nation, and the Israelis and the West exploit this by placing contracts and incentives with those who will play their game, thus creating an advantaged overclass of beneficiaries with a private interest in keeping things that way.

In July 2009 we were visited at Hope Flowers by a researcher from Oxford University, part of a team examining the broader effects of the NGO sector in Palestine. Members of the team were shocked to find that the overall outcomes arising from the NGO sector were more negative than positive. The researcher added that the funding body financing the research would not want to hear this. There had been a lively debate about the extent to which each researcher wished to present the truth of their findings, knowing that their future jobs and grants could come into question.

This industrial-scale charity and billion-size funding has become systemically tarnished and it arises from the professionalisation of this sector, the imposition of corporate-style values and its domination by a management culture accountable to head office in New York or Brussels, not to the Palestinian people. The sector is run by graduates with aid-and-development, accountancy and business degrees who are poor on real knowledge and have less emotional connection with issues and people on the ground. They stay in top hotels, fly business class, boss people around, favour their own kind, fail to see what's really needed and cost the earth. This is not *corruption* exactly, it's Western institutional mission-drift and protection of people at the top.

There is an illustration in Hope Flowers itself, though not of its own making. International funders understandably require transparency and accountability but expensive multinational agencies have to be hired to oversee accounting and auditing, at an annual price equivalent to two or three of Hope Flowers' educational projects added together. The school must contract with accountants and auditors to earn eligibility to receive funds, yet most foreign funders won't fund these professional expenses. Would that the school could spend that money on the children!

It is shameful for the Israeli government to dictate heavy terms on Palestine while letting the international community pay for social and humanitarian services, then to tell the world that Israel won't respect international law or opinion. It is a scandal that the wider world buys into this, relieving Israel of its responsibilities as an occupying power. The distortion on the economy of this foreign money and influence is carcinogenic, every bit as bad as the American arming of Israel. Few people have the guts to say so because they will lose their job or face opprobrium – so the rot spreads.

56 Down Under
return to Jordan

It was hot down in the Jordan Valley, a humid heat trap far below sea level – a fine place to live if you're a fly, and there were many that day. But I wasn't complaining: I'd just got through Israeli border control, which had been rather quiet and lax, run by people the age of students – except for the odd ex-military man in civilian clothes with a sub-machine gun over his shoulder. Now I was waiting, swatting flies, for the shuttle bus to take us through no man's land to Jordan, but it was Ramadan and regular service had been suspended.

The previous day had been one of goodbyes. Many people seemed rather shocked that I was going, though they knew that I had family and a life in England, and I had told them repeatedly that I was soon to leave. Besides, my three-month visa was up. I hoped to return soon, *inshallah*, though this would depend on my money situation and the health and welfare of my ailing parents. My mother died four months later and, a year after that, this released some funds, so it took time before I could eventually return.

There had been the usual last-minute tasks: people suddenly wanting me to take photos or sort out a diversity of remaining details. It's a familiar pattern – busy up to the very last moment, the last item of packing being my computer rather than my toothbrush. This was also a product of the firefighting mentality of Palestinians: if they're not yelling "Yalla, yalla!" at you to do it now, things are left to the future and, when the future comes, it's panic stations. So when the future became the present, a lot needed finishing.

Pictures of Palestine

In the evening Hind and Ibrahim invited the teachers and me to the Everest Hotel above Beit Jala for a goodbye get-together. The Everest sits on one of the highest points in the West Bank, with wonderful views. Once a watering-hole for British officers in the time of the Mandate, it's now a haven where Bethlehemites and Jerusalemites may meet. Although in Israeli-controlled territory, most Israelis consider it dangerous to go there – so the hotel is an *apartheid* anomaly.

The teachers are a superb bunch – well-chosen, dedicated, friendly, a sisterhood. When my turn came to speak, with Ibrahim translating, I talked about the significance of their work and what a wonderful group they were. I talked of my country, where it is possible to jump in a car and drive anywhere without checkpoints or restrictions – except cost, of course. I talked of the high sea-cliffs of Cornwall and how I would think of them when I visited my favourite clifftop haunt. I suggested that, whenever they thought of me, I might well be thinking of them.

Half of the people gathered there had never seen the sea, even though they were not far from it, because travel restrictions treat these respectable, well-behaved, decent people as suspects, criminals and terrorists. That is the peculiar nature of this land and its conflict of belief and culture, so bizarre and seemingly unbelievable unless it's a daily fact that conditions your life. I'd got used to the security walls and checkpoints – though checkpoints are less common and blatant than they once were. Still the walls remain, and the Israelis aren't about to dismantle them unless a miracle occurs.

If peace comes, many people will lose their livelihoods. Others will gain livelihoods and more – but that's not as prominent in people's minds as the potential loss brought on by change and peace; we cling to the devil we know. Tragically, conflict is a wonderful way to make money so people from the top to the bottom of society, from diplomats, soldiers and NGO workers to smugglers and workers constructing the security wall, all have a perverse, largely unintended vested interest in keeping conflict alive.

The same goes for people such as extremists – Palestinians, Israelis or Texas neocons – all mutually dependent on one another to maintain their extremism. Peace has been stealthily elbowed into a corner, re-framed as if it would bring loss. We're all at it, including media editors and TV viewers worldwide, as though we humans are addicted to hardship, strife and dismay, a comfort-zone guarded by watchtowers, gun-emplacements and checkpoints.

Yet today the angels were with me – or, if you prefer, I had luck and good timing. Whatever the cause, crossing through the Israeli controls was uneventful and not a single question was asked about where I had been or what I had been doing. This was a relief since, although I had prepared stories about the Jews I'd hobnobbed with and all the Israeli places I'd had been to, I prefer not to tell untruths. After all, I hadn't actually been doing anything *wrong*. The two Ethiopian ladies who checked my passport and entered its number in their computer came up with nothing. I had my gentleman-tourist look on and they were duly charmed, smiling and wishing me a good day. Just as well, for I was carrying a collection of photos and computer files which, although not wrong or illegal, could have been considered sensitive and, on a bad day, might have got me into trouble with an Israeli inquisitor.

To charm them, look at them with steady, friendly eyes and chatter genially with a soothing voice. If your conscious and unconscious minds are out of sync or you're nervous, you'd better watch out, but if you convey an unworried, routine, calm air, then suspicious minds gain little traction and things usually go well, even in hair-raising circumstances. Sometimes it's necessary to brighten up officials' otherwise dull lives with wit and pleasantry; after all, they're just obeying orders, doing their job.

It's remarkable nevertheless how many factors can slot together to help things run smoothly. Half an hour later a coachload of German political activists arrived and there were tense moments at passport control as armed guards emerged, watching closely. Two Israeli soldiers entered a room with a one-way mirror window to observe people in the queue and two travellers were extracted, led into a side room for questioning, while the Ethiopians were replaced by stiffer, more inquisitive officers. While we were watching this, another traveller told me that when Ramadan ended in a week's time, with crowds crossing the border, this place would become a nightmare. I had slipped through at the right moment – if I had come at the same time as the Germans, the story would have been different.

This is one benefit of operating intuitively. I had used my feelings to choose the day and time of crossing – but there were added 'chance' factors which had helped too. Ibrahim Abu el-Hawa's taxi-driving son Hamed had picked me up from the school and something funny had occurred. The week before, Palestine had changed its clocks back from summertime while Israel had not, and Hamed arrived one hour early in terms of Palestine time. He had to wait, but I speeded up my departure by half an hour, saying goodbye to everyone with a tear in my eye and trundling my bag through a swarm of kids to get away. The roads were clear and we made rapid progress so perhaps the angels were pushing from behind, to get me through the border controls while the going was good. Even if it was just 'chance', the Holy Land is a place where many such 'chances' happen.

Pictures of Palestine

Hamed is a nice guy and has driven taxis for many peacemakers over the years. As an Israeli Arab with the relevant permits, he took me through Jerusalem, avoiding two Israeli checkpoints and one Palestinian border control *en route*, each subject to delays, dropping me directly at the border crossing.

The main road down from Jerusalem through the Judean Desert is lovely – dry, barren, impressive in its heights, valleys and contours, populated only by Bedouin in small shack-encampments alongside the route. This 'peace road' from Jerusalem to Jordan was financed by the Japanese government as its contribution to the ultimately abortive 1990s peace process – and, of course, the Israelis mainly benefited. Down and down you go from the heights of Jerusalem to the depths of the Jordan Valley, the heat rising and ears compacting a little further with every few miles.

Having passed through border control, the Jordanian shuttle bus seemed in no hurry, but we were a captive audience and they weren't going to lose our custom. The German group was restive to get out, and an assortment of other travellers looked bored. My choice was either to stand in forty degrees outside or to sit refrigerated inside, and I hovered between the two for a couple of hours.

I was looking forward to the long climb up on to the Jordanian plateau on the way to Amman, out of this sticky heat into the thinner, drier upland air and the lunar landscape of the Jordan Valley. I didn't take photos because this is a security area but it's captivating if you have an eye for geology. It's a landscape of solid sandy hillocks shaped into remarkably otherworldly forms by wind and water. No wonder Jesus came here for baptism by John – it's hauntingly, heat-shimmeringly atmospheric, so barren that it's almost lively.

The land on the Israel-Palestine side is largely desert, though if you look back you can see the date palms of Jericho gaggling around its oasis, cradled below bare rock mountains behind. On the Jordanian side it is agricultural, with irrigation ditches, plantations, vegetable growing and greenhouses – with its own backdrop of the high escarpment bordering the valley.

Pictures of Palestine

The dramatic escarpments on both sides rise up boldly, acting literally as the edges of this crack between continents. Southwards you can see the blueness of what's left of the Dead Sea shimmering in mirages – it's drying up, thanks to removal of water from the rivers feeding into it. The continents are still moving apart by small amounts, and the Jordan Valley, in geological time-scales, is sinking. It does have a close-to-the-earth feeling, as if gravity is a wee bit stronger. The ancient, geophysical feeling of this landscape, indifferent to the self-importance of mere modern mortals, makes sure you feel like a humble guest.

I found myself reflecting on this dry, brown, barrenly beautiful landscape and the green, cloud-covered and rained-upon landscape of Britain. I had mixed feelings about returning home, especially to the subtly restrictive, routinised atmosphere that pervades British society. Britain is my homeland but, at this time of life, I find it less welcoming and nourishing than the Middle East. Decent, a bit bottled-up though not unfriendly, we Brits tend to live an individualised, risk-averse life, politely circumnavigating each other, carrying on in our own privatised reality-bubbles. Still, my stay in Palestine had loosened me up and I hoped that my fortunes might change back home.

The man at the hotel in Amman smiled at me as I lugged my bag up the stairs to the desk. I love the way people here remember their customers as people. Life feels different in Jordan from Palestine: by degrees Jordan is more of an *economy* while Palestine is more of a *society*. I went Downtown to find some food but, being Ramadan, I was obliged to fast until evening. As darkness came, everything closed and there was a fearful rush home for *iftar*. Every taxi was full and the roads were choked. So I trudged back up the hill to Abdali, hungry, eventually finding a Greek Christian food shop where I bought enough to tide me over.

Then, wistfully, I blogged my thoughts in my hotel room, relieved to be out of the Israeli control system, which had felt as if it could pounce at any moment. Yet I felt bereft and deflated from leaving edgy, energetic, friendly, colourful Bethlehem. When would I see my friends again? How would I find the means to do so?

415

57 Right of Return

meeting a Palestinian exile

In Amman, I met Denab, a Palestinian refugee whom I'd first got to know in Geneva. She hardly conforms with the classic image of a refugee as she's an academic who hangs out in four countries, doing sociological research concerning Palestinian refugees. In so doing, she embodies one aspect of the exile mentality: those who can get ahead go to great lengths to do so and achieve great things.

She took me around Amman, a tricky city for an outsider to see because it is spread-out, designed for automobiles and built on a series of hills overlooking a set of river valleys. Downtown in the main valley is the nearest to a city centre that you get, a traditional commercial area dense with shops and alleys and quite distinct from the modern malls, striking office blocks and freeways up in other parts of the city, the parts that most foreign visitors see.

From her I learned some of the history of Amman, an ancient city with much recent growth. One major contribution to Amman's prosperity and splendour was the immigration of rich Palestinian exiles in the 1990s from Gulf States such as Kuwait and Dubai. They had gone to the Gulf some decades ago, generating wealth in the oil trade or its derivatives, then moved to Amman in the 1990s because it is as close to home as they can get. Jordan is also a relatively agreeable country to live in. Since the decline of Beirut as a city of business and pleasure, and since the deterioration of Iraq in the 1990s, Amman had thrived.

Pictures of Palestine

Jordan has a Palestinian majority. Palestinians were originally spread across what is now Jordan and Palestine until they were separated into two countries by the British. When Israel was founded in 1948, Jordan took control of the West Bank. Its twenty-year West Bank occupation wasn't so much territorial expansion as natural affinity. It was done with quiet British encouragement to stop the Israelis taking over the West Bank, which eventually happened anyway in 1967.

In 1948 and 1967, refugees flooded into Jordan as the Palestine of Mandate times was shattered. In subsequent decades some refugees made progress while others remained stuck in poverty, disadvantage and the debilitating effects of dispossession, bereavement and exile. The refugee camps of today, of which Jordan has many, contain the left-behind ones, those who haven't progressed.

The problem of refugees has been exacerbated by two big factors. Many exile Palestinians have clung to their refugee status on the basis that, one day, they might return to Palestine, but this hasn't happened and might never happen. Refugee status has become embedded as a factor of identity in their host countries, reflecting an understandable Palestinian reluctance to fully integrate into the society into which they were unwillingly thrust. Many refugees keep the keys to their old Palestinian homes even though, in many cases, their villages have been razed or their houses occupied by Israelis.

Also, host countries such as Lebanon, Kuwait, Egypt and to an extent Jordan and Syria, have striven to retain Palestinians' refugee status as a way of, they hope, eventually getting rid of most of them. In Lebanon, giving full rights to Palestinians would have tilted an already volatile ethnic mix in a direction which would have disadvantaged Maronite Christians and Shi'a Muslims, fanning the flames of civil war – so Palestinians were not granted full status as Lebanese, and many did not seek it. In Jordan, Palestinians with Jordanian relatives or those who married into Jordanian families became Jordanian, while those retaining allegiances to Galilee and the West Bank did not.

Organisations such as UNRWA have reinforced this pattern by catering for registered refugees and thereby keeping them in that position, in a kind of poverty and identity trap. As with many NGOs, UNRWA has unwittingly built a culture of dependency, even though it does good work and it was set up with the best of intentions. It acts like a massive sub-government, specialising in education and social services for Palestinians.

Pictures of Palestine

Israel has consistently refused to countenance the idea of refugees returning, whether to reclaim properties in Israel, many of which no longer exist, or to swell the West Bank and Gaza populations and tip the overall demographics in Palestinians' favour. This isn't just a numbers game: the return of refugees involves full acknowledgement of the wilful damage Israelis brought to Palestinians around 1948 and 1967, which in itself would undermine Israel's national narrative, summed up as 'a people without a land waiting for a land without people'.

The dilemmas are now beginning to be quietly addressed in Palestine as the PA has realised that a massive return could be problematic for resident Palestinians. It would bring an influx of richer, internationalised Palestinians who could bid up property prices and elbow people out of influential positions. It would bring poor disadvantaged refugees needing housing, jobs and support. It would impact families, neighbourhoods, villages, land use, resources and population density. The PA is being forced by circumstance to re-examine this big issue, to try to separate the possible consequences of repatriation from the emotional and political principle of the right of return.

In other words, it is not only the Israelis who don't want the refugees to return, but also, secretly, many Palestinians – even though refugees may be their relatives. This is awkward. Palestinians feel that their kinsfolk should be able to return but, in many cases, those who actually think about it anticipate mixed results. No one broaches the subject: they adhere to the right of return as a fundamental redemptive principle, and there is justification to this in terms of the unresolved issues and pain of the past.

But in terms of dealing with the future, a significant return would have a big impact, potentially creating divides between those who stayed and those who had lived elsewhere – and it could vastly increase Palestine's population. The outcomes are likely to be mixed. Many refugees feel okay where they are in other countries, and many are nowadays strangers to Palestine –

but they still want to rebuild connections and visit, and this is understandable and proper.

The matter remains unresolved because the conflict is unresolved. People hang on to the principle of return because to drop it would imply a surrender to Israel and a legitimisation of what Israelis have taken and occupied. This cannot be done, except perhaps in exchange for massive concessions and a healing of past history, which Israelis currently will not make. Into this space of unresolution, the Israeli settler movement, many of them fresh Jewish immigrants, has moved, partially to block refugees' return.

The right of return, tragically, is unventilated and unprocessed, yet this toxic, undealt-with issue is becoming more crucial because Palestinians claimed recognition as an independent country in 2011. This means serious thinking about a Palestinian state. In international law, multiple UN resolutions support Palestinian independence and deem the Israeli occupation illegal, and there are existing legal precedents for such a declaration of independence in post-colonial countries like Indonesia, Zimbabwe and even Israel itself. Palestinians are entitled to independence.

The world is morally obliged to support it, on the basis of previous resolutions and legal decisions, although whether it fulfils its obligations is another matter – especially with USA applying vetos and threats. Yet the right of return can jeopardise independence, both by invoking Israeli resistance, even war, and by placing a burden on Palestinian society at a crucial moment in its history. If peace came, foreign funding, much needed elsewhere, would diminish, and Palestine's special call on the world's attention would end. So the right of return must somehow be constrained – and anyone specifying how this could be done needs a bodyguard. It has been a sacred cow for so long that no Palestinian would wish to deny a refugee their right of return, so the matter tragically remains a bomb waiting to explode – or perhaps a damp firecracker waiting to fizzle out.

Most Palestinian demands are more achievable – if, that is, the Israelis, by miracle, persuasion or force, were willing to allow them to be achieved. Emotionally, returning East Jerusalem to the Palestinians would be a hard nut for Israelis to crack and Israeli withdrawal from the West Bank and yielding of control there would be difficult too. But they are more doable than fulfilling the right of return.

Yet there is one thing not generally factored into this seized-up equation: *change happens*. The Cold War ended, *apartheid* ended in South Africa, Germany was reunited, the juntas of Latin America disappeared, Maoism in China died and ancient India modernised. *Change does happen*. Some things may look as if they are permanent fixtures, but in truth they aren't. Paradoxically, the word 'impossible' is a sign that change indeed is possible. So it is possible to say, without being too idealistic, that resolution, justice and peace will come to Palestine and Israel.

There's something else too: sooner or later, conflict and polarisation will ease worldwide and new generations will forgive and forget. Israelis and Palestinians will even get to like one another, just as the Irish and English, the Greeks and Turks, the Japanese and Koreans are gradually doing. So the matter will be resolved by humans re-humanising one another, the Israeli security wall will come down and things will move on.

It will probably come about in a completely different way than anyone ever anticipated. Rather like love, which so often arises when you're not looking for it, change will come and the issue of Palestinian refugees will somehow be resolved. But quite a few people will have to swallow hard.

58 First Great Western
welcome home, at a price

Next morning, I got up at 5.20 and took a taxi to Queen Alia airport, southwest of Amman. The security guy at the airport, examining my technology bag, stared at a small bottle of *Arak* I was carrying as a gift for my father. It was Ramadan and alcohol is *verboten*. I could see him debating whether or not to confiscate it. His colleague examined it.

"Where did you get this?"

"Beit Lahem."

"What have you been doing there?"

"Working at a peace and democracy school." Long discussion with his colleague.

"If you take that bottle from me", I said, after a lengthy pause, "My 92-year old father will be disappointed. I bought this from Christians in Beit Lahem, and it might be Ramadan but my father is a Christian". He's actually secular, but that was the best way to put it. "Besides, I am leaving your country, not entering it." He looked at me and I eyeballed him. He started rooting through my bag.

"What's this?" "Computer."

"This?" "An ethernet cable." We go through a comical list of the ingredients of a wired-up multimedia-techie's bag and eventually his mate chips in, in Arabic, probably telling his colleague to give it a break.

"D'you want me to show you what's in my computer? The Israelis sometimes like to take a look..." Now I was taunting him. This jogged him sufficiently to end this silly charade.

Pictures of Palestine

Eventually I was upstairs drinking a cuppa, but nowhere in this smart, modern airport, built to impress, could I buy a decent newspaper! I'd been looking forward to this for weeks – foreign papers are difficult to get in Bethlehem. If I wanted to buy a Givenchy handbag, no problem, but a newspaper? So I spent five hours on the plane daydreaming.

Then came the biggest rip-off of my three-month trip – not disastrously large, but rather symbolic of the British malaise. Before leaving Bethlehem, I had bought a ticket online for my train journey from London Heathrow to Cornwall. Theoretically this should be easy: you just book and pay for your ticket using plastic, then collect it from a machine at the station – except that, at the end of the booking process, there was no such machine listed at Heathrow. Surely some mistake? The website boasts 600 machines around the country, claiming how easy and convenient it is for the customer to use them, but you can't do it at Heathrow, Britain's chief point of entry. Excuse me?

I had e-mailed two train companies to ask their advice, reminding them that travellers from abroad just wanted easy transit on the

Pictures of Palestine

final leg of their journey. One company didn't answer and the other replied a week too late. The reply suggested that I should buy a ticket on the day (at double the price) and, if not, then I should order it online, get it posted to my home in Britain and have it forwarded to me. Great, thanks. I had already explained that time was too short and this wasn't possible.

So I had booked to collect my ticket at London Paddington station, planning to show my proof of payment at Heathrow, to get to Paddington. This was my big mistake. I naively assumed that, as in Palestine, human discretion would save the day. Well, I reached Heathrow only to be told that I couldn't do that. The man looked at me as if I was being plain awkward.

"Does this mean I have to pay double for my ticket to Paddington?" The man started waffling corporate-speak in reply, avoiding saying yes.

"Listen, I've had a long journey from the Middle East and I'm not interested in all this. I've paid for my ticket, I want a train and I've had enough." He continued evading the issue. To cut a long story short, I bought an extra ticket to Paddington for 100 shekels – I could have travelled the length of Palestine for that, with friendlier service too. Israelis might be pretty good at obstreperous obstructionism, but the British rail system outdid them. I won't bore you with the details of futile dialogues I later had, trying to reclaim my money, but it cost them at least 600 shekels to establish that they wouldn't refund 100 shekels since the error was, of course, *my responsibility*.

Later I sat at London Paddington, drinking a coffee to stoke me up for the five-hour journey to Cornwall. It cost the price of a full meal for two in Bethlehem. Ah, welcome back to civilisation! On the Penzance train, the sun shone through the windows, the fields and trees were green and verdant and there were no separation walls, checkpoints or sub-machine guns. Everyone sat there, wrapped in their own world, saying nothing to anyone else, playing safe. Privacy, hardly existent in Palestine, was duly restored – a lonely place.

Pictures of Palestine

At least we have trains in Britain. In a speech in late 2009, Salam Fayyad made a speech positing two characteristics of an independent country: secure borders and a railway of its own. A fine idea, although I cannot quite figure out how the Palestinians would build a railway, since the West Bank is seriously hilly and most river valleys go east-west while the railway would need to pass north-south. It would demand so many tunnels and bridges that even a mad train enthusiast wouldn't invest in it – or it would be so twisty and tortuous that a donkey would be quicker. "The Jenin to Hebron express now standing at platform four is due to arrive at Hebron when it gets there, *inshallah*. Mint tea and falafel are served in the buffet car, except at Ramadan, but we'll fix that for ten shekels if no one is looking." Somehow I don't think rapid rail transit in Palestine is likely, but Palestinians are entitled to their dreams.

The condition of Palestine is a tragedy. It's easy to blame Israel but most Israelis are decent people blinkered by their own historic trauma and the pain of decades of conflict.

It is more difficult to acknowledge how this situation reflects on civilisation as a whole, on you and me, on the international system that exists today, on the militaristic, heartless, globally-destructive culture we collectively permit to exist. It consumes people, trees, titanium, oxygen and pristine landscapes like they're going out of fashion, which indeed they probably are.

Israelis do what they do to Palestinians because they are implicitly permitted, encouraged and financed to do so and because bad press, worldwide disapproval and UN resolutions are not enough. For the triumph of badness, it is necessary only that good people do little to stop it.

Israel-Palestine is thus a microcosm of the world, a world of winners and losers, dog eat dog. The situation may be resolved only by an enormous overall change in the wider world, a change of geopolitical values, a surge of universal justice and a pragmatic confrontation with raw facts, plus a big dose of mutual human care and regard.

425

Until then, Palestinians will do the best they can with what they've got – and they might continue to do so for some time. They're experts at it, this is their strength. In conflict, they do not win and yet they are not beaten.

Thanks for coming on this journey. The happy end of this story, peace in Palestine, is yet to be written. In your own small way, you could be part of the script.

Salam alekum: peace be with our souls.

Pictures of Palestine

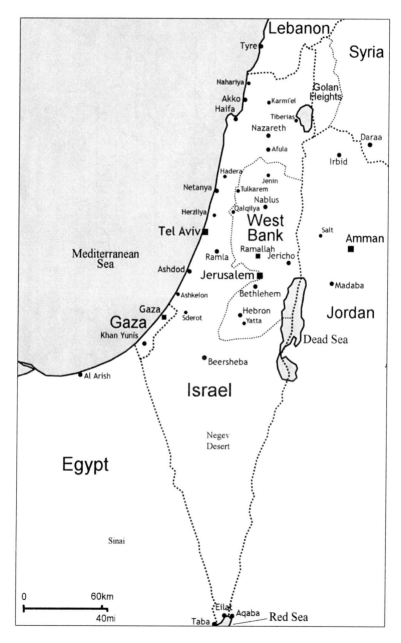

Pictures of Palestine

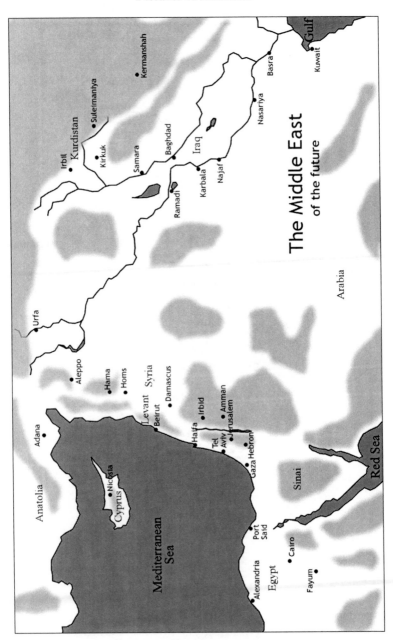

The Middle East *of the future*

Anatolia · Adana · Urfa · Kurdistan · Irbil · Kirkuk · Suleimaniya · Kermanshah

Aleppo · Hama · Homs · Samara · Baghdad · Iraq · Ramadi · Karbala · Najaf · Nasariya · Basra · Kuwait · Gulf

Cyprus · Nicosia · Syria · Damascus · Levant · Beirut · Irbid · Amman

Mediterranean Sea · Haifa · Tel Aviv · Jerusalem · Gaza Hebron · Arabia

Port Said · Sinai · Red Sea

Alexandria · Cairo · Egypt · Fayum

Lightning Source UK Ltd.
Milton Keynes UK
UKOW041832140512

192539UK00001B/12/P